P9-BYU-055

Doing Psychotherapy

Doing Psychotherapy

Michael Franz Basch

BasicBooks
A Division of HarperCollins*Publishers*

Library of Congress Cataloging in Publication Data

Basch, Michael.
Doing psychotherapy.

Bibliography: p. 181
Includes index.
1. Psychotherapy. I. Title. [DNLM: 1. Psychotherapy. WM420 B298d]
RC480.B317 616.89'14 79-3084
ISBN: 0-465-01684-7

Printed in the United States of America
DESIGNED BY VINCENT TORRE
25 24 23 22

To

Carol

and to

Gail, Tom, and John

CONTENTS

ACKNOWLEDGMENTS

This book, representing the culmination of my twenty-five years as a student, practitioner, and teacher of psychotherapy, owes much to many: to teachers who were more than kind; to colleagues who befriended me; to students who stimulated me; and, above all, to the patients whose trust, cooperation, and effort in the treatment situation gave me the opportunity to grow as a therapist. I gratefully acknowledge my debt and, albeit collectively, thank them all sincerely.

I was fortunate indeed to have the advice of Daniel Offer, M.D., while my manuscript was still in its early stages. His comments and suggestions helped me greatly in formulating its subsequent revision.

My friends Arnold Goldberg, M.D., and Constance Goldberg, M.S.W., were good enough to read each chapter as it took form. Their help and encouragement sustained me during the months that elapsed between the conception and the completion of *Doing Psychotherapy*. To say that I am most appreciative of the interest they showed does not do justice to my feelings, but I must let it suffice.

The thoughtful suggestions of George H. Klumpner, M.D., and Ruth Westheimer, M.D., proved to be most worth-while. Two others, Virginia C. Saft, M.D., and Charles M. Jaffe, M.D., gave me the benefit of their respective comments. I asked for a critique of the manuscript, never imagining that each of them would devote to that task the time and effort required to give me, literally, a line-by-line evaluation of my work. With the help of the eyes of these colleagues I was able to gain some distance from what I had written; as a result this is a better book than it would otherwise have been. I am both grateful for and touched by their efforts on my behalf.

Many thanks to Mrs. Eva Sandberg who stood by me uncomplainingly, typing and retyping the manuscript as often as I changed it. Knowing that I could count on her skill made my task much less tedious and difficult.

I want to thank my wife and my children who committed themselves to the idea of this book and to what its writing entailed. Their interest, understanding, and encouragement was and will remain vital for me.

Acknowledgments

I am grateful to the Theresa Benedek Research Fund of the Chicago Institute for Psychoanalysis for its generous assistance, and I also wish to express my appreciation to the Center for Psychosocial Studies for courtesies shown me during the preparation of this book.

M. F. Basch
September 1979

PREFACE

Students of psychiatry, psychology, and social work often wonder, Does talking really help? In this book I answer that question in the affirmative by clarifying how and why psychotherapy works. My goal is to provide newcomers to the field, irrespective of their background, with a practical guide to individual, insight-oriented therapy. Many textbooks of general psychiatry teach the art of conducting a mental status examination, establishing a differential diagnosis, and managing the acutely disturbed and/or hospitalized patient. This book focuses on the treatment of a different group of emotionally troubled individuals.

My concern is with people whose problems are not clarified by an exploration of symptoms and overt behavior in keeping with the Kraepelinian method of psychiatric evaluation, and who generally do not respond to treatment based on a biologically oriented medical model. These patients function satisfactorily, perhaps even successfully, when judged by superficial standards, but their personal relationships are usually troubled, unsatisfying, and frequently destructive. Despite the fact that they often show significant potential, their creativity, their originality, and their capacity for meaningful achievement are frustrated by their pathology. At the root of their difficulties are long standing patterns of perception and behavior which interfere with the successful conduct and enjoyment of their lives. Often severely anxious and depressed, these distressed and unhappy people require treatment in depth to resolve their difficulties. I have found that an active, goal-oriented, dynamic approach based on an understanding of the transference relationship between patient and therapist has an excellent chance of succeeding in these cases and can be taught readily to students.

Far from wanting to found one more school of psychotherapy and set it up in opposition to others, I wish to transcend factionalism and describe an approach that, though based on psychoanalytic principles, is not rigidly bound by any one method or philosophy of treatment.

Frequently psychotherapy is taught in the context of a theoretical framework with the expectation that students will adapt it to the needs of individual patients. In my experience this has proved frustrating for all concerned. Students, understandably anxious about their ability to function as therapists, want something more immediate and directly applicable. It is in the context of participating vicariously in the work of a more experienced therapist that they can acquire the principles they need and the theoretical background that they must master to become professionals. Using detailed, extensive, chronologically arranged excerpts from clinical material, I depict typical situations the psychotherapist is likely to meet. These examples are then used to derive the principles of technique and the underlying theory of development which form the basis for therapeutic intervention. By illustrating what actually happens in the course of treatment, making no effort to cover up the difficulties encountered by the therapist or the limits on the results obtained, I try to show what really goes on in psychotherapy, rather than to present an unrealistic version of what should or would happen if we were perfect and our patients all ideal. It is my hope that this approach will help the therapist build up reasonable expectations for him- or herself and for the patients being treated while learning suitable techniques with which to attain these ends.

I found that as I wrote I would think of related issues and questions I had raised but left unanswered and of clinical experiences I had had that were germane: then I knew what to write in the next chapter. I suggest that you deal with my book in the same manner. Even though I cannot provide a neat denouement, read it from cover to cover as you would a detective story, trusting that the information needed to tie up loose ends will be forthcoming.

Doing Psychotherapy

I

Introduction: Listening Like a Psychotherapist

What psychotherapists do formally in an interview is in many ways not much different from what all of us do intuitively all the time in other relationships. One continuously forms impressions of the person to whom one is talking, becoming aware of the feelings stirred up within him and of the thoughts and memories stimulated by the conversation, all the while monitoring the content of what is being said. One's final judgment about the interaction is as much based on one's inner reflections as on what the other person has actually said. In the same way, while listening to our patients, we psychotherapists form some opinion of their character, what they want with us, whether or not we feel what they want is reasonable and feasible, and we determine how we will go about communicating and implementing either our compliance with or refusal of their implicit and explicit wishes (Grinker 1959). Now it is true that patients may be quite secretive about what it is they want—indeed, they usually do not know themselves what it is they are after—and as a result we have to be prepared to be puzzled for a while and, over a period of time, seek as much clarification as we can get from them. But is that interaction really so different from everyday social interactions? We may be able quickly to identify the various levels of meaning in a conversation with a friend or family member, but that is because we already believe we know what kind of person he is, what is important to him, what experiences, both fulfilling and disappointing, he has had, and how he has reacted to them. When a patient first presents himself he is a stranger, and that much more than his symptoms makes him an enigma. It has been my experience that one way of minimizing anxiety about the initial clinical encounter is to realize that my first job is to get acquainted with the patient. I have found that it benefits the patient if, rather than focusing exclusively on a symptom or complaint per se, I make it my business to learn something about the person in whom the problem resides.

Before the therapist can hope to understand a patient, he must establish how, and how successfully, the patient goes about making himself understood. A great deal can be learned from the manner in which the patient deals with the therapist. It is just as important to listen to how a patient sounds as to note what he says. Is the patient ingratiating, matter-of-fact, insulting, condescending, admiring, indifferent, oblivious, or does he display a mixture of these and other attitudes? In order to evaluate a patient's behavior properly, the therapist should become aware of what feelings that patient stirs up in him. Does he have a reaction of pity, anger, boredom, curiosity, interest, or helplessness as the patient speaks? Does he have the urge to help the patient, to rescue him from an ununderstanding family, to win his favor, or to dismiss him as quickly as possible?

The tenor of what the patient says may be quite different from the reaction created in the listener. The therapist may hear a truly pitiable story of misfortune and shattered hopes and yet find himself thinking that the patient deserved his fate; or, per contra, he may hear what seems to be a matter-of-fact recital, and yet experience great sadness for what the patient has endured. It is the therapist's inner reaction that is most important in evaluating a patient's situation, especially if there are discrepancies between the communication the patient is trying to make and the reaction he arouses.

For the therapist an obstacle to his making full use of the patient's behavior—and of the effect it has on the therapist himself—is the myth that a therapist should be unaffected by the transaction. Implicitly or explicitly psychotherapists were given to believe in their student years that the therapist, like a blank screen, is supposed to remain unaffected by a patient's verbal and nonverbal activity: the therapist is impassive, neutral, and receptive to all that he hears or observes.

This idea has come from an unwarranted extrapolation of Freud's comment that nothing is served by making a psychoneurotic patient privy to the analyst's own conflicts and problems. Rather, keeping private the results of any self-analysis stimulated by the patient's associations, the therapist, like a mirror, should reflect to the patient only the substance and the implications of what the patient has said (1912). This suggestion has often been misinterpreted to mean that the therapist is always to remain still, silent, and unmoved by whatever the patient may say or do. The result is that too often perfectly decent, friendly, curious, and helpful people act like robots when they begin to function as psychotherapists. They literally wonder whether they should smile or shake hands upon greeting a patient for the first time, worry whether such behavior might already "contaminate" the field—as if a relationship between two living beings could be reduced to the artificial atmosphere of a physics or chemistry laboratory where comparatively simple experiments permit the focus to be on one variable at a time.

One can be oneself and still act with reasonable professional objectivity.

INTRODUCTION: LISTENING LIKE A PSYCHOTHERAPIST

There is no prescribed or ideal way for a therapist to behave. Becoming a psychotherapist is a challenging, at times arduous, task and is not a matter of play-acting a role. In encounters with patients we do not have the armamentarium of laboratory tests or X rays or an assortment of "scopes" to let us know what is going on. Our only instrument is our personality; and to pretend that we do not react as human beings while engaged in a task that embodies so many of our own hopes, fears, wishes, and ambitions, is to make the development of that personality into an effective instrument more difficult than it needs to be. Whether in psychoanalysis or in psychotherapy, Freud's (1915a) admonition not to act out or act on one's (countertransference) feelings is well taken, but nowhere does he say that therapists should remain unaffected by what they hear or behave like machines that issue interpretations upon being fed facts about patients' lives.

Especially at the beginning of his career a therapist is vulnerable to his patients' attitudes. Insecure about what to do and how to do it, his level of anxiety is high, and he cannot help but look to his patients for indirect reassurance that he can do his job while, at the same time, fearing that it will be embarrassingly obvious that he can not. These circumstances necessarily affect an apprentice therapist's work, but he can turn them into an asset and make them grist for the therapeutic mill if he embraces rather than hides from his reactions.

There are a number of other misconceptions that, although by now time-honored and regarded as dogma, at best interfere with and at worst prevent the therapeutic task from being accomplished. One of these is the belief that, given an accepting atmosphere, the patient will in due time "open up" and permit the therapist to see his problems in depth. The corollary is that the therapist's activity is an interference with that process. Though the therapist may be curious about this or that facet of the patient's life, though he may be unclear about what it is that the patient is saying, though he is puzzled by how the patient's thoughts at the moment fit with what has gone before, he may not ask for clarification or information. To do so would be to detract from the spontaneity of the associations and suggest to the patient what is wanted rather than to give him a chance to go where his unconscious leads him.

Like the concept of the therapist as unfeeling and unresponsive, this, too, is a misunderstanding of what it means not to interfere with the patient. Of course there are times when it is better for the therapist to say nothing. If the patient is clearly pursuing something very important to him, the therapist should by all means hear it out and should limit his efforts to encouraging the patient to continue. Questions and comments can wait till later, or they can remain unsaid if more important things are going on. However, most of the time a patient needs the active participation of the therapist, lest the sessions deteriorate into non-productive recitals of complaints and empty theorizing about problems. But what to ask and when? Here again, the therapist's reaction to what the patient is saying or not saying provides the best, indeed the only, clue to what to do. As one listens to the patient, one becomes aware of a nagging doubt whether something the patient said was really so, or one realizes that a sequence of events that may be significant has not been grasped, or one is unclear about what really happened in some situation the patient is describing vaguely, or one gets the feeling that something is being left out, or the patient is talking in technical language about a subject that the therapist does not understand. These and myriad other situations should move the therapist to intervene and suggest (yes, suggest) that the patient elaborate, clarify, repeat, and so forth. Many times I have asked trainees in supervision with me to tell me what they were thinking at the point in the session where things started to go wrong; and in most instances the question they wanted to ask, or the comment they felt like making, or the opinion they would have liked to give, was exactly what I, too, thought would have been the proper intervention. But, to the detriment of the therapy, it was not made for fear of influencing the patient. There is nothing wrong with influencing the patient; indeed, without the therapist's influence on the patient, there is no therapy worthy of the name. Like it or not, the therapist is influential, he cannot escape that responsibility; the art of psychotherapy lies in promoting and then using one's influence skillfully.

II

The First Contact

The dictum that the therapist should remain relatively anonymous about his personal life so that a patient can freely re-create figures from the past, does not require you to be unresponsive in the social aspects of the therapeutic situation.

I would urge you to be yourself when greeting the patient. Do not be afraid to be friendly when you introduce yourself. If in response to your greeting he or she replies, "And how are you today?" do not hesitate to say, "Fine, thank you." You have not given anything away about yourself with that answer; and it would be much more disconcerting and upsetting to the patient if you ignored the overture in the mistaken belief that you must remain totally unknown.

If you do not respond to a greeting or to some innocuous remark about the weather, you are not remaining anonymous at all; you are telling something about yourself that may be quite inaccurate. A patient is going to start wondering whether you are always so mean, or whether there is something about him that you do not like, or whether you do not care about the people you see and just want to get it over with, and Lord knows what else. In any case, whatever conclusion the patient reaches is going to influence what he says subsequently and how he says it.

That you may choose not to answer questions or engage in small talk in the interest of the treatment, and not because you are unfriendly, is something that has to be explained at an appropriate time. You can not assume that a patient already knows this or will accept what may seem to him peculiar behavior without reacting negatively.

By responding courteously and observing accepted social amenities at the opening and closing of sessions, you implicitly keep your part of what will be the therapeutic bargain. During the session the patient will of necessity sometimes behave in ways that would be totally unacceptable in any other situation. He will be asked to speak without forethought of the consequences of what he says, and in the process often expose himself in regressed or otherwise unflattering ways. Yet when he leaves he must be an adult again. Your readiness to extend yourself politely helps him make that transition and acknowledges that whatever he may have said during the session has not diminished him in your eyes.

This does not mean that the therapist should overlook the fact that seemingly superficial amenities may have hidden significance. One responds on the social level at the time but notes what is said, how it is said, how it influences the session itself, whether there is a pattern to the opening and the closing of sessions that has the quality of a defensive ritual, and so on. But in the initial interviews one can take these things at face value and need not get too concerned about them.

Upon ushering the patient into your office indicate where he might hang his coat and where you would like him to sit. Chairs for yourself and the patient should be placed across from each other at a conversational distance. How close that is depends on what you think will be comfortable and, of course, on the size and shape of your office. I feel most at ease sitting somewhat farther from the patient than I would in a purely social situation. In this way I acknowledge that there is a gap between us that must be bridged by what we say, that the closeness that may develop must be achieved by what we do together, and does not come automatically. I am also diffident about forcing myself on another person who may not care to be or work with me. Even if we agree to be therapist and patient, I prefer to give both of us room, literally as well as figuratively, to negotiate the relationship each time we meet, to permit each of us some privacy even while we are together.

Occasionally a patient, who is seeing me for the first time moves his chair either closer to mine or away from it with some comment about his discomfort with its placement. I make no issue of it, although obviously we have already started to talk to one another in action. Perhaps there is something about me, as expressed by my office arrangement, that is not to this patient's liking; maybe that patient has to leave his mark on my office, taking over just a bit, unable to let me control him even to the extent of "dictating" where he should sit; and so forth. There are many possibilities for a patient's reaction to the setting, and the therapist's first interpretation may be far from correct. I note what has happened and wait for further developments to make clear what, if anything, has to be said about it.

Usually a psychotherapist does not sit across a desk from his patient, the reason given being that the latter will be more relaxed in a more informal atmosphere. I, too, think it a good idea to dispense with a desk, but for a different reason. The trappings of the medical consulting room carry with them the expectations of a patient-doctor relationship in which the physician actively prescribes while the patient passively receives. The arrangement in a therapist's office subtly sets the stage for the patient's having to relinquish such expectations and to become an active partner in the treatment process.

However, my thoughts about the manner in which a therapist meets the patient and sets the stage for the work to follow are just suggestions and no more. It is nice if the patient is comfortable, but it is much more important for him in the long run that the therapist be comfortable enough to pay attention untroubled by the uneasiness engendered by trying to copy a style that is not suited to the needs of his personality.

Having met and seated your patient, the formal aspects of the initial interview begin. If the patient begins to speak, you, of course, listen to what he has to say, but generally it is up to you to get started. I like to take the first few minutes to check that I have the spelling and pronunciation of his name correct, and to make sure I have his address and telephone number in case I need to contact him. This gives the patient a chance to familiarize himself a bit with me and the surroundings and to settle down for the business at hand.

What you say to the patient is not nearly as important as why you say it. In the initial interviews you must establish whether the patient is indeed one who will be amenable to and benefit from psychotherapy. An open-ended, neutral question such as "Please tell me what brought you here," or "How is it that you came to see me?" gives him the opportunity to tell you his complaint.

In the clinic setting where most students begin their training, the patients have been previously screened for suitability, but it can't be assumed that further evaluation is unnecessary. A mistake may have been made in the diagnostic procedure or the patient may have changed radically between the time of his application and of your seeing him for the first time. If it turns out that in answer to your question the patient displays a serious thought disorder, gives evidence of being suicidally or psychotically depressed, has a toxic or organic brain condition, or indicates in other ways that he can no longer function independently with safety, then the immediate crisis becomes the focus of the interview and the goal is to arrange for appropriate hospital care (Redlich and Freedman 1966; Freedman, A. M., et al. 1975).

Let's assume that this is not the case, and you hear instead a story that can be approximately summarized by one or more of the following descriptions:

1. The patient complains that he either cannot establish, maintain, or enjoy relationships of one sort or another.
2. He has set goals that he cannot seem to reach.
3. There is an inner turmoil and/or dysphoria that he can neither understand nor control.
4. Though he is successful by the world's standards, he feels unhappy with himself and the position in life he has succeeded in achieving.

Upon hearing this sort of presenting complaint I tell a patient that the nature of his troubles suggests that psychotherapy may well be the treatment of choice, since it seems that there is something about himself and his behavior that he needs to understand better before he can go about dealing more effectively with life. (Of course, to settle this issue may take more than one meeting.)

My next steps would be to see if the patient accepts my recommendation, and, if he does, to settle the logistics of the sessions, and then to proceed with therapy.

The Initial Interview

The psychotherapeutic process is significantly influenced by the initial interview which tends to set the tone for subsequent sessions. In my opinion, misconceptions about its function may create unnecessary difficulties that then affect the course of the treatment adversely.

As commonly taught, interviewing technique is based on the model of the medical anamnesis: The general physician tries to get as complete a history as possible from a patient on the first visit. The onset, the description, and the vicissitudes of symptoms are carefully investigated with the expectation that the pattern that emerges will reveal the nature of the illness and determine its specific treatment. The psychotherapist is led to believe that this sequence holds also for his patients and that he must strive to obtain a similar history from them. If a patient seems to be suffering from a psychosis or an organic brain disease there is reason for obtaining such an anamnesis from him and/or from available informants; otherwise the effort can be pointless and even counterproductive. If a therapist attempts to gather detailed information about symptoms, it may interfere with his ability to see where and how far the patient will choose to go when given the opportunity to express himself. Furthermore, it can reinforce the patient's tendency, understandable but mistaken, to focus on his symptoms as the cause of his suffering. It is pointless to insist on a complete symptomatic history initially because neither the determination of the need for treatment nor the course of psychotherapy is based upon symptom patterns. That is not to say that symptoms don't have to be studied; they do—in great detail—for what they reveal about the patient's character formation and adaptive capacities, but this can be done much more effectively if the details emerge in the course of treatment (Freud 1913). The context in which they appear gives invaluable clues to their underlying significance; this is not the case when information is artificially isolated and extracted according to a preconceived formula or outline.

The apprentice psychotherapist is further burdened unnecessarily by the demand that he be able to produce a so-called dynamic formulation of his patient's personality after interviewing him. This means that in addition to the symptomatic history he must elicit the patient's recollections of what his childhood and adolescent development was like and what impressions he has of his relationship to his parents, siblings, and other important figures from his past. The student is then expected to "explain" the patient's symptoms on the basis of what disappointments, upsets, and injuries the latter has suffered, or believes he has suffered, by chance or at the hands of the people who raised him. When and if it is achieved, a meaningful explanation of how a patient's childhood experiences came to determine his character and account for his behavior as an adult—a so-called genetic reconstruction—is the hard-won result of many hours of careful work during which a patient's growing insight sheds increasing light on his psychological development. Such a process has nothing in common with the impressionistic, syncretistic guessing game based on didactic preconceptions students are encouraged to engage in after one, two, or three interviews with their patients. Apart from being useless, this sort of speculation is detrimental if it brings the therapist to premature closure regarding his understanding of the structure of a patient's personality and how it came to be what it is. To come to specific conclusions about such matters before knowing the patient in an ongoing therapeutic process interferes with the therapist's freedom to learn what there is to be learned from the patient over the course of time.

In addition a tendentious investigation of the patient's past with a view to explaining his problems by blaming them on what in essence has been visited upon him by life, reinforces the belief, often already present, that he is a "victim" entitled to compensation and relief. The therapist is then elected to fill the impossible role of rescuer and, what is worse, may believe that this is indeed a reasonable expectation. To learn how your patient orders or fails to order his world you have to give him a chance to work at ordering it with you; he should not be presented with a series of preconceived questions that relieve him of the tension of having to adapt himself creatively to you and to the session.

Once the presence of a psychiatric emergency has been ruled out, the psychotherapist's immediate task is to become aware of his impressions and to *avoid* coming to premature conclusions about his patient and the patient's problems. Nor can the therapist afford to jeopardize the treatment by acquiescing to pleas or demands for immediate help or advice for problems having a background that needs to be understood. The task of the initial interviews is to let the therapist become acquainted with the patient and to give the patient the opportunity to react to the therapist.

Not every patient is able to express himself spontaneously in a coherent and meaningful fashion. Indeed, such spontaneity is an uncommon gift and, especially during the first interviews, guidance from the therapist is often essential.

The difficulties the patient has in talking about himself and his problems may be due to anxiety precipitated by actually coming face to face with a psychotherapist, may reflect a general inability to communicate verbally, or may be a defense against coming to grips with what is troubling him. In any case he needs help from the interviewer, who, especially if he is inexperienced, is counting on the patient to get things moving. Probably the greatest fear of the beginner is that questions he may ask or comments he may make will muddy the waters by directing the interview to what the therapist wants to hear instead of keeping the focus on what the patient has to say. This concern is exaggerated. If the patient isn't saying what he has to say, there comes an impasse that must be resolved by the therapist's activity. If one can mobilize the patient to speak of himself he will usually get around to what is important, or else it will become obvious that he is avoiding something; that can then become the focus for the therapist's comments.

At this point, rather than continuing to simply talk about technique I would like to present a number of examples that illustrate the conduct of psychotherapy in various phases, interspersing comments about theoretical and technical issues where I think them to be helpful and appropriate. I have chosen this way of presenting my thoughts because I remember well that as a student I always wanted to know what the therapist actually did. It never helped me much to hear or read that this or that was interpreted to the patient, or that the patient was confronted with such and such. What I wanted to know was what the therapist actually said, and how he got to the point where he said it, and then what happened? Most important, what was said that didn't work and how did one get the treatment back on the track after making inaccurate, unproductive, and/or mistaken attempts at confrontation, clarification, or interpretation, as I always seemed to do? As far as I can tell from my present vantage point as a teacher, students still have these questions.

Confronted of necessity with the demand to function as a therapist before he or she feels confident in that position, a beginner is oriented toward practice. Theory only seems to make sense if it can be shown to be relevant to a student's immediate concern with patient management.

I have chosen my clinical examples from cases that I either treated or whose treatment I supervised. These excerpts are not meant to be guides to or paradigms for the therapy of specific types of patients or particular disorders. They are reconstructions, sometimes amalgamations, of interchanges I consider particularly illustrative of various phases and vicissitudes of the psychotherapeutic relationship. The patients have of course been disguised in such a way as to preclude recognition. Since I am more interested in conveying the flavor of a transaction than in presenting the sort of verbatim account that would be required if a particular patient's treatment was the main consideration, wherever possible, I have eliminated what I felt to be extraneous material. This makes the case studies more readable and focuses attention on particular therapeutic issues.

I have no doubt that other therapists would have suggested management that differed in one or another respect from what I advocate here. However, that is beside the point. Each therapist must develop his own style based on his own character and experience. As a complex mathematical problem can be solved in different ways, so any given patient's difficulties can be approached differently by different therapists. Yet I would expect that in the hands of equally experienced therapists, the insights gained by the patient and his understanding of himself, would be essentially the same. My aim here is not to advocate a particular style of therapy but (1) to illustrate what I have come to consider helpful, basic principles for the practice of psychotherapy and (2) to give the newcomer to the field an opportunity to experience vicariously what actually has transpired between a patient and a therapist in the consulting room.

III

An Uncomplicated Case: Initiating Therapy and Maintaining Its Momentum

Session 1

Mr. Harry Arianes, a thirty-five-year-old foreman for a construction company, was referred from the general medical clinic because no physical basis could be found for the gastrointestinal symptoms that were troubling him. He acknowledged the therapist in a friendly manner when the latter introduced himself. He seemed somewhat ill at ease and tended to speak in short sentences, pausing to look at the therapist as if to see what to say next.

Therapist: [*Looking at the patient's record*] I see you come from the medical clinic. They seem to think that your stomach discomfort might be due to an emotional problem.
Mr. Arianes: I figured it was nerves.
Therapist: You're aware of some psychological problem in yourself?
Mr. Arianes: When my wife and I fight my stomach gets tied into knots.
Therapist: Tell me about it.
Mr. Arianes: What's there to say? All married people fight. I just can't take it I guess.

It is clear that the patient is not about to elaborate on his complaint, and that the therapist is going to have to do something. A number of questions, however, are dead-end streets and leave the therapist no better off than before he asked them:

1. Therapist: Sure, there's more to say.
   Mr. Arianes: No, there isn't.

or:

2. Therapist: What do you mean "you can't take it"?
   Mr. Arianes: It makes me nervous, that's all.

3. The therapist can challenge the patient's statement:
   Therapist: "All married people fight," is that really so?
   Mr. Arianes: All the ones I know.

Not only has the interview not progressed, but the therapist has probably antagonized the patient by making a statement that can be interpreted as suggesting that he, the therapist, comes from a more genteel social class than the patient, a class where fights between husband and wife are unknown. The patient may doubt that he can be understood by such a person, and may even think that he is now held in contempt. Not an auspicious start.

4. The psychiatrist can choose to say nothing. Many beginners in their anxiety about not knowing what to do or fearing to do the wrong thing, hide behind what they believe is an "analytic silence." However, to say nothing is not to do nothing. Silence on the part of the therapist leaves the patient without feedback about what the therapist wants or feels. Like a stimulus deprivation experiment, the therapist's silence raises the patient's anxiety and forces him to arrive at an order based on his inner resources alone. This technique has a place in therapy, but its use is ill advised until the patient understands the process of letting his associations emerge unrestrictedly and has given evidence that he can profit from it. Nothing is to be gained from using this maneuver during the initial evaluation. The patient will either become more frightened and less able to cooperate or conclude, correctly, that the therapist does not know what he is doing.

A variant of this technique is to tell the patient, "Say what you are thinking" or—another time-honored ploy—"Say what occurs to you." If you have reason to believe the patient can indeed go on by himself, and that your attempt to guide him will only play into his defenses, giving open-ended encouragement is a valid technique. However, that is not the case when you first talk with a patient. At that time the only result you can expect is that the patient will become more anxious than he needs to be, and will think that maybe therapy is not going to help after all.

5. The therapist can direct the patient:

Therapist: Tell me more about yourself.
Mr. Arianes: Like what?
Therapist: Well, where are you from, what's your family like . . . ?
Mr. Arianes: I was born right here in the city. My father, he was a drunk and died when I was fourteen years old, so Ma, she had to go to work. . . .

Important as this information is, at the moment it leaves incomplete the patient's attempt to describe his present situation. The interview is becoming too diffuse and will probably end in confusion for both therapist and patient.

If the principle to be followed when greeting the patient is, Don't be afraid to be yourself, then the principle that should guide the evaluatory, diagnostic interview is, Become a master of the obvious. Rather than trying to figure out and imitate what somebody more expert might ask or say under the circumstances, imagine what you would say to a friend who told you that fights with his wife were upsetting him to the point of physical illness. You would likely ask: "What happened, when did it happen, what was it about?"

Therapist: When was the last fight with your wife?
Mr. Arianes: Oh, yesterday. What difference does it make?
Therapist: If the fights are enough to make you ill, then it's important for me to know about them in detail, so that I can be sure that I know what you mean. After all, it makes a difference whether you were glaring, yelling, or striking out at one another, doesn't it?

Here the therapist is doing more than justifying his need for information. He is giving the patient an example of psychotherapy as a coöperative effort by acknowledging that he, the therapist, does not know what he needs to know unless the patient helps him. By giving the patient an example of the kinds of fights people have, the therapist indirectly reassures the patient that he, the therapist, knows and is prepared to talk about such matters and does not consider himself above discussing the quarrels, even violent ones.

Mr. Arianes: Oh, I don't hit her or anything like that. Felt like it though, I'll say that. How would you like it if you came home every night looking to relax and found her jabbering in the kitchen? No supper. Nothing.
Therapist: Jabbering? With whom?
Mr. Arianes: Her sister. She got a divorce and had to go to work. My wife gets stuck with her kids all day, and then when she gets off of work she comes by the house to pick 'em up and they get to talking. Christ knows what she finds to talk about to that sister of hers every day. Has to hear all about the job, and is the boss nice, and what happened to the old lady in the bookkeeping department who tripped over the Xerox machine—people she doesn't even know! Never asks me what happened from one week to the next at work, just make sure the damned money is on the table Friday night, that's all she cares about me. Say, Doc?
Therapist: Yes?
Mr. Arianes: Just talking about it gives me that pain. I get a burning right here. [*Points*]
Therapist: You sure looked mad talking about it.
Mr. Arianes: Well, I had enough of that shit when I was a kid. Pardon my language. All my life. When the others were playing after school, goofing off and stuff, I had to come right home and babysit for the little ones, even weekends.
Therapist: Your mother wasn't home?
Mr. Arianes: She had to work. Father died when I was fourteen, and she had to support me and six other kids.
Therapist: Your father died when you were fourteen?
Mr. Arianes: Hit by a streetcar. Drunk as usual.

When historical material emerges in a spontaneous manner, as it does here, it is much more meaningful for both the patient and the therapist than when it's elicited by direct questioning.

Therapist: Sounds like you've had it with taking care of kids?

The therapist here guides the patient away from talking more about his father because (1) he, the therapist, wants to hear about the equation the patient has set up between the children who interfered with his life as an adolescent and the ones who are depriving him of his wife now; and (2) the end of the session is approaching and the therapist does not want to have the patient open up a new, emotionally loaded topic only to have to bring the discussion to an end.

Mr. Arianes: Better believe it, Doc. I told her when we got married three years ago. I told her, I said: "Shirley, it's going to be you and me for a good long while, no kids, I want to be able to enjoy myself for a change. If we want to see a movie, we go, and no worrying about who's going to watch the brats. We want a vacation, we go, I don't want to hear nothing about how the money has to go for shoes and coats for the winter." Shirley, she agreed. She comes from a big family, too, and knows what it's like. So everything is fine for a couple of years and now, BOOM, I come home to this. Damned house even smells like the old place—diapers and baby food. Walk up to the front door and you're lucky you don't fall flat on your can tripping over a tricycle. Roller skates, skateboards, scooters, kids got too damned much stuff nowadays anyway.

It is now ten minutes before the end of the session. The therapist wants to give himself the opportunity to come to a reasonable closure and, having concluded that therapy seems indicated and feasible, wants to see if the patient will accept a treatment plan.

Therapist: Well, Mr. Arianes, it's almost time to end for today. I agree with you that your stomachaches are emotionally caused. I think we ought to get together—let's say once a week for now—to explore the situation further.

Mr. Arianes: It's O.K. with me, you're the doctor. But do you think just talking will really do anything?

Therapist: It has helped others in difficulties similar to yours. I certainly think it's worth a try.

Mr. Arianes: How does it work? I mean, you can't change what's going on at home for me, can you?

Therapist: Look, you came here because you've got a problem that's clearly caused by emotional tension. You've started to talk to me about it, but I know there's a lot more to be learned. You can see how this works. Originally you believed all you had to tell me was that you fought with your wife, but you ended up saying a lot more than that, didn't you?

Mr. Arianes: That's for sure.

Therapist: All right, that's how we work. We start talking and we see where we go. It's basically no different from how it is in your business or any other business. Something doesn't look right on the job, so you investigate it. If there is a problem, you want a solution, but first you have to look at it from all angles, really study it till you are sure you understand it. Once you do that, you can figure out what to do about it, at least you've got a chance. Otherwise you're just making stabs in the dark hoping you'll hit on the right answer. We have to understand what's happening with and to you. It's my job to help you do that. Your job is to do just what you did today: talk openly with me, say what you are thinking, don't pull any punches, and we'll find out soon enough whether we're getting where you need to go.

Mr. Arianes: I'd like to try it. Anyway, I got to do something.
Therapist: How about the same time next week?
Mr. Arianes: Yes, that'll work out.
Therapist: [*Standing up*] O.K., I'll see you then.
Mr. Arianes: [*Standing up*] Glad to have met you, Doctor. [*Extends his hand*]
Therapist: [*Shaking patient's hand*] My pleasure.

The therapist uses his closing remarks to set the stage for the treatment to follow. He believes that this patient can be helped, and there is no need to hide this feeling out of fear that he will be making "promises" to the patient. No need to fob off the patient's questions with a mysterious "Well, we'll see," or "Let's discuss that next time, if you like." The patient is entitled to hear why the therapist wants him back—and to an explanation in terms he can understand of what therapy is going to involve. The therapist again uses this opportunity to emphasize what he can offer the patient and what the patient's share of the task is. He is encouraging to the patient by telling him, without being obvious about it, that he, the patient, is already doing what needs to be done, and doing it well.

It may be argued that I have picked or constructed an "ideal" case to illustrate the points I want to make about interviewing technique. Mr. Arianes, when asked to detail the nature of the argument with his wife, was stimulated to pour out an emotionally loaded description of his situation; it provided momentum for the rest of the session and laid the groundwork for the therapy to follow. What if he had not responded so readily after only a little prodding by the interviewer? The principle remains the same: unless you have good reason to go in a different direction, continue to explore the main complaint. Not, as was pointed out before, to get a complete factual history, but to help the patient to express clearly what it is he came to tell you. This in itself is already therapeutic for him and prepares him to go on.

1. Therapist: Tell me more about the fight with your wife last night.
   Mr. Arianes: That's pretty personal, isn't it. I'm not here to blow the whistle on her. She's not a bad person, you know. We just fight once in a while, that's all.
   Therapist: But you still think of her as a good person. Let's talk about that. I agree with you, there sometimes is a tendency to remember only the unhappy things and forget the rest. What do you find rewarding in your relationship with your wife?
   Mr. Arianes: She's a terrific girl, great sport. I like football, she never nags me when I watch the game on TV, like so many of 'em do. Always makes a fuss over me. When it's my birthday or Christmas, she's always got nice presents for me. Treats me right you know, at least she used to.
   Therapist: Used to?
   Mr. Arianes: Yeah, till her sister got that divorce and started coming over all the time.
   Therapist: Her divorced sister comes over all the time?
   Mr. Arianes: Yeah, with her kids. That's what the fights are about. . . .

There is seldom any need to pursue a point relentlessly in an interview. If the patient has aroused your interest and then balks or takes a different tack, follow him. If the detour he takes turns out to be worth-while, by all means go along with it. You can always come back later, or some other day, to the matter that was left hanging. If the patient seems reluctant to go on, as in the preceding example, find out what his objection is and then work within that framework to reach your goal.

2. Mr. Arianes: I don't know what you want, Doctor. I told you my wife and I fight, and it makes me sick, and that's all there is to say.
 Therapist: What do you fight about?
 Mr. Arianes: I can't remember. Nothing, I suppose.
 Therapist: Well, I don't get the impression that you are the kind of person who is just looking for a fight and uses any excuse to have one.
 Mr. Arianes: I don't want to fight. I always tried to avoid that.
 Therapist: Maybe you dislike the fighting so much that you want to forget all about it and it feels as if you don't remember. But you are here to get some help, and in order to make that possible I have to talk with you about those things that are important for you. Obviously the fights are important, you have good reason to think that they are what makes you sick. So even though it's painful for you, I have to ask you to help me reconstruct what happens. Tell me if you can remember at least when the last fight took place.
 Mr. Arianes: Last night.
 Therapist: About what time?
 Mr. Arianes: Around six o'clock.
 Therapist: Where did it take place?
 Mr. Arianes: In the kitchen, I guess.
 Therapist: You were eating supper?
 Mr. Arianes: No, supper wasn't ready again. I guess that's what I lost my temper about. . . .

If a patient behaves like an angry or suspicious child who is not going to tell anyone about what he did, the therapist often finds it useful to handle him as if he were, for the moment, such a child. The therapist becomes concrete: "Exactly where were you? Who was with you? What time was it? What were you wearing?"—and so forth. Once the patient begins to answer these factual questions, he shortly finds himself elaborating spontaneously, just as the therapist had wanted him to do in the first instance.

There is no sharp dividing line between the initial interviews and the beginning of treatment. There can already be considerable therapeutic benefit from the patient's determination to do something about his unhappiness or discomfort and his actually coming to see a psychotherapist. The opportunity to have one's difficulties taken seriously and to review them in the presence of an expert who does not get upset by what he hears is also potentially helpful. But in the formal sense insight-oriented psychotherapy begins when the therapist has determined that it is both necessary and possible for the patient to gain self-understanding, and the patient has provisionally accepted the idea of participating in the process.

Self-understanding is a goal to which everyone subscribes but one that is seldom defined clearly. Rather than trying to establish a definition of "self" at this point I suggest that we deal with this issue operationally. To say someone understands himself means he is able to take distance from his actions and wishes and to evaluate his motivation in terms of past, present, and future. The unhappiness of which many patients complain stems from an inability to think and behave in ways suitable to their present needs. Beginning with the work of Freud clinical experience has repeatedly confirmed that the cause of self-defeating conduct, whether in the form of an isolated symptom or of a more pervasive attitude or behavior pattern, is the sufferer's inability to become cognizant of the underlying purpose served by the symptom, attitude, or behavior pattern in question.

Practically speaking, what prevents anyone from understanding his thoughts or overt behavior are the limits of his perceptual set. One's experiences and the way one interprets them build up patterns of expectation—often unconscious patterns—that one then uses to adapt to new situations. One can only see what one is prepared to see. As a person develops he builds perceptual frameworks with which to conceptualize not just the concrete aspects of the world, but also the significance and implication of his relationship to others. Under optimal circumstances these perceptual frameworks are flexible and capable of being changed as a result of experience. In everyone's life, however, there are percepts generated in transaction with others whose repetition seems too painful to tolerate because they are associated with fear, shame, or guilt. Then it often happens that perceptual flexibility is sacrificed to defense, that is, in the interest of avoiding anxiety. As a result the brain's capacity to do its work, to organize signals and communicate messages, is impaired. Quite literally there is functional brain damage. If a person's circumstances require him to deal with areas that in some way touch on the experiences that need to be avoided, he finds himself unable to perceive what he should and can bring to bear on the problem only a now inadequate perceptual framework, geared to avoiding rather than encompassing information.

Sometimes we see a patient whose difficulties have obvious solutions, but even if these solutions are already known by or made known to the patient, they cannot be implemented because he is not free to deal with the problem except in an inappropriate frame of reference. Many times, of course, the underlying problem that lies behind the presenting complaint—or its solution—is not so clear. In any case, the first task of the therapist is to learn how the patient perceives the situations that are the occasion for his difficulties. Ultimately the help the therapist can give depends greatly on the degree to which he can enable the patient to comprehend his situation without distortion. Such perception promotes the understanding that makes choice possible where none was possible before. To find the solution to his problems is up to the patient; given perceptual freedom he may arrive at a very different resolution than what the therapist might have worked out for himself under similar circumstances. The therapist's task is to restore or promote the ability to experience and organize that which had been selectively eliminated from recognition during development.

Becoming acquainted with the patient during the initial interviews means giving him the opportunity to tell how he perceives his situation, that is, what theoretical framework he uses to interpret what is happening to him and around him. If he cannot proceed spontaneously, the therapist assists him in the process of putting into words what he is struggling to express or trying to conceal. Therapy continues this process, but also demands that the therapist be alert to what the patient either does not perceive or distorts in the perceiving. The therapist selectively interprets to, clarifies for, or confronts the patient with his understanding of the patient's perceptual problems and deficits. The aim is both to further the patient's thoughts on these matters and ultimately to restore his perceptual capacity.

Too often the search for the significance of the patient's complaint is permitted to drift under the misapprehension that it is the job of the patient to say all his thoughts as they occur to him and the job of the therapist to fathom and interpret the meaning of what he hears. This approach generally fails in the early part of the treatment because in order to get a clearer picture of what is happening in the patient's life, the therapist needs to know what it is the patient is *not* saying. Contrary to common belief, the missing material will not emerge spontaneously no matter how patient the therapist may be, and it must be elicited directly by him. If it is not, the treatment tends to become circular with the patient repeating in various ways and in different contexts the accommodation he has made to and through his symptoms. This repetition usually takes the form of placing blame. Some patients blame themselves for their troubles; more blame their circumstances or the influence of other people, past and present, for the dilemma that brings them to treatment. You should certainly listen to what your patient has to say in this vein because it acquaints you with his defensive maneuvers. But even if he is correct in his evaluation, how will allocating blame alone help the patient with his problems? His unhappiness has to do with what he is doing or not doing in the here and now, and it is that behavior, or lack of it, that has to be clarified.

Past history is important, but it is erroneous to think that establishing what were the past influences on the development of the personality is in itself curative. The function of eliciting the patient's past history is the clarification of the perceptual set the patient developed that now causes him to look at life in a particular way—it determines his life style, that is, his typical reactions. But it is what he is missing as a result of his perceptual set that he needs to understand. As long as he remains in his perceptual mold he can't go beyond it. The therapist must establish what that set is and by seeing what is missing help the patient to see it too, thereby enlarging his perceptual framework.

Session 2

Mr. Arianes: Hello, Doctor.

Therapist: Hello, come in and sit down, please.

Mr. Arianes: Well, what should I talk about today?

Therapist: I don't have any specific agenda in mind. Is there anything you've been thinking about since I saw you last?

Mr. Arianes: I don't know exactly what happened last time, but I don't feel so nervous any more.

Therapist: Knowing that someone else is working with you, trying to understand your problem, can take off a lot of tension.

Mr. Arianes: I guess that's true. Shirley, my wife, noticed a difference right away after I came back from here.

Therapist: You were discussing your appointment?

Mr. Arianes: Not exactly. That night when we were getting ready for bed she mentioned that I looked a lot more relaxed and acted like it too. . . . [*Looks at therapist for further direction*]

Therapist: Go right ahead speaking and don't feel you have to wait for me to respond or ask questions. If I need to know or want to tell you something, I won't hesitate to interrupt you. Otherwise you go right on with whatever comes to your mind. We'll follow wherever that leads us. So you were saying that you and your wife were talking at bedtime. . . .

Mr. Arianes: Like I said, she said I was more relaxed since I was here. We talked some about why I'd been so tense. I told her I didn't appreciate her sister taking over my home the way she was doing. Shirley got kind of mad about that, said I should be more understanding and, anyway, it was only for the summer till Grace, that's her sister, got the older kids in school and a regular sitter for the baby.

Therapist: You hadn't mentioned to her how annoyed you were with the arrangement, and your wife hadn't made it clear that it was only for the summer?

Mr. Arianes: I guess we didn't ever really talk about it.

Therapist: And your wife didn't see how angry you were and put two and two together?

Mr. Arianes: That's a funny thing, you know. I sort of asked her that, too. You know what she said? She said I didn't act any different now than I always do. "You're always angry about something," she told me.

Therapist: You sound hurt.

Mr. Arianes: [*Ruefully*] At first I got mad and started to tell her off, but she said, "That's what I mean, no matter what I try to tell you, you fly off the handle." She sort of stopped me with that.

Therapist: Do you think she has a point? Is there some truth to what she told you?

Mr. Arianes's situation is not uncommon. Often a visit to a therapist is enough to alter the relationship of a patient with his immediate family. Now that a professional has entered the picture, it is no longer necessary to maintain the mutually protective defenses that have been used to gloss over or minimize the underlying difficulties. The patient's wife has confronted him with a different perception of himself and in the process has given the therapist a potentially different view of the patient. At first one couldn't help feeling sorry for the poor fellow taken advantage of by his wife. Now one sees her as the injured party. Just as the therapist did not take sides in the first interview, so he remains noncommittal now and focuses on learning as much as he possibly can as he sees the patient from different perspectives. The goal remains one of helping the patient ultimately to understand himself better, not of serving as a referee or counselor in family squabbles. Not that the therapist does not make value judgments and react emotionally to what the patient tells him. But what makes therapy different from ordinary social intercourse is that the therapist does not necessarily share his opinions or act on them in his relationship to the patient. As the preceding interchange shows, the picture received at any given time from a patient is of necessity distorted, and any conclusions the therapist reaches must be recognized as provisional, surely incomplete, and in all probability erroneous in significant respects.

Mr. Arianes: Well, if she had my job she'd be plenty mad, too. Everybody craps on the foreman. You get it from all sides. The boss kicks you in the butt so you should finish faster already, the city inspector gives you hell if everything isn't up to specifications, and the guys working for you call you a slave driver.

Therapist: How do you manage?

The therapist makes a decision to let the patient go on talking about his job. The man needs to justify himself before he can speak more about his wife's view of him as chronically angry. In the justification he is indirectly acknowledging the truth of his wife's allegation. There will be plenty of opportunity to take up the specifics of his anger, and it will be more productive if the patient feels the therapist understands about the tension he is under at work. This line of talk will also give the therapist a beginning look at another aspect of the patient's life. Another very important consideration is that the patient and his wife seem to have started a dialogue that may prove salutary; the therapist doesn't want to interfere with that process or place himself in the middle.

Mr. Arianes: Well, they haven't fired me yet. They give me all the tough jobs too, and me the youngest foreman ever in the company.

Therapist: It sounds as if it's a tough job, but I think you welcome the challenge and enjoy it in its own way.

Mr. Arianes: Oh yeah. I wouldn't know what else to do anyway. This is the only work I've ever known. Except for one year I've been with the company since I was sixteen years old.

Therapist: How did you get started in that line?

The therapist continues to help the patient protect his self-esteem by letting him talk about his achievements, which do sound genuine and impressive. It is important to remember that though therapy requires a patient eventually to look at himself clearly and often in ways that are not flattering, there is no need to strip him naked and cause him more embarrassment than is absolutely necessary. The patient will be in a better position to gather the courage to look at the difficulties he creates for himself and for others if he realizes that the therapist is not just interested in faultfinding and problem-finding but wants to understand him as a total person who has assets and accomplishments. Never let a patient present himself as exclusively negative; he also has to face what is good about himself. Surprisingly it is sometimes harder to get a patient to "confess" to his assets than to his faults. Behind this is the patient's nonconscious intent to seek a regressive solution for his problems. If he can paint himself as all bad and incompetent then it is up to the doctor to rescue him. Once he faces his assets as well as his liabilities he has to accept the fact that, with whatever aid the therapist can give him, he is potentially capable of doing something for himself.

Mr. Arianes: I don't know, really. I told you about my dad; money was always short. Even as a kid I hung around the construction sites and tried to earn a couple of bucks running errands for the guys, bringing them sandwiches, cold drinks, and stuff. When I got old enough to get a work permit they put me on, first in the summer and then, when I dropped out of school, full-time.

Therapist: You dropped out of school?

Mr. Arianes: Yeah, when I was sixteen. Later I went and finished high school, nights at the Y. I saw that if I didn't graduate I'd only be a laborer all my life.

Here the patient tells more than the content indicates. Past history can be used to provide the therapist with the base line of a patient's functioning before his present problem became overt. This enables comparisons to be made between the former and the present state; also it bears on the patient's potential and helps the therapist formulate treatment goals. In this case Mr. Arianes reveals that he has the ability to rise to a challenge, can face his shortcomings, and, once he understands his situation, can behave in an adaptive manner. Such a past life style augurs well for psychotherapy. One would predict that the patient will rise to the present challenge, too, once it becomes clear to him.

Therapist: It looks to me as if you have achieved what you set out to accomplish. Granted your job is a difficult one, still it's the job you wanted and I would imagine it has its satisfactions.

Mr. Arianes: Sure. It's nice once things fall into place. Sometimes I just take a ride on a Sunday and go look at the buildings I worked on and say to myself, "You did that." I mean it's something you can point to. Someday if a kid of mine asks me what I do for a living I can tell him, "Get in the car and I'll show you what I do."

The therapist notes the patient's intention to have children of his own someday. It seems his aversion to fatherhood and its responsibilities is not all-encompassing. However, this is not the time to point this out to Mr. Arianes, though it need not be forgotten and can be referred to at an appropriate time in the therapy.

Therapist: Yet in spite of the pride in your accomplishment, and the over-all satisfaction from your work, according to your wife, as you told me, you always seem angry. Do you think she has a point or is it all her imagination?

The patient is now brought back to the focus of the session. He has had a chance to explain himself, to convey a significant, positive perception of himself to the therapist. Now he may be ready to face himself as he appears in his wife's eyes. One should not assume, however, that his wife's perception of him is necessarily correct; and, therefore, the therapist has declared himself ready to accept the patient's evaluation of her statement.

Mr. Arianes: I never saw it her way before, but she's not all wrong, I don't think. I'm impatient. I have to yell at people all day long, "Do it this way," "Not that way." On every job you always have somebody doping off and you have to be after 'em every minute. Maybe it's hard to stop that when the bell rings at quitting time.

Here the patient is offering a rationalization for his behavior pattern that the therapist should not be quick to accept. A bad—that is, a counterproductive—habit might require only some reconditioning; but before attributing Mr. Arianes's anger to such a superficial cause, the therapist should investigate it further for the possibility that it represents the expression of underlying attitudes and conflicts that require interpretative management.

Therapist: How and about what would you show your temper before your sister-in-law provided the focus for your irritation?
Mr. Arianes: Oh, I don't know. I guess I'd yell at Shirley and call her stupid if she didn't catch on to something I was saying. If we had an argument, I'd pick up and leave and slam the door behind me. Once I stayed out all night, I was so mad.
Therapist: What kind of things do you argue about?
Mr. Arianes: To tell you the truth, most of the time I can't remember.

Here, again, it is important to have the patient become specific, and not just so the therapist knows what actually happened. The patient's knowledge that he and the therapist have discussed the details of his situation gives the events in question a kind of reality that is qualitatively different from the reality they had when they were vague and private in the patient's mind.

Therapist: Well, give yourself a chance to remember. Try to imagine your mind as a blank screen or an empty stage and see if any pictures or scenes regarding those quarrels with your wife show up against this background.

Mr. Arianes [*Reddening in the face and quite flustered*] I don't see nothing, Doc. I'm no good at this I guess.

Therapist: O.K., that's no problem. Let's see if we can explore this from another direction. You mentioned when I first met you that you had the feeling that your wife, though she was interested in her sister's comings and goings, wasn't interested in you as a person, only in your pay check. Might this feeling of yours have led to quarrels with your wife.

Mr. Arianes: Well, I only said that when I was mad.

Therapist: Sure. I know that and you have made it clear that you have very fond feelings for her. Still, what comes out under emotional pressure often has some basis and isn't just made up out of a clear sky.

Mr. Arianes: I'll have to think about that, I guess.

Therapist: [*Noting that the time for the session is almost up*] O.K., then. Let's stop for today, unless you have other comments you'd like to make or questions you want to ask.

Mr. Arianes: I don't think so. Should I come back?

Therapist: Yes, of course. I'm sorry if I didn't make that clear. Let's consider this a standing appointment if it still fits your schedule.

Mr. Arianes: That's fine with me.

Therapist: [*Standing up*]. See you then, good-bye.

Mr. Arianes: Good-bye, Doctor.

When the patient seems at a loss as to what to say about the quarrels with his wife, the therapist tries to get the patient to participate in unassisted introspection, so-called free association. The patient becomes quite anxious under this stress, and the therapist—correctly—backtracks, does his best to minimize the patient's sense of failure and actively to guide him to a new topic.

When the patient flounders or runs out of things to say, it gives the therapist an opportunity to follow up leads he has picked up earlier in the session or in previous sessions, leads that were not explored at the time. Often the beginning therapist is afraid to guide the patient's associations lest he play into the patient's defenses and help him to cover over what might otherwise emerge. However, without such guidance many patients, especially in the initial phases of therapy, become overly anxious. Nondirective encouragement to permit thoughts to emerge at random creates an optimal level of anxiety in an introspective patient, but to another patient it may be destructive and generate a near-panic state.

The therapist's suggestion that Mr. Arianes think further about the friction with his wife does not result in pertinent associations. No matter. Once broached, the topic can be reopened at a later time even if the patient does not bring it up spontaneously.

It was probably a mistake anyway to try to open up this new avenue so close to the end of the session. Had the patient begun to associate productively in response to the therapist's question, he would have had to be given sufficient time to develop his ideas until there occurred a reasonable point for interruption. But, then, there is nothing sacrosanct about the forty-five-, the fifty-, or the sixty-minute "hour"; a few minutes one way or the other as dictated by circumstances is perfectly acceptable. A patient's reactions to time variations, whether overt or covert, positive or negative, simply become a matter for therapeutic examination. The rule of thumb is that one does what seems most appropriate at the time, and one is prepared to deal with any complications that are generated by treating such reactions as one would any other associations that the patient may have to the treatment situation.

The last part of this session has an unsatisfactory feel to it. Probably the therapist is made anxious by the patient's visible upset at being asked to free-associate. Although the therapist quickly recoups, the hour ends on an awkward note with the patient seemingly not sure whether he has another appointment. Again, the therapist handles the situation in a matter-of-fact, but not unfriendly, manner, geared to minimize the patient's anxiety. Anyway, distressing as it may be for the therapist to feel he has bungled, the fact of the matter is that psychotherapy is so complex that even for the most experienced among us the therapeutic session with a perfect beginning, middle, and end is a memorable rarity. The therapist has to get used to the idea that a session need not be ideal in order to be productive. Usually the patient bears with the therapist, as the therapist does with the patient, and as long as one is willing to make the inevitable misunderstandings, blunders, and other errors grist for the therapeutic mill, there is usually no harm done. Inactivity on the part of the therapist for fear of being wrong is a much more serious error than any mistakes he may make in actively trying to help the patient to see himself clearly.

Session 3

After mutual greetings the patient comes in, sits down, and does not say anything; he looks expectantly at the therapist.

Therapist: Well, how are things going since I last saw you?

Mr. Arianes: Pretty good. I don't have those stomach-aches much any more.

Therapist: But you do have them sometimes?

Mr. Arianes: I still get some twinges when I first get home, but I tell myself it's nerves and try to relax.

Therapist: Relax?

Mr. Arianes: Instead of going right in the house I stay in the back yard a little bit. Smoke a cigarette and fool around with the flowers. That's sort of my hobby. I've planted most everything we have back there. I got some nice rosebushes, but you really have to watch it with roses. They're like kids—you have to feed them right, when they get sick give them medicine. Next year, though, I'm going to put in some vegetables too—tomatoes, beans. Maybe we can save some money, everything is so high at the store.

Therapist: Your sister-in-law and her kids don't upset you so any more?

The therapist actively brings the patient back to the events that, ostensibly, precipitated the initial complaint. To let him go on about his garden or to elicit how the interest in his hobby developed would be to lose the focus of the treatment. Right now the importance of the gardening hobby is that it permits him to alleviate tension. It testifies to the patient's resourcefulness and adaptive capacity. Having established this, the therapist wants to return to the vicissitudes of the marital relationship because he believes that it is in this context that the patient can best begin to face what he must in order to understand himself. Were the therapist not clear about what was important at the moment, he would let the patient go on to see if a focus could be extracted from the associations; but just to let the patient ramble is not productive. A student therapist is frequently frustrated with the treatment process as a consequence of acting on the conviction that one must not impose direction on the patient. The result is chaos, as the patient wanders from topic to topic or becomes boringly repetitious, while the therapist maintains the forlorn hope that out of all this will come some unifying concept that will make sense out of the mélange and set the patient on the road to insight.

Mr. Arianes: I've got to hand it to Shirley, she's really trying to make things better. Now she gets supper ready on time and, anyway, they leave pretty soon after I get home. Sometimes they're even gone by the time I get there.

Therapist: It does sound as if your wife is trying to accommodate your needs. Yet as I mentioned last time, you have indicated that you felt she wasn't that interested in you as a person.

Here the therapist uses the opportunity to get back to the unfinished business of the last session which he still believes holds a key to helping the patient see himself clearly.

Mr. Arianes: I thought a little about that too after I left last time. I asked Shirley about it when we were talking about her sister the other night; we're talking more now and it's sort of nice. She was telling me some funny story Grace had told her about the people at her office and I said, "You know all about everybody at her office, but I'll bet you ten dollars you can't even tell me the name of my two bosses at the company." She started to get mad at me then and said there was no talking to me when I always came in with a chip on my shoulder. If she asked anything about my day I'd snarl and tell her she wouldn't understand anyway. So how should she know what I did or who I did it with. Then she clouded up and it looked like we were going to have a fight right then and there, but I told her she was probably right, that I didn't mean to be like that, and I've tried to change things. She cried a little, but not angry-like, and told me she could tell I was trying.

Therapist: You've been trying to change your behavior with your wife in some ways?

Mr. Arianes: I'm really trying to talk to her now. If something bothered me at work I tell her about it. I think she doesn't really understand it all, but it feels better to have talked about it to someone anyway.

Therapist: It sounds as if you really are on the right track to a much better relationship with your wife and to a better feeling about yourself. Once you've surmounted a problem it's often easier to look back and get an understanding of how it developed in the first place. I get the impression that your feeling that she didn't care about you was based on a lack of communication between the two of you.

The therapist validates the patient's increased self-esteem while also letting him know that his improvement does not vitiate the need to understand the difficulties that originally brought him to treatment.

Mr. Arianes: I think you've got it there, Doc. We weren't communicating. I wouldn't tell her what was wrong or what I wanted from her. Maybe I expected her to understand me without saying anything.

Therapist: Like the expectations a child has of its mother.

Mr. Arianes: Not my mother!

Therapist: Oh?

Mr. Arianes: No, I always thought she had too many troubles of her own to pay attention to mine. I remember once I got hurt on my bike and came to her all bloodied up. When she saw me she got mad and yelled at me for making more trouble for her when she already had her hands full with my father.

Therapist: Do you remember how you felt then?

Mr. Arianes: I can't remember, but I know that after that I never brought my troubles to her again.

Therapist: How old were you?

Mr. Arianes: Nine. I know that because I got that bike for my ninth birthday. It was a little too big for me still, that's why I got hurt on it.

Therapist: Perhaps you carried this attitude into your marriage.

Mr. Arianes: What attitude?

Therapist: The feeling that your wife, like your mother, would be unsympathetic to your difficulties. That there was no point in telling her about your experiences because she was too preoccupied or too busy to care.

Mr. Arianes: But she's so different from my mother. I come first with her.

Therapist: On one level you know that. On another, deeper level there may well be the fear that people—or maybe only women, or maybe only women you're close to—are all the same, and you can't take a chance at being rejected again in your need.

Mr. Arianes: Maybe you're right, Doc, but all that was so long ago, and I should be over that by now.

Therapist: That's not the way the mind works. If a shock, or a disappointment is strong enough it can permanently freeze our picture of ourselves and our expectations of the world. The rest of us grows up—that is, we let ourselves learn about life from experience and from what we see, hear, or read of the experiences of others, but that one area where we really got hurt stays unchanged. So what I mean when I say you might be carrying that attitude into your relationship with your wife is that when it comes to your hopes of being understood and catered to when you feel hurt or abused by life, you still feel very much like that nine-year-old boy who was rebuffed in his need and gave up hope that anyone would or could respond to him.

In this session the therapist suggests to the patient that he may be approaching aspects of his adult life with attitudes developed in childhood and essentially unchanged since then. The key statement that initiates this deepening of the patient's perception of himself is the therapist's comparison of the patient's expectations of his wife with the expectation of a child of its mother. The beginner will ask how one knows when to make such comparisons. What rules govern such interventions? The answer is that there are none. The therapist has the thought that the patient is like a little boy who expects to be understood and comforted without having to explain what is the matter. That is how children behave. There is only one way that one knows such things, and that is from one's own experience in growing up. Indeed, it is likely that there flashes through the therapist's mind's eye a comparable episode of his own life where he behaved like a child though chronologically an adult. Then there comes conviction that this recollection fits the patient's situation and that Mr. Arianes is moving along well enough in his daily life and in his therapy to hear about it.

This may sound unscientific, but it is not. We are all shaped by our early upbringing. There are enough commonalities in our childhoods, even though we may come from different subcultures, to draw parallels between our own development and that of any other person raised in a Western country dominated by the concept of the nuclear family. The expectations that such a constellation engenders and the disappointments, optimal and traumatic, created when the expectations go unfulfilled are similar, even when there are differences in the actual situation in which children are raised. Throughout our lives we signal implicitly by behavior, appearance, and attitudes the hopes, the wishes, and the fears of childhood which we try explicitly to hide from ourselves and from others by assuming so-called adult roles. Our happiness depends to a great extent on how successfully we manage to blend those early needs with the expectations we and others have of us as adults. A person who becomes a patient in psychotherapy is saying in effect that in some significant way he or she has failed to achieve this goal. Another approach to the therapeutic task of helping the patient to gain a different and clearer perception of himself is to say that the therapist must help the patient to see how the expectations he built up of himself and of those around him in childhood are affecting his present conduct. In the case of Mr. Arianes the therapist is making an educated guess that the patient, who seems in so many respects to be positive and well adapted, is failing to meet his emotional needs—though his marriage seems well suited to meeting them—because he approaches his wife expecting to be rejected. His behavior is a self-fulfilling prophecy: his attitude ensures his rejection and, painful as it may be, confirms over and over again an emotional set of many years ago. The therapist is able to make such a hypothesis when he has the freedom to use himself as an instrument that resonates empathically with the patient's communications, spoken and unspoken. Most psychotherapists have a great capacity for empathic listening; or, rather, it is usually the person who is empathic, and who values understanding and being understood above everything else, who chooses to become a psychotherapist.

I think few students, if presented with Mr. Arianes's associations, would not have similar thoughts. However, the beginning therapist may be unable to become fully aware of and utilize such ideas because his didactic training has committed him to too narrow a view of development—that is, to the Oedipus complex and psychosexuality. In the first place, he is not prepared to recognize that his empathic response to his patient touches on other, equally important developmental lines that have much more to do with his patient's difficulties than does the psychosexual one, which is of primary and practical importance in a limited number of cases (see pages 38–40 and chapter 9). Second, believing that there is only one correct statement for him to make, he dares not hazard a guess. He must realize, sooner or later, that most psychotherapeutic interventions are informed guesses; seldom is one absolutely convinced about the accuracy of an interpretation.

Although there is an educational element in all psychotherapy, the therapist should not think of himself as being in a professorial role with the patient in the role of student—the former always having to be impressive and right so that the student will be convinced of his professor's superior wisdom. It is not neglecting or underestimating the therapist's expertise to say that often he and his patient find themselves in the position of two mountain climbers. Roped to each other and dependent on each other, they struggle to scale the peak. Either one can slip, and each must be able to count on the other to take those steps that will save the situation. If one loses ground, they lose ground together, then regain their footing and go forward, much closer for having been in danger and helped each other out of it.

Naturally this type of cooperation does not always come as a matter of course. Some patients insist that the therapist be an all-knowing savant. That insistence deserves to be examined rather than catered to, and in the process the patient is helped to become a partner in the task. Do not be afraid to be wrong or have a patient think you are in error. Here is where the mountain-climbing analogy, like all analogies, breaks down. Unlike a mistake in mountain climbing, one in psychotherapy is seldom—very, very seldom—fatal. On the contrary, the examination of some misunderstanding between therapist and patient can ultimately be turned to good account and can lead to unsuspected insights. If a patient must exaggerate the consequences of some error of omission or commission on the therapist's part, and cannot let him forget it in spite of what the therapist may do to acknowledge and correct it, then the patient's need to behave this way can profitably become a focus for the therapy. The patient who leaves the therapist who makes a mistake, inadvertently hurts his feelings, looks stupid, or foolish, or otherwise disappoints him, most probably cannot get along with any other therapist either. Where is the perfect therapist? The need for the perfect parent cannot be fulfilled; that need can only be studied, understood, and interpreted.

Mr. Arianes: You know, I just remembered something I hadn't thought about for a long time.

Therapist: Yes?

Mr. Arianes: It's funny. It's a smell more than anything. The smell that comes from a drunk sleeping it off. I used to tiptoe into the bedroom where my dad was and just look at him lying there passed out.

Therapist: Somebody else who couldn't talk to you or help you if you needed him at that time.

Mr. Arianes: Could be.

Therapist: Go right ahead. Let your thoughts just come out without worrying for the moment whether they make sense or not.

Mr. Arianes: [*Chuckles to himself*] He wasn't such a bad guy sometimes, the old man. When he was sober he'd let me work with him fixing things around the house. I got the feeling he liked me, even though he never talked much.

Therapist: Life isn't all black and white, is it? The drinking problem wasn't all there was to your father. He had other meanings for you too.

Mr. Arianes: I suppose he couldn't help himself; he was all right in his own way.

Therapist: I think this is very interesting and important. I'm sorry that we do have to stop now, but perhaps we could go on with this next time we meet if your thoughts go in that direction.

Mr. Arianes: I'd like to. Good-bye Doctor.

Therapist: Good-bye, Mr. Arianes.

The recollection of his rejection by his mother leads the patient to memories of longing for his father. What this might mean is not at all clear yet. The therapist's comments are meant to underscore what the patient has said and perhaps lead him to think about that relationship between sessions.

Session 4

Mr. Arianes: [*Sits down, looks cheerful and animated*] I want to tell you, Doctor, I don't know when I've felt this good. Everything is so much better now that me and my wife are really communicating. She really is interested in me if I give her a chance.

Therapist: In other words, you have learned something very important about relationships. Once you sort out the present from the past things go much better.

Mr. Arianes: Shirley is certainly a lot more understanding than my mother ever was. I can't believe I treated her so mean when all she wants is for us to get along.

Therapist: Of course your wife doesn't have an alcoholic husband, a houseful of kids to raise, and no money.

Here the therapist tries to prevent a simplistic cause-effect explanation for the patient's difficulties based on blaming his mother. There is potentially much more to be learned about Mr. Arianes's relationship to his mother. It is unlikely that he would be able to gain so much from therapy and mature so well in his relationship to his wife if the earlier mother-child transactions had always been as traumatic and frustrating as was the one incident he described.

Mr. Arianes: That's true. She had her hands full. I think I knew that for as long as I can remember. That's why I tried to be a good boy. I did an awful lot for her—watched the kids, did the dishes, went grocery shopping.

Therapist: Was your mother appreciative of your efforts?

Mr. Arianes: Oh yes, in her own way. She'd sometimes say she wouldn't know what to do without me; called me the man of the house—the way I looked after her and showed her I cared. But you know, when you're a kid you don't understand everything the way you do later. When she was crabby, like she usually was, no matter what you did she'd get mad. You should have done it sooner, or different—nothing satisfied her then. I used to think she didn't like me. [*Tears well up*] Look at me, I can still feel it hurt now just thinking about it.

These associations help the patient arrive at a more balanced picture of his relationship to his mother. You might see this as an opportunity to recover and interpret oedipal material—that is, the son replacing the father in mother's eyes. This would be a mistake. Nothing in the material indicates phallic competitiveness for the mother. It is the mother's understanding that this little boy wanted. He suffered, not because he did not possess her, but because he felt he was only a target for her moods—moods that he could not control by being good and helpful.

Therapist: Yes, exactly. That's what I meant. Old feelings and the attitudes they create are still very much in evidence in all of us.

Mr. Arianes: When will I get over that, Doc?

Therapist: In a way we never really get over our childhood experiences. They are the building blocks of everyone's personality, it's what makes you you, and me me. But as you found out, when we learn to understand the reason for our behavior we get a new control over our feelings and can stop ourselves from being self-destructive. You, for instance, based on certain early experiences, have come to expect disinterest where your emotional needs are concerned. That attitude hasn't disappeared, but knowing about it makes it possible to prevent its spoiling your relationship with your wife.

Mr. Arianes: Not only with her, Doc. I've been noticing what I do in other places too. I used to think no one ever appreciated what I was trying to do at work, I only heard them complaining. Now I can hear it when they say "thank you," or when the boss tells me the job went good. It's funny how you can have your mind made up to something and never know it, even when it gets you into trouble.

Therapist: It's a revelation when you first see it, isn't it?

Mr. Arianes demonstrates that he has achieved a new perspective on his behavior. That his knowledge is not just intellectual, superficial, or merely an attempt to please the therapist is shown by his ability to use it productively in various situations. His vitality and excitement is in response to the feeling of freedom and choice that comes with a newly found ability to order his experiences in a more flexible and productive perceptual framework than he has had available heretofore.

The therapist can now ask himself: (1) What made it possible for the patient to accomplish so much in so few sessions? (2) Should treatment be stopped at this point? (3) If therapy is to continue, what should be its goal? In order to answer these questions, the phenomenon of transference must be considered.

IV

Transference: Definition and Use

Hope, wish, and fear are names for patterns of expectation that either develop directly through experience or are taught by example. Once established, these anticipatory configurations are mobilized in response to situations that resemble, or seem to resemble, the original conditions that gave rise to the pattern. This process is called *transference*.

A pattern of expectation may change with maturation and experience, or it may remain unaltered. Since the transference process is the basis for goal-directed behavior, motivating one positively or negatively in any situation, it makes a great deal of difference whether the expectation transferred to a new situation or relationship is appropriately adapted.

The basis for all dynamic psychotherapies is Freud's discovery that the reasons for a given behavior are often not known to the actor. What he says he wants or wishes may not coincide with the goal-seeking behavior he actually displays. *Intrapsychic conflict* is a condition in which a person's avowed goal is frustrated not by environmental exigencies, but by a contradictory and unknown pattern of motivation that takes precedence in determining behavior. Operationally speaking, as Grinker (1959) has pointed out, a patient's explicit role may differ from the one implicit in his actions: what he consciously avows to be his aim may not coincide with the transferred pattern of expectation.

In the case of Mr. Arianes the investigation of the presenting complaint led to the uncovering of a transference pattern that accounted for his difficulties. The patient was distressed by the fact that his wife cared about the vicissitudes of her sister's life while disregarding his needs to be comforted, supported, and coddled a bit when he felt exhausted and drained by the responsibilities and disappointments of his workaday life. However, without realizing it, he had transferred to his wife an aspect of his childhood relationship with his mother—that is, the conviction that any appeal for her understanding would fail, leaving him disappointed and humiliated for exposing his need. His transferred negative expectation became a self-fulfilling prophecy when, instead of making his wishes known to his wife, he behaved in a short-tempered, angry, and supercilious manner toward her, as if she had already treated him unfairly and rejected him. The patient's improvement came about when he became aware of the nature and inappropriateness of the transference behavior, and recognized that he had no need to protect himself in his relationship with his wife as he had had some reason to do with his mother. In a successful treatment a patient learns to perceive himself differently; or, to say it another way, a transference pattern—an expectational set—is altered through therapy.

It would be a mistake, however, to limit the phenomenon of transference to pathology, as is often done. Transference is the basis of all meaningful relationships, including the therapeutic relationship. Mr. Arianes was helped so quickly because the self-defeating aspect of his transference was not pervasive. He did not deal with the therapist as if the latter were an enemy who had to be defended against or outwitted. In his relationship to the therapist he did not act as if he expected to be rejected and to have his needs unmet. He was friendly, receptive, cooperative, and able to learn from the therapist. In other words, he brought to the treatment an underlying capacity for a positive and an appropriate relationship, trust that the therapist would help him, and readiness to do his part of the work.

Up to this point in his treatment, the positive transference has been used to good advantage, and there has been no need to question its nature or origin. This is often not the case. A patient may from the outset involve the therapist in a negative transference: without being aware of it, he imputes to the therapist certain attitudes associated with figures from his own past and then defends himself against the expectations these unconscious phantasies engender. The upshot is that he acts as if the therapist were an enemy, and the treatment situation may become a battle from which only one participant will emerge alive. In this case the task of treatment is to help the patient to see what his assumptions are, and then to explore what fears lead him to behave so defensively (see chapter 4).

What should be the next step in Mr. Arianes' treatment? The problem that brought him to therapy seems to have been solved. He and his wife are building on his therapeutic gain and are improving what appears to be a sound marriage. Should therapy now be brought to a conclusion, or should the therapist look beyond the presenting complaint and into other aspects of the patient's personality? There is no hard and fast rule for making such a decision. The most reasonable course is to let the patient's associative material be one's guide. In any case, therapy should never be simply halted then and there because the problem under consideration seems to be solved. If treatment is to be ended, it should be done gradually, giving the patient and the therapist an opportunity to see if the patient is really ready to apply what he has learned about himself without further help. More time also gives the therapist an opportunity to assess the nature of the patient's transference to the therapist and to determine whether the patient is ready to relinquish that relationship. That is, can the patient resolve or deal in some other salutary manner with the hopes and wishes from childhood that have come to be attached to the person of the therapist in the course of their work together?

Session 5

Mr. Arianes: I don't know what to talk about today. Everything is going real good.
Therapist: Why don't you talk about that?
Mr. Arianes: I mean, I don't have any problems to tell you.
Therapist: Our job is to understand you and what you are doing. If things are going well that's great, but we can certainly learn something about you in that state too. So why don't you just go ahead as you always do here. Say what's on your mind and we'll take a look at it.
Mr. Arianes: Gee, I don't know, there's really nothing.
Therapist: Something will come up, just give it a chance.
Mr. Arianes: [*Blushing*] This is embarrassing.
Therapist: Mmhmm?
Mr. Arianes: It's about you—it really has nothing to do with me.
Therapist: That we can't tell ahead of time, can we? So go ahead.
Mr. Arianes: I don't know how you can do what you do, day after day, listening to people complain.
Therapist: Any idea why you are thinking about that today?
Mr. Arianes: You look a little tired today.

As far as the therapist can tell, he is not tired or feeling any different than usual; therefore, the patient must have his own reasons for seeing the therapist as tired.

Therapist: I think it's possible that you may be stopping yourself from telling me something, thinking to yourself that I look tired and perhaps shouldn't be bothered.
Mr. Arianes: Not that I know of.
Therapist: Let's not give up trying to figure this out just yet. It might be important. When did you first get the idea that I looked tired?
Mr. Arianes: When you came out to get me in the waiting room.
Therapist: What were you thinking about while waiting for me?
Mr. Arianes: [*Blushes again*] Oh, nothing.
Therapist: You look uncomfortable and you are blushing a bit—something's cooking. I gather that whatever it is that's on your mind, it is embarrassing for you to tell me. But for the sake of our goal bring yourself to say it anyway. So far you've done well. Let's not undermine your progress now by an evasion of your thoughts.

Here the therapist is using a "carrot and stick" technique. To encourage the patient to deal with whatever is troubling him, the therapist gives Mr. Arianes praise for the work done so far and, at the same time, predicts that the good work cannot continue if he stops being straightforward with the therapist. But the therapist's comment also has deeper, transference implications. At first, when the session begins, it seems that the patient is just uncomfortable in not having any particular difficulties to report. Many patients have this reaction and think of a psychotherapist as a "problem doctor" whose interest and concern they will lose if they are not troubled in some way. The therapist tries to help Mr. Arianes by explaining that he, the therapist, is not disturbed by the absence of problems. A therapist can work perfectly well with the patient's positive achievements; furthering the patient's understanding of himself does not require that the latter be miserable. In this way the therapist is laying the groundwork for a number of sessions in which he will test the patient's capacity to manage his life more successfully; after that, the therapist may set about bringing the treatment to an end. It turns out, however, that the patient's reluctance to speak has a different basis than the one he first announced—that is, it has something to do with the therapist himself. This indicates that the relationship between the two of them, the transference, is about to become focal for the therapy, rather than simply supplying the underlying incentive that makes therapy possible. Accordingly, the psychotherapist works to help the patient to speak as openly about these issues as he has about other life situations, and uses the heightened transference itself as leverage to effect this result. When the psychotherapist praises the patient for his work to date, the implication registers with the patient, unconsciously if not consciously, that the doctor is pleased so far, but that failure to be open will lead to his displeasure. In terms of childhood life, which is the basis for the transference, if a child does what Mother and Father want (the therapist does not at this point know whether he is dealing with a mother or a father transference, or, possibly, with a transference from some other important figure in early life), they will continue to be smiling, cheerful, and interested in the child; but if that child disobeys, they will frown, their tone of voice will change, and they will become punitive in other ways. In more abstract terms, compliance with parents' expectations brings love; disobedience brings withdrawal of love. It is this incentive, and this alone, that sustains therapy, permitting it to go forward when all the adaptive mechanisms the patient has acquired to date pull him in the opposite direction and provide ample rationalization for his evading "just this once" the fundamental demand for honesty in the treatment process.

The transference is the basis for all dynamic therapy, be it psychoanalysis or less intensive psychotherapy. The more sophisticated its management, the better the results of treatment will be. There is a pseudo problem that often prevents a student from learning how to deal effectively with transference phenomena. The fear is that, by encouraging the emergence of transference feelings, the therapist may open a Pandora's box of sexual and aggressive feelings that cannot be controlled. This fear, however, is based on a confusion between transference, a ubiquitous phenomenon, and transference neurosis, a rare variant form, iatrogenically promoted for the specific purpose of carrying out a psychoanalysis. The transference neurosis is exactly what its name says it is. It is the transfer to the person of the analyst of incestuous oedipal wishes, which had previously been dealt with by neurotic symptom formation. The fear that the psychotherapist will inadvertently precipitate a transference neurosis and put himself and the patient in an untenable therapeutic posture has led to the idea that transference in psychotherapy should be avoided if possible and, if it does manifest itself, should be minimized by avoidance or generalization. So, for example, in the present case, when the patient says he has some embarrassing thoughts that deal with the therapist, he could be told: "O.K., if it's that embarrassing, by all means let's not bother with it at this time. After all, we're here to talk about you, not me, aren't we? Why don't you tell me what's been happening in the relationship to your wife since I saw you last." Or, when the patient acknowledges that he saw the therapist as tired, the therapist could respond by saying: "Funny you should think of me as tired. I'm not tired a bit. Must be those yellow lights in the waiting room that make everything look sort of gloomy and dragged out." Neither one of these statements is necessarily wrong or antitherapeutic. There are times when the therapist for good reason decides that the treatment is better served by steering away from the transference. However, such a decision should be based on something other than the therapist's fear that he cannot manage such a relationship.

Transference neurosis is only one possible manifestation of the transference. In my experience, to develop it requires not only that the patient have a psychoneurotic character structure, which is rare, but also that he be in psychoanalysis, a situation in which both the frequency of sessions and the technique of the analyst fosters the emergence of transference neurosis. In practice, it usually takes at least a year, often much longer, of preparatory analytic work before signs of a transference neurosis appear. The danger of this reaction occurring in psychotherapy is, for practical purposes, nil. In the unlikely event that repressed infantile sexual transference material does emerge in a psychotherapy, it is still not an unmanageable crisis. An oedipal transference neurosis does not emerge full-blown; quite the contrary, its beginnings are marked by tentative moves that can be readily handled before further development takes place. In such a case the therapist should, of course, consider the advisability of psychoanalysis for his patient and should obtain appropriate consultation if he is not qualified to make that judgment himself.*

The therapist who makes warding-off comments the moment the patient expresses thoughts and feelings about the former as a person is not preventing transference complications; he is signaling that he is not competent and/or is too frightened to cope with the material that is coming to the surface. The result may be that the patient gets—and complies with—the message that he must back away from such material; the treatment then remains on a superficial level, and it does not deserve to be called dynamic psychotherapy. Or else the outcome that was feared by the therapist actually occurs: the transference feelings, prevented from gaining therapeutic expression, become mobilized in less manageable forms and are directed either toward the therapist or toward people outside the treatment situation.

The therapist's inability and/or unwillingness to deal with the transference is probably the most common reason for the failure of psychotherapy—the cause of its becoming a boring, circular, repetitive recounting of symptoms, with emphasis on placing the blame for them on external situations, past and present. The beginning therapist who thinks about transference in the narrow terms of the Oedipus complex may become fearful of being confronted by the patient's aggressive and sexual wishes in all their infantile intensity. On the other hand, if the therapist thinks of transference as the remobilization of the parent-child relationship in all its possible forms, he will likely be less perturbed. After all, there is nothing unusual or frightening about a patient's wish to be understood, comforted, stimulated, admired, preferred, or forgiven. Such wishes commonly appear in the psychotherapeutic relationship and form the focus for the transference.

Mr. Arianes: Sure, I'll tell you, Doc, but it has nothing to do with me. I was thinking about this building here.
Therapist: Yes?
Mr. Arianes: It's hard to say this, but this place is very poorly constructed.
Therapist: What's wrong with it?
Mr. Arianes: Well, it's settling poorly. The foundation was poured improperly—you can tell by how uneven the floors are.
Therapist: Oh?
Mr. Arianes: Yes, look at your desk, Doc. See how the drawers sag on one side? That's from being on an uneven floor.
Therapist: Say, you're right. I'd never noticed that before. Though I have been an-

*In terms of diagnosis Mr. Arianes has a psychoneurotic character structure. This means that he should be able to form a transference neurosis under the appropriate therapeutic circumstances. Yet, as his treatment demonstrates, this created no untoward complications in the psychotherapy. Further discussion of this diagnostic category and the choice of treatment will be found in chapters 9 and 11.

For further discussion of the management of repressed infantile sexuality in psychotherapy, see chapter 8.

noyed by the way the drawers stick. Now I know why that happens. This is very interesting, but you seemed so upset about telling me. Is this what you were so embarrassed to speak about?

Mr. Arianes: Yes, I don't want to run down what you have. You've never done that to me. . . .

Therapist: Apparently you feel I'd take your critical observation about this building as a personal insult?

Mr. Arianes: Well, it's like you got taken. They put one over on you. That foundation should never have passed inspection.

Since the therapy is taking place in a clinic that is part of a larger hospital complex, it is obvious that the therapist does not own all or even part of the building. The patient for the moment talks as if he didn't realize this fact, not because he is stupid, but because he apparently needs to see the therapist as having been taken in by the duplicity of the builder. This indicates that the patient is constructing a scenario involving the therapist in order to justify the transference of some past attitude. However, for the therapist to state the "facts" at this point—to make clear that his prestige and economic well-being are not affected at all by the office in which he finds himself working—would be to abort the development of the transference.

Therapist: Sounds like you're disappointed that I'm working in a less-than-perfect environment. As if it rubs off on me and I become defective through being associated with this place. As if there's something wrong with me now.

Mr. Arianes: I didn't want to say it, but it's like you're a loser.

Therapist: A loser?

Mr. Arianes: Somebody who doesn't get the breaks, never has any luck. You know, loses out all the time even though he's not a bad fellow and tries hard. We see a lot of those in construction. Some of them are very smart fellows. Operate the big machines, earth movers, earn lots of money but always end up messing themselves up. I guess I haven't told you that I was overseas for a year in Arabia, did I? Well, I was. They're always looking for guys to work over there. I was single then. Ma needed the money and I was looking for adventure, I suppose. They offered twelve hundred dollars a month, your plane fare, and your keep. That was a lot of dough back then, so I went over. We were enlarging a harbor so they could get the big new oil tankers in. The heat was something else there. We'd work ten hours and then back to the barracks, but nobody much palled around with you there. Whisky was cheap, and all these guys had a case of booze under their bed—just lay there all night drinking till they passed out. Losers, every one of them. One guy I did get sort of friendly with, we worked together on a rig for a couple of months. He told me he'd worked the desert for twenty years. Each time he'd start out on a tour of duty with the idea that he'd make enough to buy some little business when he got back—I forget now what kind of a shop he wanted—but each time he hit the States someone'd take him for a sucker. He never learned, he'd always blow his bundle on a pie-in-the-sky deal that some con man'd talk him into. Finally, he ended up a drunk, just like all the rest. He told me how when he gets back home the first thing he does is buy an expensive car. Not to ride around in, but so's he'll have something he can sell to tide him over between the time his money runs out and when he can sign up for overseas again. A real loser, but not a bad guy and not a dumb guy. Knew earth moving like no one else I've ever met.

As the patient talks, the therapist finds himself thinking back to earlier sessions when the patient described his father as a drunkard.

Therapist: You've mentioned that your father was an alcoholic. Did you think of him as a loser too?

Mr. Arianes: Oh, yes. Dad was a dreamer. He had his big plans. Always some big deal waiting just around the corner. They all came to nothing. Some of his ideas weren't bad either. He was trying to get into the fast-food business before McDonald's and all those chains got going big. It worked for them, but not for him.

Therapist: Did your father start to drink when his plans didn't work out?

Mr. Arianes: Mother said he sort of fell apart with the family responsibilities. You can't be dreaming when you keep getting more mouths to feed. When his plans didn't work out he just sort of laid down and quit, I guess.

Therapist: Now that you've started to count on me, I wonder if you have to see me, like your father, as a loser who can't face up to the strain of his responsibilities. It's as if you are preparing yourself for the inevitable disappointment in store for you if you let yourself depend on any man.

Mr. Arianes: I see what you mean, Doctor, but I haven't thought that, really. . . .

As the patient's associations unfold, the therapist feels that a father transference is manifesting itself, and he interprets this to the patient. In psychotherapy, where the patient is being seen at much longer intervals than in psychoanalysis, it is technically important for the psychotherapist to be more active than the analyst needs to be, and to be ready to take more chances on making interpretations. Each psychotherapy session should be thought of as an entity, posing particular problems that have to be dealt with during that session. In this particular segment of the treatment it is demonstrated to the patient that the therapist is ready and able to deal directly with transference feelings. Whether the therapist is correct in his interpretations remains to be seen. As in psychoanalysis, whether the patient agrees or disagrees with the therapist's hypotheses is not the criterion of accuracy (Freud 1937). If Mr. Arianes brings up material in the next session which deepens his insight into his relationship with his father, it will be an indication that the therapist's notion about the meaning of the present session is probably correct.

An alternative way of dealing with this hour would be to interpret the material to Mr. Arianes by explaining that on the basis of what he has experienced with his father in the past, he now thinks of men as inadequate and tending to escape responsibilities. For the time being no reference would then be made to the fact that the therapist is now the man upon whom Mr. Arianes's fears are focused. Although this would pave the way more gradually for transference interpretations, it might also register as an evasion. The patient is already disturbed by the intrusion of his uncomplimentary ideas about the therapist; so the therapist, by dealing with these ideas directly rather than generalizing them to men as a group, indicates in the only convincing way possible that there is no need for the patient to be worried or embarrassed; the therapist can handle the situation. Indirectly he shows the patient that the latter can safely vent his fears and anger on the therapist in the transference—that he can treat the therapist as weak and inadequate if some inner expectation necessitates it—precisely because the therapist is secure enough in his self-concept to deal with this content in a therapeutic fashion rather than taking it personally and being crushed by it.

Sessions 6–31

Mr. Arianes: Am I glad to be here. It's the first chance I've had to sit down all day.
Therapist: Working hard?

The therapist hears the first part of the sentence, "I'm glad to be here," as an acknowledgment of positive transference feelings. He thinks to himself that in all probability his having dealt in a straightforward manner with the patient's doubts about his capacity in the last session had the desired effect. The patient is reassured on some level that he can trust the therapist to be adequate to his needs. The therapist takes the patient's statement at face value and invites him to continue talking about his day. Not saying anything would serve no purpose and might be seen by the patient as insulting. At this point silence on the part of the therapist would interfere, not enhance, the momentum of the associations. On the other hand, the therapist's ideas about what the patient really means by his opening statement are still just speculation and do not permit interpretation in depth.

Mr. Arianes: Oh, yeah, we've really got a tough job on our hands. . . .
[*The patient goes on in considerable detail, encouraged by the therapist's occasional comments which convey genuine interest, to describe in animated fashion the particular assignment he is fulfilling for his company. After twenty minutes or so the patient catches himself and is a little embarrassed by his own excitement in telling his story.*]

Mr. Arianes: Boy, I've been talking a blue streak, haven't I? You must be bored by all this, Doc.

Therapist: Not a bit. I find what you say interesting in itself, but, more important, it's your life you're describing, and that's what we need to know about. Hearing of your job in some detail makes me feel that I know you better.

Mr. Arianes: I guess I'm not used to having someone really hear me out. I mean, I've got friends and all that, but when you talk to them you can just see they're waiting for you to finish so's they can go you one better. But I suppose it doesn't matter whether they listen or not. It doesn't change things.

Therapist: I think you know that's not true. It makes a great deal of difference when someone who is important to you attests to the fact that you, too, are important to him or her by listening to what you have to say.

Mr. Arianes: That shows you that you haven't gone off the deep end with your ideas, sort of.

Therapist: Right. It validates you, gives your ideas credibility that they don't have when they are just in your head. Also, in explaining yourself to someone else, very often you end up seeing yourself differently, too. When you bounce ideas off another person you hear them in a new way yourself.

Mr. Arianes: Yeah. When I was talking to you about my plans today I ended up feeling pretty good about myself. I think I've got a good idea for that project, even better than I thought it was.

Therapist: You know, I think it must have been very frustrating for you in Arabia, among all those men and yet all alone because each one of them was so withdrawn into his own world.

Mr. Arianes: I didn't think of it that way, but it makes sense. I know I didn't go back there after my contract was up, even though the money was good and the work was O.K. Somehow I couldn't take it any more.

Therapist: Could it be that it was that way with your father, too? Your wanting to talk to him but finding him troubled and withdrawn into himself and his alcoholic stupors?

Mr. Arianes: I told you how I used to go to his room and just look at him. Sometimes I'd call to him, "Dad, Dad," but he was out of it. He'd be pretty nice to me sometimes, after he sobered up. He'd lift me up and make me promises that he'd take me to the zoo, or that we'd go down to the river and fish, just him and me together, but when the time came he never quite made it. I don't think he was lying when he promised. He meant it then, I suppose, but he was weak and always ran away, even from the promises he made a little kid.

Therapist: I think that's why last time you became afraid I was tired and thought of me as a loser. Talking to me as you have been reawakened the feelings you had as a child for your father and with it the same expectation of disappointment—sooner or later I had to fail you, too, as your father had done. You had to picture me as a loser, someone who would become so preoccupied with his own failure that he wouldn't have time to be concerned about you.

Mr. Arianes: Why would I do that though, Doc? If I wanted it so much, wouldn't I be happy that you were helping me and listening?

Therapist: I think you are that, but I wouldn't be surprised if there was a voice in the background saying, "Don't count on it to last, prepare yourself for the inevitable letdown. Didn't your father also promise you that things would be better? Do you want to get hurt again like you were when you were a little boy and believed that maybe everything would be all right?"

Mr. Arianes: I do tend to get suspicious when things are going too well. You think it comes from that?

Therapist: We think we leave childhood behind us, but how we look at the world when we are adults is very much tied to the way the world looked to us then.

The original complaint is no longer the subject of the sessions, and the relationship to the therapist has become focal. This is a hallmark of dynamic psychotherapy. Although the tension the patient experienced with his wife, which through attendant somatic symptoms brought him to treatment, seems to have been resolved, Mr. Arianes makes no mention of ending the therapy. Instead, he mobilizes patterns of expectation in the session that open up for examination areas of his personality which were not previously evident. Specifically he manifests a wish to have the therapist be a father surrogate who has the time and the interest to listen and who does not withdraw because he is overburdened by his own failures and problems.

Just as the patient derived benefit from his relationship with his wife once he could recognize that, given a chance, she would respond differently from the way his mother had responded, so it works out with the therapist. Although the therapist relates the present situation to the patient's past whenever such interpretation is possible, the therapist also encourages the patient to make full use of the therapeutic relationship in satisfying his need to have a more successful transaction than he was able to have with his father. In a very real sense the therapist gives the patient an opportunity to fulfill a childhood wish. Many students become uncomfortable when this happens because they have heard that unconscious wishes are to be interpreted and not indulged. As a result they tend to interpret to the patient that his wishes for a relationship with the therapist in the here and now are *only* infantile wishes in adult clothing. This reinforces the shame many patients have about their dependent longings and prevents those longings from being relived in therapy.

When one is dealing with repressed infantile incestuous wishes, it is indeed important to limit oneself to interpretation and as much as possible to avoid symbolic gratification of such wishes. There are two compelling reasons for this. First, gratification interferes with the recovery of repressed material; only frustration, "abstinence" as Freud (1915a) called it, provides the atmosphere in which such content can be raised to consciousness in verbal form. Second, incestuous wishes cannot be directly gratified even in derivative form; they belong to childhood and to phantasy. They must be interpreted, recognized for what they are, and given up by the patient. The void that this leaves needs to be dealt with by the reapportionment of interest toward attainable and meaningful adult goals. However, usually the therapist is dealing not with repressed infantile sexual wishes but with longings that have as much a place in adult life as in childhood. These are precluded from adult gratification because they have not been correctly formulated by the patient, due either to his developmental arrest or to a perceptual set that creates so much anxiety around the issue that the patient disavows it whenever it is broached. Once the therapist helps the patient correct this defect there will be a period when the heretofore unrealized potential for growth manifests itself in the context of the transference. In this case the patient's wish for fulfillment in the transference is not a resistance to facing his childhood situation; here fulfillment and insight go hand in hand.

The third question (page 34) can now be answered. This treatment can have a goal that goes beyond relieving the original complaint. Mr. Arianes shows every indication of being able, interested, and in need of exploring with the therapist the formation of the perceptual sets that he brings to his adult relationships. He seems able to gain this understanding without becoming involved with an examination of the even deeper unconscious infantile wishes that formed the backdrop for his characterological development.

In the next twenty-five sessions, which will not be detailed here, the patient quite spontaneously looked at his childhood with different eyes. He usually began the session by reviewing the week's events and then would proudly recount some new insight into his behavior or present some evidence for his increasing self-control and heightened self-respect in tension-producing circumstances. Then telling about some event in his daily life or about a nighttime dream would, with the therapist's assistance, lead him to reminisce about his early experiences. What emerged was the picture of a family whose members were deeply committed to one another in spite of all the quarreling around the father's alcoholism. Though the family's fortunes steadily declined in the face of the father's incapacity, there was never any question that the father was the head of the household, and that the family would remain intact. In the context of the history as it emerged, the patient's having been called "the man of the house" seemed to have been more the result of his mother's desperation than of her rejection of his father and, by implication, the patient's oedipal victory. Pardoxically, the mother's complaining always carried an undertone of affection and respect for what her husband was and might have been. The puzzling thing for the little boy was the contradiction between his mother's oft-voiced assertion that her life had been better before children came and the arrival of a new infant every two years.

The patient dealt with these displacements by emphasizing his role as the oldest child and taking quite a bit of responsibility for his brothers' and sisters' behavior; this action, as he mentioned, found favor in his mother's eyes and led her to reward him with praise. In retrospect he felt cheated by all the household and baby-tending chores he assumed as a child. As he had said earlier, and emphasized in these sessions, children were an unwanted burden to his mother and, he felt, his brothers and sisters had robbed him of much of his childhood. He was not going to give up his pleasures to parenthood now.

One can legitimately speculate, on the basis of what psychoanlysis has uncovered about the phenomenon of sibling rivalry, that what the patient resented on a deeper level was his father's sexual dominion over his mother. He attempted to compete by being his mother's helper, responsible where his father was not, but even though he received appropriate rewards for his efforts in the form of praise and appreciation, he did not—fortunately for him—dethrone his father, as evidenced by the arrival of the next baby. His conscious resentment of the burden that children represent may well reflect a deeper resentment at suffering an oedipal defeat.

These formulations are, however, only speculative, and it would have been meaningless to involve the patient in them. What is of practical importance here is that there seemed to be no active conflict around the oedipal issue. Mr. Arianes had adapted to his sibling rivalry by not having children, thus keeping the woman, his wife, all for himself. At his work he remained in the position of foreman, the oldest son, the best foreman the two bosses had. Even though these issues were not dealt with directly, they were affected by the work the patient did at other levels. Mr. Arianes successfully used treatment to correct a deficit in his development. He used therapy as an opportunity to examine himself in a way he never had had a chance to do as a child. He had grown up hungry for direct parental help, but his family had neither time nor interest for it. His father had been unable to carry out his promises to spend time alone with the boy and to give him the opportunity to reflect on life with his admired parent. His mother had been too burdened to saddle herself with her son's personal problems; rather than being taken care of by her, he had done what he could to ease her load. In treatment Mr. Arianes had the chance to work with someone he respected, the possibility of examining himself and his hopes and experiences with an attentive man who was not preoccupied with his own difficulties. Mr. Arianes made up for lost time and used the therapy to establish and utilize a positive parental transference. This shifted the balance of his personality. It permitted a better relationship with his wife and coworkers. His satisfaction with life increased. As will be seen, the closing hours of the therapy found his fundmental perception of himself undergoing a change.

Session 32

Mr. Arianes: [*Patient has come twenty minutes late, which has not happened before*] Sorry I'm late. We're really busy now it's starting to get warm again, so I couldn't leave early like I usually do to get here on time. [*Pause*] There didn't seem much to say the last few times and today isn't any different.

Therapist: Actually you've not been at a loss for what to say. I think what you mean is that you're no longer coming here to get answers. Now you find them yourself and let me know what you have done without depending on me as much as you used to do in the beginning.

Mr. Arianes: Things are going pretty good now. . . . [*Long pause*]

Therapist: Yes?

Mr. Arianes: I was wondering how much longer I have to come. . . .

Therapist: At this point you are able to think through problems effectively, to do for yourself what you previously needed me to do with you, so it's not a question of your *having* to come here, but of whether you have reasonably done all you can do to help yourself through psychotherapy. It comes down to whether you are satisfied with your achievements here.

The therapist resists the patient's unconscious attempt to make the therapist responsible for the decision to end treatment. The patient has to face the termination of psychotherapy as an active step he is taking. From one point of view, termination is not an end but the beginning of a new phase that the patient has helped to bring about and must now implement. In the process of dealing with this aspect of therapy, the therapist reinforces the patient's self-esteem and supports the idea that he can promote his own well-being and exercise control over his fate.

Mr. Arianes: Well, the way I see it, things are about the way I'd want them to be and, what with work being so busy now, maybe I could stop coming now.

Therapist: I think your decision is basically a reasonable one. But like every conclusion we've come to in therapy, let's give it a chance to see if it holds up under scrutiny. When were you thinking of stopping?

Mr. Arianes: I was thinking that if I don't have much to say maybe today could be it.

Therapist: That doesn't strike me as such a good idea. I believe we should have time to talk about your decision and to see if, having made it, it generates associations that we could profitably examine together.

Mr. Arianes: How much longer should I come then?

Therapist: I'm not sure. Why don't we see what happens before setting a definite date? I am thinking in terms of two, three, or four more sessions.

Mr. Arianes: That'll be O.K., but we're getting awfully busy.

This kind of interchange can be quite painful for a therapist. It sounds as if the patient, in whom a lot of time and interest has been invested, is prepared to relinquish treatment as if it were only a luxury that could be dispensed with once it could no longer be scheduled conveniently.

However, Mr. Arianes has always been polite, appreciative, even deferential, and it is unlikely that he has become contemptuous of the therapy or of the theapist now that he feels he has derived sufficient benefit from the sessions. What often happens is that a patient becomes uncomfortable with thoughts of termination because (1) he feels the therapist will resent his wish to become independent and (2) he experiences resistance to facing what the prospect of separation from the therapist stirs up within him. The therapist should not take at face value the often inconsiderate things a patient says under such circumstances, any more than he would other statements a patient makes. Instead, the therapist should recognize the possible legitimacy of the patient's wish and encourage him to work through its significance.

Session 33

Mr. Arianes: So, what do we do now?

Therapist: We continue as we always have by your saying what's on your mind and the two of us looking at that.

Mr. Arianes: [*Smiling to himself*] Life is funny. Remember how in the beginning I used to get all upset about my wife's sister's kids?

Therapist: Yes.

Mr. Arianes: You know I was in the garden yesterday, getting things ready, cleaning up, and darned if my nephew Bobby—he's the six-year-old—didn't follow me around like a shadow. I said, "Bobby, you don't have to hang around here. Why don't you play with your pal Jimmy next door?" He just shook his head and stuck with me till dinner time.

Therapist: How'd you feel?

Mr. Arianes: That's what surprised me. I didn't mind. He wasn't in the way and I guess he's sort of cute now. More like a person and not such a baby like when they're little.

Therapist: Do you know if Bobby sees his father much since the divorce?

Mr. Arianes: Not much. The guy sort of bugged out. It's all she can do to get the support money out of him.

Therapist: Looks like Bobby is turning to you now that he needs a man to copy and model himself after.

Mr. Arianes: I was figuring that, too, but it makes me uncomfortable.

Therapist: How so?

Mr. Arianes: I'm not exactly sure how to handle it. After all, I'm not his father.

Therapist: Can you describe a specific situation for me in which you became uncomfortable with Bobby?

Mr. Arianes: Well, like I said, the kid had been following me around for a couple of hours and then we went inside to wash up. I thought he'd go in the TV room with the others, but when I sat down at the kitchen table to drink some coffee and look at the paper, he was right there. [*Pause*] And he leaned up against me, you know, sort of rubbed up against me.

Therapist: Was it the body contact that made you uncomfortable?

Mr. Arianes: Yeah, I mean is there something wrong with the kid? I don't want him to be one of those homosexuals, you know. It worries me.

Therapist: Good God, no. He probably just wanted to sit on your lap or have you rub his hair a little. Didn't you feel the urge to put your arms around this cute little guy who obviously thinks you are the most wonderful man in the world?

Mr. Arianes: [*With a relieved laugh*] I guess so, but I don't want him turning queer or nothing.

Therapist: The possibility of Bobby's becoming a homosexual is much greater if he continues to be deprived of reasonable affection, including physical affection, from a male. I think that Bobby is experiencing the same thing that you did when you stood at the doorway of the bedroom and looked longingly at your father.

Mr. Arianes: That makes sense.

Therapist: I think Bobby knows intuitively that you have the makings of a very good father or, in this case, uncle. He trusts you.

Mr. Arianes: What do you think I should do now?

Therapist: There's no set way of behaving in a situation like this. But you are a sensitive person, and I think we ought to trust your intuition to guide you properly. Do what you think is right with and for Bobby. Maybe talk it over with your wife, see what her point of view is. Above all, have some fun with the boy. Don't be afraid to enjoy him—a child's love is a unique and wonderful experience.

Mr. Arianes: I was going to tell you that maybe next time would be my last visit for a while, but now I'm not so sure. It looks like we found something else to talk about, doesn't it?

Therapist: As I said, let's play it by ear. Exactly when we should stop will become clear, I'm sure. Let's just see how it goes.

As the patient is undergoing separation from the therapist, in a sense preparing himself to give up his father—that is, to relinquish the father transference gratifications of the therapy—he finds himself identifying with the therapist. It is no accident, in my opinion, that his nephew is now coming to him. There is a readiness in this man to turn from needing a father to becoming a father. The concerns of the present session should not be interpreted as indicating that the patient is not ready for termination; on the contrary, it is not unusual in the closing phase of a successful treatment for a patient to dare to expand his horizons and to invest the interest that has been focused on the problematic aspects of his development in new ventures that will further his development.

This is not necessarily a smooth unfolding, any more than was true for other phases of therapy. The therapist's active intervention is required to help the patient bring into focus what needs to be worked on.

In this case the turning point of the session was the therapist's insistence that the patient become specific about what was troubling him rather than keep the discussion of fatherhood on an abstract level—that is, by comparing the patient's need for a father with Bobby's similar need. The fact that termination of therapy is in the offing is no reason to be more content with generalizations than one would be in the beginning or the middle phases of treatment.

The therapist's direct advice to the patient regarding his relationship to his nephew has several levels of significance. It shows the patient that the therapist is not ashamed of his own "homosexual" feelings—that is, his affectionate, as opposed to homoerotic or homogenital, feelings. By advising Mr. Arianes directly, he gives credence to the patient's identification with him in the role of therapist. Mr. Arianes will give up the therapist as a father, but he will carry with him the implicit knowledge that he, too, can now do what the therapist does: he can further the development of others. The fear of interfering with a patient's spontaneity both in and away from sessions can make a therapist afraid to give advice. However, there is no blanket dictum that you may not guide or advise a patient when you think it is indicated. The important thing is to know why you are giving advice, and what the significance of the intervention is likely to be for the patient at that particular point in his treatment.

As a matter of course the question of termination has fallen into place; the patient is realistic about it, and his feelings are appropriate without the belligerence that accompanied his first introduction of the issue.

Session 34

Mr. Arianes: I think everything is going O.K. again. I got things straightened out with the kid. We're having a good time. I promised to take him to a game next

Sunday. You never saw a boy so excited. My wife and her sister are very happy about Bobby taking to me that way. My wife still can't believe it. She thinks I'm going to get mad at the kid any minute. I explained to her how he needs a father or somebody like that to use as a model and that I wouldn't disappoint him, me knowing what it's like to be disappointed that way. She said she's proud of me, but I told her I was having fun, too, and wasn't just doing it to be a good guy.

Therapist: It sounds very nice. Pretty soon the other kids are going to be after you, too, I think.

Mr. Arianes: Well, he'll have to learn how to share. I guess I can explain to him what it's like to be the oldest. You might say I'm the expert at that.

Therapist: With you to help him I think Bobby will have a better time of it than you had.

Mr. Arianes: I hope so. If I could make it better for him, then what I had to go through wouldn't be wasted, would it?

Therapist: Not only that, it also makes the past easier for you when you use it productively instead of letting it eat away at you.

Mr. Arianes: I do that now, or at least I try to. But I've been thinking that it's easy to get tripped up. I could have messed it up with Bobby if I hadn't talked it over with you. I want to stop now—as far as I can tell I really am ready to go on by myself—but how do I know that things won't come up that I need to talk over?

Therapist: What would you like to do?

Mr. Arianes: Could I come back to see you if I needed to?

Therapist: Of course, I'd be happy to see you again. We could handle that in one of two ways. If you want, we could make an appointment now to get together in a month or two, or we could leave it up to you to call whenever you feel the need to talk to me.

Mr. Arianes: Right now I'd just as soon not tie myself down to a specific time. I'd like to call you if I feel something is coming up that needs to be looked at.

Therapist: Fine with me. In any case, even if there aren't any problems, I'd still be interested to hear how things are going with you.

Mr. Arianes: Well, I guess I'll be going then. I appreciate what you've done, Doc. I feel a lot better about everything, not just my stomach, I mean.

Therapist: Good, I'm glad to have been of help. You certainly did your part and it was a pleasure working with you.

Mr. Arianes and Therapist: [*Shaking hands*] Good-bye.

Mr. Arianes: Thanks again.

Therapist: Good luck to you, Mr. Arianes.

The therapist has mixed feelings about the way in which termination came about. Although there is a temptation to prolong the therapy so as to help the patient deal with the new-found maturity he exhibits in his relationships, and to explore the meaning of this development, the therapist deems it best to let Mr. Arianes go with the expectation that the groundwork laid in treatment will now enable him to progress independently. Like many patients, Mr. Arianes evades working through the sadness that comes with leaving therapy. What makes parting painful is not so much losing contact with the therapist per se as it is relinquishing hope for the fulfillment of unconscious phantasies that attach to the therapist. Instead of confronting the disappointment of the wish to have the therapist for a father who could undo the past, Mr. Arianes deals with his longing by doing for his nephew what he wanted his own father, and now wants the therapist, to do for him. Also, it may well be that in this particular case termination has mobilized the patient's feelings about his father's death, but that he is not ready to deal with them and thus chooses to end his treatment speedily. In any case, the patient's father transference is unresolved—a situation that the therapist and the patient manage by agreeing to meet again when and if the latter wants to do so.

That the passive transference wish has been turned into active identification is, however, significant and attests to the success of the treatment. Mr. Arianes no longer sees himself as overburdened and beleaguered by life and its responsibilities, but finds himself in a state of narcissistic surplus where giving is equated not with drain but with gain. The insistence that if therapy is to be considered successful, the bond between the therapist and the patient must necessarily be completely dissolved through interpretation at termination interferes with the therapist's freedom to let the patient use the relationship in a manner best suited to him.

In any case there is no way one can ever do a "complete" job in either psychotherapy or psychoanalysis. It is impossible to anticipate everything the patient may encounter in the future and to prepare him for it. All that therapy can do is to help the patient understand himself sufficiently so that when he is faced with the inevitable stresses of life, he does not simply repeat old defensive patterns but, instead, exercises choice in his response based on the present and past significance of the situation at hand.

V

Management and Transformation of a Negative Transference

There are many patients whose difficulties are not as clear-cut as were those of Mr. Arianes. The following interview illustrates a not uncommon situation in which the patient presents himself in such a way that the evaluation becomes a challenge for the therapist both intellectually and emotionally.

Session 1

Miss Lena Banks, a twenty-seven-year-old graduate student in social psychology, has had psychotherapy in another city and applied for further treatment when she transferred to the university.

Therapist: What brings you to the clinic, Miss Banks?

Miss Banks: [*Officiously*] I have been in therapy for three years. I have an unresolved Oedipus complex. My previous therapist and I came to the conclusion that my father much preferred me to my mother. My mother was always depressed. I, on the other hand, was the entertaining and intelligent companion he had always wanted. You can imagine the superego guilt that I built up. As a result I have not been able to form lasting and meaningful heterosexual relationships. In spite of the fact that I understand what's wrong with me, I still can't seem to find anybody who meets my standards and could be a suitable partner for me. It must mean that I need to analyze out something even deeper, so here I am. Frankly I don't know if you can help me. You look very young—and, besides that, I might need a female therapist now.

As opposed to the patient in the preceding discussion, Miss Banks does not approach the therapist as an authority to whom to appeal for help. She is outspoken, makes the professional jargon her own, doubts the ability and suitability of the doctor, and asserts that she knows what is wrong with her. Her manner is calculated to challenge any therapist, especially a beginner, who may well be made anxious by the prospect of having to deal with such a seemingly sophisticated patient—that is, by one who can compare him with other therapists and catch all his mistakes.

The therapist, both hurt and anxious at having his ability questioned, can respond in various ways.

1. He can take the patient's doubts at face value:

Therapist: [*Coldly, with ill-concealed anger*] Since you feel that way, maybe you'd better apply for a therapist more to your liking. There doesn't seem to be any point in continuing with me.
Miss Banks: I don't see why you are so angry. I have a right to express my feelings here. You are supposed to be a psychotherapist, aren't you?
Therapist: [*Now guilty in addition to being angry*] I am not angry. You have made it clear that I am not the person to treat you, and I am going along with what you've said.
Miss Banks: I didn't say anything like that.
Therapist: Yes, you did.
Miss Banks: Well, I guess I better go then.
Therapist: I'll return your chart to the admissions department, and you can talk to them about reassignment.
Miss Banks: [*Looking both angry and tearful, gets up to leave*]
Therapist: Good-bye.
Miss Banks: [*Stalks out of room and slams door behind her*]

2. The therapist can respond in kind to the challenge to his competence:

Therapist: What do you mean you have an "unresolved Oedipus complex"?
Miss Banks: Don't you know?
Therapist: Yes, but I want to know if you know.
Miss Banks: My analyst explained all that to me, and I don't feel I want to start all over with this again.
Therapist: How many times were you being seen in your previous treatment?
Miss Banks: Once, sometimes twice a week.
Therapist: [*Triumphantly*] That's not psychoanalysis!
Miss Banks: [*Angry, hurt*] I don't care what you call it, it helped me a lot.

The therapist's attempt to deal with his anger at his patient's depreciation of him, by discrediting her in turn, has succeeded only too well. The two are now facing each other as antagonists, a position not particularly conducive to their becoming better acquainted either with each other or with the patient's complaint.

3. He can ignore his feelings and focus on the patient's wish for a more experienced and/or a female therapist:

Therapist: Why do you believe you need a woman therapist?
Miss Banks: Men can't really understand what a woman is all about. In our society men have a prejudiced attitude toward us, they see us as inferior and imagine that we see ourselves that way too. That's what all that talk about penis envy adds up to. I don't want to be a man, and I don't want to have to feel that all my problems stem from not being one.
Therapist: I haven't prejudged your problem that way at all.
Miss Banks: Maybe not consciously, but those feelings are unconscious ones. How many cases like mine have you treated, so that I can be sure you are able to handle me properly?

Although the therapist does not respond with anger to the patient's attack on him, he implicitly defers to her view of their relationship. He is now in the position of having to justify himself to her. A pattern is being set whereby she will keep questioning his competence; and, given the level of her anxiety, it is likely that no matter what he says he will be able neither to satisfy nor to reassure her. She will continue to externalize her difficulties and avoid facing what ever may be the underlying problems that brought her to see him.

4. The therapist can note that he feels angry, anxious, and depreciated and can confront the patient directly:

Therapist: You seem to be belittling me and my competence.
Miss Banks: No I'm not.

or:

Miss Banks: I'm sorry, I didn't mean to do so.

or:

Miss Banks: If you feel that way, it's your problem. Maybe you need treatment more than I do.

It is sometimes therapeutically desirable to confront a patient with the effect he or she has on the therapist. Here, however, such an approach serves no purpose but to keep the focus on the problem Miss Banks thinks she has with the therapist rather than on her real difficulties.

5. The therapist, though hurt, can say to himself: Maybe I'm not the therapist for her, perhaps she's right about that, but if she had her wish and were seeing an experienced woman therapist, which of her complaints would still be left? It would be that she doesn't have good relationships with men.

Further thought: If she treats other men the way she treats me, who would want to be with her? Who could tolerate her kind of attack on his self-esteem day after day?

At this point the therapist feels his anger disappear to be replaced by the beginning of some understanding and the formulation of a provisional hypothesis. Maybe the patient's attack on him is not personal, has nothing to do with him per se; if he were a different, more experienced therapist, the patient would probably have found another way to hurt and anger him. In her daily life, too, perhaps this patient antagonizes men who might be interested in her, but is unaware of what she is actually doing and rationalizes her poor relations with men as being the result of her superiority.

Right or wrong, the therapist has managed to raise himself above his emotions without ignoring them and has formulated a testable hypothesis.

Therapist: [*Ignoring the provocation*] You say you can't find a suitable partner. Are there any men in your life now?

Miss Banks: Well, there's a guy in one of my seminars. We often have coffee together after the class.

Therapist: Do you see him at other times, too?

Miss Banks: No. I think his conversation tends to be quite limited, it's always about work and his theories.

Therapist: You mean you don't go out on dates because he's so wrapped up in his work?

Miss Banks: He's living with a lab assistant from the biology department, she's a couple of years older than he is. Probably he has a mother fixation.

Therapist: Any other men in your life now?

Miss Banks: No. . . .

Therapist: What do you do with your free time, weekends, and so on?

Miss Banks: Oh, I don't know. Go home mostly, I guess. That's one reason I transferred to the university. It's only an hour or so away from my parents.

Therapist: And before you transferred, what was your social life like?

Miss Banks: For a while I dated Bill. The mistake I made was living with him, I think. After two months of that we broke up and never seemed to get back together again.

Therapist: Can you tell me about that relationship?

Miss Banks: Well, we got together after he broke up with a classmate of mine. We'd sort of see each other in the cafeteria. Neither one of us had anyone to sit with, so we started eating together. We'd walk to class and talk between periods, we seemed to get along all right. One night we both worked late and, you know how things go, he ended up spending the night at my place, that's all.

Therapist: You describe it as if you and Bill came together by default. I mean you didn't "date" in the usual sense. Go places together.

Miss Banks: I wanted to, but he didn't want to go where I wanted to go, and he wouldn't dress right or treat me thoughtfully. We just ended up fighting about it all the time. . . .

Therapist: Yes, what happened?

Miss Banks: He started staying away nights. Drinking beer with his friends. At least that's what he said he was doing. Eventually we just drifted apart, and he didn't come around any more.

Therapist: Before Bill, did you have boy friends in high school or college?

Miss Banks: I didn't date in high school much. Once in a while I'd get fixed up, but it never worked out.

Therapist: And in college?

Miss Banks: Not really. I guess I was always too bright for the men around me. I've always been a high achiever and men resent that. They want someone who isn't going to compete with them, who caters to them and makes them feel that they're wonderful.
Therapist: Well, it's getting close to time to stop for today. If you wish, I can see you again next week at this time.
Miss Banks: But you haven't said anything yet. How do I know you can help me? Do you think a woman might be able to understand me better?
Therapist: At this point I don't know enough about you to offer an opinion on either one of your questions. As I said, we can talk further. Whether we do will have to be your decision.
Miss Banks: I guess I will come back. No sense in being put on the admission office list again and waiting to be assigned, unless this won't work out.
Therapist: [*Standing up*] All right, I'll see you then. We'll consider this to be our regular appointment time if that fits your schedule.
Miss Banks: [*Leaving*]
Therapist: Good-bye.
Miss Banks: [*Leaves without answering*]

The therapist wisely does not try to bring the interview to a more satisfying closure. He does not know whether Miss Banks will be suitable for insight therapy; her problem is not particularly clear to him. It is nevertheless a productive interview because the therapist does not permit himself to be placed in an untenable position by the patient's antagonistic attitude. He is able to formulate for himself a way of looking at her behavior which leaves him free to pursue the appropriate goal of the initial interview—that is becoming acquainted with his potential patient. Tacitly he conveys to her that he can deal with her aggression in a therapeutic manner, and so makes it possible for her to return for further work.

Session 2

At the appointed time the therapist comes into the waiting room. Lena Banks, who does not see him, is slumped in a chair with an anxious look on her face; she is twisting a handkerchief nervously in her hands. She spots the doctor and gets up, her face tight and angry.

Miss Banks: [*Sarcastically*] Well, I'm here! Surprised?
Therapist: Come in please.
[*Both are seated in the office*]
Miss Banks: I'm not at all sure that I'm going on with this. I still have the same doubts that I had last time. Some of my friends with whom I discussed our session have encouraged me to give you a chance, so I came.
Therapist: O.K., here you are. Let's go on then.

Miss Banks: My former therapist always had me review my thoughts about the previous sessions for him. Is that what you want me to do?

Therapist: If that's what's on your mind, go right ahead with it.

Miss Banks: Look, I asked you a question and you answer me with that "say what's on your mind" crap! That approach won't work with me. I've read all the books, too, you know!

Therapist: Then you also know that, cliché or not, what you're thinking about is what I need to hear. We've only met once before, and I have no way of knowing what might be important for you at this time that would enable me to make productive suggestions about the focus of our interview. Maybe last week's session is indeed what you want to and should talk about, but then again thoughts of the future or events in your daily life might be occupying you and, if so, that's what we ought to be listening to.

Miss Banks: I didn't mean to argue so much. I know what you say is true, but it's just that my other therapist always seemed to know what to do to get me started.

Therapist: It must be difficult to start with someone new.

Miss Banks: Dr. Ralph understood me so well. . . .

Therapist: And now you have to make yourself understood all over again.

Miss Banks: There's no help for it, I guess.

The patient's tone and attitude have changed dramatically. She now sounds sad and resigned. It is not so much what the therapist has said as it is his ability to remain thoughtful and reasonable in the face of her challenging and depreciating manner that seems to have reassured her sufficiently to enable her to come forward with what is really troubling her at the moment—the loss of her former therapist. A significant indicator of her readiness to engage in therapy is her volunteering the man's name.

When a patient refers to people in his life by name, especially if he has not done so previously, he is making the therapist part of his reality instead of just telling about it. Psychotherapy is not a spectator sport with the patient sitting on the sidelines talking about what goes on in his real life on the field. Psychotherapy and the psychotherapist are very much a part of that life and should be seen as such. Stilted, formal, affected, vague, or indirect language—as opposed to an informative, conversational style—shows a need to keep the therapist at arm's length, and it vitiates the unique intimacy of the therapeutic situation. I have had patients who talked about their various and anonymous girl friends in this fashion: "Remember I told you about that girl I met at the party last Sunday? Not the one I picked up at the concert, though, who turned out to be a friend of that guy who I met through that other girl I told you about who I dated in high school." And the patient expects me to know and follow what he is saying. Another patient tells me he got "a very substantial raise" without mentioning a figure; someone else bought a new car but says nothing about what make or model it is; and so forth. When I call such noninformative statements to a patient's attention, sometimes he is genuinely surprised, and it turns out that he has an unspoken assumption or a demand that somehow I would know what was happening in his life even though I was not a witness to the events. Another patient feels that he has an obligation to protect his friends' and family's reputation from my voyeuristic propensities by keeping identities concealed, especially if I know the individuals involved. Still another patient feels that mention of finances will make me jealous and angry, perhaps lead me to take advantage of him by immediately increasing my fee. Usually behind a patient's concealment or distortion of information, however he may rationalize these processes, is a fear of acknowledging the need for the therapist—a need he, consciously or unconsciously, anticipates will be disappointed. For this reason a patient's avoidances, evasions, and circumlocutions should sooner or later be confronted in an insight-oriented therapy unless, as in Miss Banks's case, the problem resolves itself spontaneously as the patient is drawn into the transference relationship.

The therapist recognizes the change in Miss Banks not just from the words she speaks or from her tone, but also from the relaxation of his muscles as he listens to her. He realizes that from the time he found her in the waiting room, his body has been tense as in anticipation of an attack. Indeed, he now understands why he slept poorly the night before. The expectation of being subjected to this patient's scorn had apparently made him very uncomfortable. Psychotherapy is not a spectator sport for the therapist either!

The patient's declaration that she does not mean to argue acknowledges that she can, potentially at least, trust the new therapist and make him the object of her emotional needs. This is an important prognostic sign. The emotional fluidity or flexibility that Miss Banks demonstrates is a sign of inner strength. The person who has to cling rigidly to one emotional attitude or position and twists all experiences to fit it is much more difficult to treat; indeed, such a person may not be amenable to insight therapy at all.

Therapist: You mentioned that you were in therapy for three years—all that time with Dr. Ralph?

Miss Banks: Yes.

Therapist: How and on what basis was the decision made to end or interrupt the treatment?

Miss Banks: I transferred to the university here, I told you that.

Therapist: Right. But how did Dr. Ralph and you come to the conclusion that it made sense for you to stop psychotherapy and leave the city, rather than staying on and working further?

Miss Banks: I wasn't going to him any more when I decided to move closer to home.

Therapist: Oh?

Miss Banks: [*Bitterly*] He left his job at the clinic and went into private practice. . . . [*Pause*]

Therapist: You didn't go with him, I gather.

Miss Banks: [*Her former sarcasm and anger replacing the softness that had come into her voice*] You "gather" correctly, Doctor. I couldn't come up with the cash, so "good-bye and no hard feelings"—that's the way you guys operate, isn't it?

Therapist: From what you've said he doesn't sound like that kind of a person at all. Can you tell me what happened?

Miss Banks: [*With tears running down her face, she gets up so suddenly that the chair overturns; she screams*] I'm sick and tired of this. I didn't come here to get upset. You've made me feel worse than when I came in. Goddamn all of you! You always stick up for each other, don't you?! Well, I don't have to take it and I'm not going to! [*Strides across the room to the door*]

Therapist: [*Startled*] Say, let's talk . . .

[*Door slams behind the patient; the therapist notes that she has left her sunglasses on the side table.*]

It seems likely that Miss Banks's outburst is the result of the therapist's inquiry into the events attending the termination of her previous treatment, including her emotional reaction to leaving Dr. Ralph. Her upset testifies to the strength of her feelings, further investigation of which was prevented by her precipitate exit from the office. The therapist now faces the practical problem of how to react to her behavior.

Should he attempt to reach her by telephone? And say what? Offer her another, extra appointment to talk it over? Is she so upset that she might suicide? If he can not reach her by phone, should he send the police to her home? Should he get in his car and go to her home himself to evaluate the situation? Or should he consider her running out of the office as a nonverbal message that needs to be deciphered when she comes next week for her scheduled appointment?

From what is known of the patient it seems improbable that she will turn on herself and suicide in despair; she has shown that she has no difficulty in relieving herself temporarily by blaming others for her unhappiness. If she tries to punish anyone it will probably be the therapist rather than herself. Last time she complained to friends about him; quite likely she will do so again.

There is a tendency to label as "borderline" a patient with poor control over his emotional impulses. Often this is simply a pejorative attesting to the fact that the therapist is angry at and unsatisfied by a patient who will not play the game by the rules and leaves the therapist at a loss as to what to do next to make therapy effective. If a patient is "borderline" the implication is that he is essentially a psychotic individual who manages to adapt marginally to the demands of life but is in ever-present danger of disintegrating if his brittle defenses become strained.

Had the therapist diagnosed Miss Banks's behavior as clinically borderline, there can be no doubt of his next steps: He would have to contact her, if necessary take the blame for her leaving and apologize for upsetting her, induce her to return for treatment, give up at least for the moment, any notion of conducting an insight-oriented psychotherapy, do his best to shore up her defenses against her inner turmoil, and help her adapt to the limitations of a psychologically marginal existence. There has, however, been no evidence of any loosening of Miss Banks's thought process, of misinterpretation of consensually validatable sensory reality, of persecutory or other quasi-delusional phantasies, or of affect inappropriate to the stream of associations she has expressed.*

If she is not borderline, how can Miss Banks's impulsive, angry behavior be provisionally explained? Here again analogies to childhood development and its vicissitudes are useful. When a child, instead of facing some frustration realistically, is overwhelmed by helplessness and becomes enraged, it is said he is having a temper tantrum. Paradoxically, he becomes furious with the persons from whom he expects help; his temper outburst is not simply a way of relieving his tension but also a way of conveying his desperation and need for outside assistance in restoring his equilibrium. Behind the tantrum is the child's unrealistic expectation that he will have a smooth passage through the world, and that if such a passage is not forthcoming, there is someone to blame—and that someone must then be forced to set matters right again.

The trick is to fathom and address the child's need without condoning his behavior, to help him without seeming to be controlled by his rage, lest he come to the conclusion that he must depend on inspiring fear and guilt in order to establish contact with people. A child, no matter how great his rage, still is dependent on and under the control of the caretaking adult—a situation that limits the child's options and thereby enables the adult to handle the situation with firmness and directness. When an adult displays tantrums as a habit pattern, the situation is complicated by the fact that, although his behavior is childlike, he is not a child and cannot be controlled as if he were one.

The therapist assumes that Miss Banks's angry outburst, like her threat to punish him by not coming for treatment ("you're a bad daddy and I don't like you"), is the equivalent of a foot-stamping, breath-holding temper tantrum; it testifies, he speculates, to her need to get help in her unhappiness and her inability to promote such help effectively. The therapist decides to do nothing and to wait for the patient's next move. She will likely come for her next appointment, for she left her sunglasses behind as a kind of promissory note. To pursue her now in a well-meant attempt to assuage her immediate distress would probably be interpreted by her as a sign that the therapist is frightened by her anger. If she can control him with her fury, then he cannot help her to face its nature and significance. It is even possible that her rage, though perfectly genuine, is also a test of the therapist. She may unconsciously be asking whether he can tolerate her "badness" and help her work through a depreciated concept of herself as ugly and destructive. This question cannot be resolved if

* For further discussion of the diagnosis and treatment of the borderline personality, see chapters 9 and 10.

the therapist, for his own comfort, needs her to be nice and lovable in the therapeutic situation.

Could it be that Miss Banks's outburst is a response to an incorrect move by the doctor in focusing on her reaction to leaving her former therapist? Whenever a patient reacts negatively to what one says, the immediate tendency is to blame oneself for some error of omission or commission. Such soul searching is certainly indicated. However, if the therapist concludes that whatever his shortcomings, his words are motivated by the patient's material and not by some short- or long-term problem of his own, he may assume that the patient's reaction is for reasons of her own. Maybe Miss Banks's angry interruption of the session is actually a positive rather than a negative sign. Perhaps having found the therapist to be dependable, kind, and capable, she has made the unconscious decision to say, "All right, you seem to be able to understand me. Now I'll show you how horrible I am and why I am so unhappy."

But what if she does not come back for her next appointment and drops out of treatment? This consideration cannot be a factor in conducting insight psychotherapy. A process geared to helping a patient to face and understand what he has spent a lifetime trying to forget, disavow, or otherwise overlook is not without difficulties. Everyone cannot meet the challenges that inevitably arise as the goal is pursued. How far a particular patient can go is not always clear at the outset. Times of distress, such as the one Miss Banks experiences, are pragmatic tests of whether the patient has the ability to trust the therapist and the therapeutic situation sufficiently to continue in the face of disappointment. Lest he lose the independence required for his work, it is important for the beginning therapist to realize that his concept of himself must not depend on the patient's evaluation of the outcome of the therapists' efforts. If a therapist operates out of concern about what the patient, his relatives, and the community at large will think of him in a given situation, he cannot help but be influenced by irrelevant considerations; he will end up working to win love and admiration instead of single-mindedly striving toward the legitimate goal of insight psychotherapy: promoting the patient's increased understanding of his or her own character and its motivations. As a professional, and not simply a technician, a therapist is expected to rise creatively to a particular occasion. By the same token his efforts cannot simply be measured by their outcome as are the efforts of someone carrying out a purely mechanical task.

Session 3

Miss Banks: Well, are you mad at me for walking out on you last time?

Therapist: I'm sorry you were so upset, but the issue of your leaving treatment with Dr. Ralph and its effect on you is still something I believe we must talk about.

Miss Banks: I suppose so.
Therapist: Why don't you tell me in your own way the details of your parting with him. I gather it was connected with his going into private practice.

The therapist finds himself inadvertently using "gather," the word that triggered the patient's outburst in the previous session and is undoubtedly associated with her distress at that time. At the moment he is about to say it, he has a slight feeling of hesitation. He does not stop himself because (1) it is impossible to control oneself artificially for any length of time, and in any case everyone has verbal habits and if the therapist thinks he must avoid this word with one person and that phrase with another, his attention is taken away from the meaning of what the patient is saying; and (2) on some level he must feel that the patient is now able to participate in the session, and his use of the word "gather" is a way of expressing his confidence in her ability to deal more effectively with what previously upset her.

Miss Banks: Yes, I was one of his first patients when he started his training in psychotherapy. At the end of three years when he completed it, he decided to go into his own practice.
Therapist: You discussed the psychological and practical implications of his move for you before it actually took place?
Miss Banks: Oh yes. He told me about it six months before he left, once he was sure he knew what he was going to do. [*Pause*]
Therapist: Yes?
Miss Banks: We knew I probably wouldn't be finished with the analysis of my feelings for my father. There was no doubt that treatment should continue, perhaps for a number of years, but the money became an issue.
Therapist: In what way?
Miss Banks: Well, I was a college student—just as I am now—and I couldn't pay the kind of money that people in private practice charge.
Therapist: So what happened?
Miss Banks: We had arguments about it. He wanted me to approach my father for it, and I wouldn't.
Therapist: Do you mean you felt your father couldn't afford to help you?
Miss Banks: Oh no, my father is a physician and very comfortable financially, but I wasn't going to him for this.
Therapist: How come?
Miss Banks: Well, Dad doesn't believe in therapy. I've never even told him I'm in treatment to this day.
Therapist: And Dr. Ralph felt you should talk to him?
Miss Banks: No, no, actually I didn't discuss my father's attitude with Dr. Ralph. I didn't feel that was necessary. My point was that he owed it to me as a patient to continue on the same financial basis as before. After all, he used me to get through his training, and he never paid *me* for that.
Therapist: You told him that?
Miss Banks: Yes, and he got mad at me. I can't remember what he said, but it was such a change. He'd always been so nice before. Later he apologized for losing his temper, and we continued for a few months. But it wasn't the same. I decided to stop then, even though he felt I should go on at least till he left the clinic. I know I needed more treatment, but I guess maybe I felt I couldn't trust him any more to understand me.

Therapist: It sounds to me as if the prospect of having to tell your father about being in treatment and asking for his support frightened you but, instead of making that fear a part of your therapy by talking it over with Dr. Ralph, you camouflaged the issue by making him angry and then letting that become a reason for quitting. That way you didn't have to let your father know you needed money for therapy. You essentially sacrificed your treatment and suffered the pain of that loss in order to avoid something that apparently you felt would be even more traumatic.

Miss Banks: What could have been more painful than having to give up the one thing that meant so much to me?

Therapist: See what occurs to you as you think about talking to your father about psychotherapy and asking him to help you pay for it.

Miss Banks: Dad has a terrible temper; if you cross him there's no telling what he'll do. I'm sure he'd be furious if he knew I was seeing you.

Therapist: I got the impression at our first meeting that you and your father were very close—would he really get so angry with you?

Miss Banks: You don't know Dad. He can hold a grudge for years. He's always held my mother responsible for my brother, he's three years younger than I am and was born retarded. Dad always blamed it on mother's family which had a history of mental illness.

Therapist: Even if there were a genetic cause-effect connection, that's hardly your mother's *fault* is it?

Miss Banks: It's not only that. When he realized that Henry was a mongoloid, he wanted to have him institutionalized right away, but mother wouldn't hear of it. She withdrew from everything and everyone and devoted herself to the baby. Eventually, though, we had to put him away when he got to be a teen-ager and mother realized she couldn't cope with him in the house any longer.

Therapist: What do you think of all that?

Miss Banks: I don't, or try not to. Maybe it would have been better to have faced the facts earlier, but that's hard for a mother to do.

Therapist: Especially if she feels to blame for what happened.

Miss Banks: That's what I meant.

The patient's ability to begin coping verbally with those issues that had caused her to react so violently in the previous session is a good prognostic sign. That the therapy is advancing is shown by the spontaneous emergence of significant aspects of her personal history.

In this treatment situation the initial goal of becoming acquainted with the patient is linked to the management of the transference. The patient's reactions to the therapist clearly have little to do with him as a person but are the result of her preconceived attitudes carried into the therapy. Therefore, the process of helping her deal with the therapist as therapist and to reveal and examine her difficulties is therapeutic as well as diagnostic. Rather than interpreting the possible significance of her behavior, the therapist remains advisedly content to modulate her overreaction; rather than responding in kind to her behavior or criticizing it, he creates an atmosphere of tolerance. On the other hand, he does not accept her attitude at face value—that is, blame shortcomings in himself, her former therapist, or in psychotherapists generally for her difficulties. Sometimes a patient engages in verbal or other behavior that is impolite and/or socially unacceptable in the belief, spoken or unspoken, that a patient has the right to impose upon a therapist in this manner. This privilege actually obtains, however, only so long as the patient also agrees to subject what he is doing or saying to scrutiny in the session. In other words, a therapist is under no obligation to tolerate invective or insult just because the patient feels abusive and is under the mistaken impression that the therapist is paid to accept him, no matter what. Only if behavior leads to further understanding of the patient's character and problems is there any reason for enduring in a therapy session what one would not tolerate outside the office. In Miss Banks's case this therapeutic bargain is not an issue since she tacitly accepts it, as demonstrated by her behavior in this third session.

Session 4

Miss Banks: I don't know if it's productive to go on with what we were talking about last time.

Therapist: What specifically of all the things we talked about?

Miss Banks: The Oedipus business.

Therapist: Oedipus business?

Miss Banks: The relationship to my father, of course. In my previous therapy it was explained to me that my mother's preoccupation with my sick brother undoubtedly caused my father to turn to me. I won an oedipal victory. I, not my mother, was the center of my father's affection. As a result I have not been able to establish a meaningful relationship with a man now that I am an adult. Not only does no man measure up to my father as he was seen through the adoring eyes of a little girl, but there must also be terrible guilt that does not leave me free to form a union with a man of my own, even if I were to find one I could admire.

Therapist: I believe that the best thing for you to do is not to prejudge your thoughts but to mention whatever occurs to you. Where it will lead to, or if it's a dead end, we'll soon find out. That way there is less of a chance of missing something important. If you happen to be thinking about your father today go ahead with that. After all, no matter how much you may have discussed that in the past, the fact that it occurs to you today may mean that there is more to be understood about that. So why don't you go ahead now.

A patient, especially one employed in the mental-health field, sometimes deals with his anxiety by falling back on clichés and stilted formulations, as Miss Banks does here. Rather than trying to deal with her question head on—it would only lead to arguments about the meaning and value of hypotheses that, in her mind, are linked with Dr. Ralph who means a great deal to her—the therapist sidesteps the challenge, avoids expressing an opinion about the patient's notions regarding her "Oedipus complex," but declares himself ready to listen to whatever comes to her mind at the moment. This is an appropriate technique whenever a patient tries to pit a current therapist, directly or indirectly, against what a former therapist supposedly said or did. Rather than take offense at the thinly veiled hostility that is often behind such remarks, the therapist must realize that this kind of maneuvering is motivated unconsciously by the patient's need to defend himself against examining what is actually troubling him.

Miss Banks: Oh, there's nothing specific, just thoughts about that trouble I had asking for money for treatment. It bothers me that you and I will be going through that in three years.
Therapist: How so?

Note that the patient has committed herself to the therapist. Although her complaints about treatment and her periodic announcements of discontinuing it may well recur, they should not be taken at face value but should be understood as distress signals and dealt with on that basis. The transference relationship can now be counted on as viable; it is the therapist's strongest ally and his most useful tool.

Miss Banks: When do you finish here? Are you going into private practice?

It would be nice if Miss Banks stuck to the topic under consideration—that is, her relationship to her father; that, however, is often not the way things go in actual practice. Thoughts have a way of intruding and seemingly diverting the process from its apparent direction. There is no telling yet whether this new direction will help or hinder the patient's learning to understand herself. The therapist must let himself be led until he can chart the course once more, perhaps better off for the digression the patient has forced upon him.

Therapist: I will be going into private practice in June.
Miss Banks: So you won't be here after that?
Therapist: That's right.
Miss Banks: But that's only eight months away. . . . [*Pause*]
Therapist: Yes?
Miss Banks: [*Starting to cry*] Oh, that's awful. I'll have to start again with someone new. Maybe I should stop now and just quit trying.
Therapist: What about the time we have between now and June to do some work. Let's see what we can accomplish.

Too many patients, and too many therapists for that matter, assume that psychotherapeutic results based on insight can be achieved only over a period of many years. However, there is no necessary correlation between the length of treatment and its efficacy. Often what a patient needs to understand about himself relates to problems of development and conflict that are not strongly defended against; that is, they are potentially available to consciousness, and there is no reason why it should take much time to promote understanding of and insight into them.

Miss Banks: But I don't even know whether I can trust you. Whether we can establish a therapeutic alliance. First I have to know what kind of a person you are. Will you really be able to understand me?

Therapist: What I think I understand about you so far is that you are frightened. As far as I know I have given you no cause to be scared of me. I must assume that there is a fear that you bring with you to the treatment, a fear that is present regardless of what kind of a person I am. So I don't think it's now a matter of my convincing you that I mean well. Let's take that for granted unless proven otherwise, and see instead what it is you imagine I might do, or not do, that makes you so anxious.

One can never "prove" oneself to a patient apart from the work done together. The patient must extend the therapist provisional credibility—that is, a belief that he can help. If the patient cannot so believe, that inability has to be confronted as the patient's problem. There is never any point in trying to convince a patient of one's good will or ability. Instead, as the therapist does here, one tries to get the patient back on a track that holds more promise for the treatment. Incidentally, in this session the therapist shows the patient again that neither her doubts nor her antagonism have deterred him from his goal of helping her. Letting her know that she cannot control him with either her anger or her despair is the greatest reassurance he can give her.

Miss Banks: I can't think of anything, except——

Therapist: Except what?

Miss Banks: It doesn't make sense.

Therapist: Say it anyway.

Miss Banks: That you'll lose your temper and get mad at me for nothing I have done, that you won't understand that I'm trying my best.

Therapist: Have I given you any reason to believe I'll do that?

Miss Banks: No, I told you it doesn't make any sense.

Therapist: Let's not be so quick to say that. If it doesn't apply to me, perhaps it does to someone else in some other situation. Can you think of anything that would fit?

Miss Banks: My father, I suppose. If he was in a bad mood he'd yell at me and find fault when all I was trying to do was to be nice.

Therapist: What particular incident occurs to you as you think about his losing his temper without justification?

It is always a good idea to get a patient to give specific examples that define how she uses emotionally loaded terms like "bad," "love," "angry," "depressed," and so forth. It ensures that you know what the terms mean to the patient; abstractions and generalities should be anchored in experiences that both the patient and the therapist have talked about.

Miss Banks: I remember that he came home late once, and I had the table set and served him the supper that I had kept warm in the oven. When he took a bite, it turned out to be too hot and he burned his mouth. He picked up his plate and flung it against the wall over my head and yelled at me as if I had done it on purpose.
Therapist: How old were you at the time?
Miss Banks: Ten.
Therapist: Ten years old? And you were in charge of his supper?
Miss Banks: Oh yes, I was expected to help out. Mother was usually busy with Henry and didn't want to be around Dad anyway. When they were together they always fought and argued, and I learned early that I could keep things more peaceful if I stepped in and relieved her of the chores.

As the therapist listens to this, his attitude toward the patient changes further. He feels that he is now on the track of learning why the patient has difficulties in relating to others. Also, he sympathizes with the little girl who meant well and got yelled at. He no longer has to remind himself not to take personally the patient's mistrust and anger. He sees her carping more clearly now as the outcome, in some way, of the difficulties she has had, and as having nothing to do with him.

When dealing with a patient who makes himself unlikable, the therapist's comprehension of such behavior and the change in his attitude toward it is often a prerequisite for promoting the patient's understanding and an attendant change in the latter's perceptual set.

Therapist: Was your father's explosive behavior toward you unusual or typical?

This question encourages the patient to say more about her relationship with her father. It is also important to see whether a particular example adduced by a patient is only an isolated incident he has seized upon because he needs to see a situation in a certain way.

Miss Banks: We all dreaded weekends when Dad was home. He was so irritable. You never knew what would set him off. There was no reasoning with him once his mind was made up to be angry about something.
Therapist: I'm confused here. I got the impression that you felt you had a very close and special relationship with your father. If so, how does that jibe with what you are telling me now?

In this way—without being accusing—the therapist is able to confront the patient with the apparent contradiction in her material.

Miss Banks: I'm confused, too. I never talked about the things you are asking me now.
Therapist: In your previous therapy, you mean?
Miss Banks: Yes.
Therapist: Still, you must have talked about your father to come to the conclusion you did about your "specialness."
Miss Banks: Well, that's the Oedipus complex. When two parents drift apart, the

daughter moves into the vacuum left by mother's withdrawal. Isn't that right? Aren't you a Freudian? Dr. Ralph was—is—I guess.

Therapist: You mean these are inferences that were made about your relationship with your father, and you don't actually remember being so special to him?

Miss Banks: No, of course not. The Oedipus complex is unconscious, you know. On the conscious level I remember mainly how we argued and fought a lot. Probably we were both defending ourselves against underlying positive feelings—you know, the incest barrier. I'm really uncomfortable about this. Your questions are on such a superficial level. Why do you stay on the surface when the important material is unconscious?

Therapist: It sounds to me as if your memories will be helpful. Let's not be too quick to dismiss what you remember just because you remember it.

The patient falls back on her initial defensive arrogance, although now much more mildly. It is her way of coping with unrecognized anxiety, probably precipitated by her beginning to confront her actual, rather than her rationalized, relationship to her father. In spite of her anxiety, however, she is now able to permit herself to associate to the therapist's suggestions and comments, with the result that she is surprised by what occurs to her. This freedom to associate indicates that Miss Banks's initial unconscious fear of being hurt by permitting herself to depend on the therapist has been sufficiently allayed to let her enter the next phase of her treatment—one where her transference to the therapist can be mobilized and used to further her therapy.

VI

Genetic Investigation and Interpretation

Session 5

Miss Banks: Since I saw you last my mind has gone back a lot to what it was like in my childhood. Are you interested in hearing about it?

Therapist: Of course I am. If you've been thinking about it, we should be hearing about it.

Should the therapist admit that he is interested? Will such an admission direct the patient and suggest what she ought to be talking about rather than let her proceed by free association?

The term *free association* should not be taken literally. The technique of psychoanalysis and of dynamic psychotherapy generally is based on the fact that, at least insofar as psychological conflict is concerned, there is nothing free about the patient's speech in the sense of its being random or unplanned. Everything a patient says is determined by and related in some way to his or her unconscious goals. Once the therapist has become a meaningful object for the patient—that is, a significant transference figure—he is the target of those unconscious wishes. Only the hope of fulfilling infantile wishes can mobilize a patient for the therapeutic task. In adulthood, as in childhood, only the hope for love and the fear that love will be withdrawn can overcome the resistance to examining defensive patterns that have, after all, been established to avoid anxiety.

A patient who has a positive transference to the therapist wants to please him and will talk about what she thinks will interest him. Transference repeats development. A child obeys and produces because he wants to be praised and loved now, not because he is moved by future and abstract goals. A patient lets himself be known, even though he fears exposing himself to humiliation and punishment, because he wants the therapist's affection and approval, not simply because he wants to get well. To know this about a patient is to be alert to the dangers of the transference relationship. The patient in a positive transference will, unconsciously, do his best to conform to the therapist's wishes as he, the patient, understands them. If the therapist wants to talk in terms of the Oedipus complex and incestuous sexuality, the patient will do his utmost to bring out material in such a way that it will fit that set; if another therapist approaches the same patient in a different framework, the latter will oblige that therapist in turn. But, as Freud (1937) pointed out long ago, all a therapist can do is set the wheels in motion; whether he is on the right track is indicated by what happens to the patient. If the material comes to have a life of its own and pulls both therapist and patient along, all is well. Under such circumstances the patient and the doctor feel that they are working hard and productively; therapy is interesting, affectively toned, and leads the patient to insight and behavioral change both in the sessions and away from them. If, however—as will often happen—they have feelings of circularity, boredom, and lack of change, these are an indication that the therapist's focus was not accurate, and that he must lead the patient's introspection in a different direction.

Miss Banks comes to the treatment with the expectation that her problems will continue to be seen as organized along the axis of the oedipal conflict, as it seems they were in her previous therapy. The therapist indicates by his questions that he wants to hear about things that she has considered trivial—that is, as not of interest to her previous therapist. At first reluctant to comply, she now deepens her commitment to the new psychotherapist by announcing she has been thinking about the things that he seemed to want to talk about at the last visit. If the therapist were to remain noncommittal, he would be rejecting the transference and making it more difficult for the patient to work with him. Whether the tack that patient and therapist are taking leads to meaningful understanding remains to be seen.

Miss Banks: I just remember being very lonely and different from everybody else. I don't recollect anything really before Henry was born. Maybe things were all right before that. Afterwards, though, I knew my house wasn't like that of other kids. I guess I was ashamed of the way the house looked. Mother kept the shades drawn all the time, everything was a mess. There was never anything in the refrigerator, so I never brought friends in to play because I thought they'd want to snack, like I did at their houses, and we didn't have anything to eat that was fun. Mom didn't really cook for years. We sent out or went out for most of our dinners. God, do I hate Chinese food to this day!

Therapist: It certainly sounds as if your mother was depressed following the birth of your brother.

Miss Banks: She was and still is, even though it got better with the years.

Therapist: How long was it before your home situation improved?

Miss Banks: I was eight years old, I remember.

Therapist: You're so definite about that. Did something special happen that left such a vivid impression?

Miss Banks: Yes, but I don't want to talk about it. [*Pause*] Oh, I guess I have to tell you, but it's embarrassing. . . . We started having Christmas again that year.

Therapist: Had Christmas again——?

Miss Banks: After Henry was born we never had a tree or presents till I was eight years old. Then all of a sudden that December Mother had a tree delivered. Some organization, I think it was the Salvation Army, came door to door selling trees for charity, and Mother said O.K., send one. We even went shopping for decorations and gifts.

Therapist: You know, my reaction to hearing this is one of sadness for the little girl who had no Christmas, but you experienced embarrassment at telling me about it, so you must feel there's something to be ashamed of here.

Miss Banks: Yes, I think what bothered me most was not what I didn't have, but knowing that my parents weren't like the other kids's. When the kids would talk about what they thought they'd find on Christmas morning, I would make up stories about the packages under our tree. I think they knew I was lying, though, because they never asked to come to my house and see the stuff as they asked each other to do. What probably happened is that the parents on the block knew something was wrong at my place, felt sorry for me, and told their children to be kind and not upset me further. I think I knew that they knew I was making up stories, but I couldn't stop myself even though while I was doing it I felt ashamed—mad, too, that they let this happen and put me in that position—my parents, I mean.

Therapist: Did you let your parents know how upset and angry you felt?

Miss Banks: It didn't do much good. If I said anything about anything to my mother, she'd cry and complain to me as if I were a grownup about how difficult her life was with my brother and my father. I remember I was invited to a birthday party and I begged Mother to take me to the store to buy a present I could take, but she didn't do it—she just wasn't up to it or was too disorganized to get around to it, I suppose—and I ended up giving the child an envelope with some money in it. It was so humiliating, all the other kids had brought packages, of course. I knew there was no point in saying any more about it to Mother. After that I just didn't accept any invitations to parties—I'd make some excuse—until I was old enough to go out and buy a gift by myself.

Here the patient is giving information that is prognostically significant and encouraging. Instead of collapsing and withdrawing into herself when faced with disappointment and adversity—behavior for which she would seem to have had a model in her mother—the then-little girl bided her time, did not give up, and corrected the problem as soon as she could—when she could go to the toy store by herself, she started going to parties again. This hints at a core of strength that therapy can draw upon. Also noteworthy and potentially helpful are both the gift she has for observing herself even while she is suffering and her ability to evaluate the effect her behavior has on others even though facing it is often painful.

Therapist: And how would your father respond when you approached him about Christmas, if you did?

Miss Banks: I don't remember if I ever talked to him specifically about that, but he had a very typical response whenever he was challenged about the way we lived. He'd blame Mother and her sickness and my brother's condition and feel sorry for himself and say I shouldn't burden him. Then as an afterthought he'd get mad and tell me I should count myself fortunate that I had it so good, thanks to him. That he worked like a slave and put up with living like a pig to keep the family together for my sake. Any other man would have left my mother long ago and made a life for himself, he'd say. He made me feel so guilty and scared, I'd put out of my mind whatever had been bothering me and try to do what I could to make him feel better.

Therapist: What do you think about that now?

Miss Banks: What choice did I have? There was nobody else I could go to. Neither of my parents had any relatives here, so I couldn't run to anybody. Besides, I do love my father, you know. He really didn't have it easy. I think he was very embarrassed by the home situation, just like I was. He couldn't bring people home either. All the other physicians entertained, and he never went because he couldn't reciprocate. Anyway, he couldn't take Mother out because of her ways. You'd never know when she'd have a crying fit, or what she'd say, or if she would talk at all. But there were some patients of his that he was very close to, who became our only friends—they really loved him and he was very devoted to them. One couple, especially, it's to their home we went on holidays like Christmas. They were Jewish, though, and didn't have a tree either, but they'd have presents for all of us. They didn't seem to expect anything in return; my father's being there was enough for them. Mrs. Rubin would be very nice to my mother—she liked her too, not just my father, I think. Dad was very different with them—pleasant, making little jokes and laughing. I could see a very different side of him when he was the "doctor" and felt comfortable. Then he could be charming and it was easy to see why he always had a good practice and a following in the community. I only saw him get angry one time there. That was when Mrs. Rubin asked him once when Mother was having a terrible time why he didn't take her to a psychiatrist. He started getting red in the face and said there was nothing wrong with her that a psychiatrist could cure. Her spells, as he called them, were hereditary and would go away by themselves eventually. He said psychiatrists never did any good, but when problems went away they took the credit for it. Besides he wasn't going to have her locked up like an animal with crazy people, he knew what places like that looked like. You could see he was really upset, maybe more hurt than angry, but Mr. Rubin smoothed it over and they never talked about it again. Mrs. Rubin was really very nice. She'd take Mother shopping for clothes, take me too. God knows how I'd ever have gotten ready for school if she hadn't taken over.

Therapist: Our time is about up and we'll have to stop for today.

Miss Banks: What does everything I said mean? You haven't interpreted anything I talked about.

Therapist: Perhaps what you really want to know now is what I think of you after what you have told me about yourself. My guess is that it was difficult to get much feedback from your troubled parents, so you turned to others for reassurance that you were worth-while.

Miss Banks: I was very aware of doing that in school. It was such a surprise to me to find that when I did what the teacher wanted, I'd get praised. It was so simple, like turning on a faucet and the water coming out.

Therapist: Perhaps that's how you see our relationship, too. I am the teacher, and you want to know whether you have been a good student.

Miss Banks: Well, was it worth-while?

Therapist: Very much so. I certainly feel I know you much better than I did. But what I'm trying to say is that you may well be bringing, not just here, but into all your social intercourse, a need to undo a feeling of insecurity about yourself. Since you initially defined your problem as an inability to establish normally satisfying relationships, perhaps this will shed some light on your difficulties.

Miss Banks: I'll have to think about that.

Therapist: Fine. I'll see you next week.

In this session the therapist reaches the goal of becoming acquainted with the patient. This does not mean that he has learned all that he needs to about her—far from it. It does mean that Miss Banks has become a person for him rather than an assortment of facts and symptoms. He now has confidence in his ability to guide the patient in further exploration of her character and its development.

The therapist's commitment to the patient is no more automatic than the patient's to the therapist. When Miss Banks first came, she was antagonistic and supercilious; quite possibly this was a defense against permitting the regression that would enable her to transfer to the therapist a child's hopes for love and understanding. From what the therapist knows so far of the patient's early life, he thinks it likely that she had constantly to be on guard against the disappointment of such wishes. The patient has to overcome her fear of regression in order to commit herself to the therapy. The therapist faces the opposite problem. In order to commit himself to the patient, he must struggle against regressive wishes to be loved, admired, and validated by the patient. By recognizing within himself the negative feelings that the patient's initial behavior precipitated, he was consciously able to rise above them by pitting against them his ambition to be a good therapist and to live up to a therapeutic ideal. This resolve on the therapist's part led him to act in such a way that the patient, after testing him in various ways to see if he would weaken before her onslaught, was able to trust him not to hurt her unnecessarily. She then demonstrated by the manner and content of her associations that she had mobilized her hopes and attached them to him. The therapist's feeling of confidence vis-à-vis this patient is based not on the facts he has elicited from her, but on the recognition that he has won a victory over himself. The patient's needs and not his own have won the day; in his inner struggle he has emerged closer to his ideals for himself. This is the basis for an effective therapeutic situation.

Analogously, a parent or a teacher may be hurt by the inconsiderate behavior of a child, but the initial impulse to retaliate is immediately opposed by the ideal image of himself functioning as either one. By trying to understand what is going on within the child to make him behave in a certain way—rather than by reacting to the provocation—the adult achieves control over both himself and the transaction.

Terms like "therapeutic alliance," "working alliance," or "therapeutic contract" have often come to imply a mutuality of goals between patient and therapist that it is unrealistic to anticipate and that should not be expected as the basis for treatment. Furthermore, in practice these terms are often used to mean that the therapist must get the patient to like him and must, in turn, like the patient. Psychotherapy is not a popularity contest. A patient's fear of intimacy, the expectation of being hurt, and other reasons may cause him to behave antagonistically toward his therapist and to present himself so as to be unlikable.

I believe that the therapist is mistaken if he makes his primary goal the establishment of "rapport." (Nor, by the way, is he guaranteed easy sailing by immediate mutual appreciation and admiration between himself and a patient; such feelings can be as much defensive and countertherapeutic as their antitheses.)

Rather than working toward getting the patient to like him, the therapist needs to work toward being able to like himself as he is functioning with the particular patient in the particular session. (Such an achievement is, incidentally, also the best antidote for negative feelings the therapist may harbor for his patient.) Failure to be satisfied with himself is a clear signal that something is amiss; and, unlike the question of whether the patient cares for him, this area of his behavior as a therapist is one that he can be expected to control.

Session 6

Miss Banks: I think I covered everything I had to say last time. Today there's nothing on my mind.

Therapist: Give yourself a chance and see what occurs to you.

Miss Banks: Honest, nothing does.

Therapist: My guess would be, based on our last meeting, that you're worried that what you might say may not hold interest for me, please me, or what have you.

Miss Banks: Not that I'm aware of.

Therapist: Have you given any thought to what we spoke about last time?

Miss Banks: What specifically?

Therapist: I didn't have anything particular in mind, but it was a very active and full session, and I'd be interested in what aspect of it stayed with you afterward.

Miss Banks: I'm sure when I left last time what we talked about must have been on my mind, but that was a week ago. Since then I've been so busy with other things that it's hard to remember any more. I know I talked a lot about my parents and the Rubins whom I hadn't thought about for a long time, but I told you all that I recall about them.

Therapist: So you've had a busy week. What's been happening to you?

Recognizing that his line of inquiry is not productive, the therapist picks up on the patient's first statement that promises to undo the impasse. It is true that her comment, "but that was a week ago," could be understood as meaning, "I don't see you enough," and as such should be kept in mind; but before he actually makes this interpretation to the patient, the therapist should have a lot more evidence.

Miss Banks: Well, for starters, my roommate decided to move out on me, so now I've got to find someone else because I can't afford to pay the rent by myself.

Then, after not seeing my advisor for months, he suddenly wants to talk to me about wrapping up my thesis, and I've got to get all that material ready.

Therapist: How come your roommate is moving?

The therapist, correctly, does not wait to see whether the patient will tell him more about the roommate: he is interested, so he asks. He chooses to ask first about the situation with the roommate rather than about the thesis because the former may shed further light on the initial complaint—that is, difficulties in interpersonal relationships.

Miss Banks: I never should have taken her in in the first place, but I needed somebody to help pay the rent. She's much younger than I am and just lives differently. She doesn't care whether her share of the work is done or not, or how the place looks. I can't live like that, so I tell her about it and she resents that. I think she's been looking for an alternative for a while and must have found it.

The therapist might be tempted to relate the patient's dislike for a messy apartment to the memories of her childhood and the state of her home during the acute phase of her mother's depression. Although there may be some connection, there is no evidence for it in the session; thus, there is no reason for the therapist not to take her statement at face value for the moment. Instead of forcing the patient's thoughts to fit a so-called dynamic formulation, the therapist takes the opportunity to learn something of her reaction to stress and her capacity to adapt in her daily life.

Therapist: What will you do now?

Miss Banks: There's a woman in the agency where I'm doing the research for my thesis who I think is interested in sharing expenses. Her apartment building is being sold and she has to move in a couple of months anyway.

Therapist: What makes you think that the two of you will hit it off living together?

Miss Banks: We're closer in age and we seem to have the same outlook on many things. Since I've been at the agency we've spent a lot of time together, and I think it will turn out all right.

Therapist: What's the nature of your work at the agency?

Miss Banks: I'm part of a study researching adoptive parents. I'm doing follow-ups of placements to see if predictions that were initially made of their parenting capacities have validity.

Therapist: Is this part of a Ph.D. program?

Miss Banks: I plan to go on to a Ph.D., but right now I'm finishing up my master's. If my advisor likes what I've done, I could get it this summer. That's why I'd like to have had more notice to prepare for this conference with him. By the way, do you mind if I don't come next week in case I need the time to get ready to see Dr. Simmonds?

Therapist: It's your session and you may choose not to use it, but I wonder if you wouldn't be better off coming for the appointment anyway?

Miss Banks: You mean if I get too worried or upset it would do me good to come here before going into the conference rather than afterward?

Therapist: Exactly.

Miss Banks: I guess I will come then. What do you make out of what I told you today? I suppose I should apologize for just talking about such mundane and uninteresting matters, not psychological problems, I mean.

Therapist: I didn't find it uninteresting at all. That you are able to deal effectively with demanding situations is encouraging to see and important for me to know about.

There are a number of things worth looking at in this session. It seems relatively uneventful, only because one has been led to measure therapeutic achievement in terms of the overt connections made for the patient between the events of today and those of the past. Actually, quite a bit happens here to clarify the patient's condition and help the therapist set treatment goals and prepare the patient to reach them.

First, it becomes clear that the patient's anxiety is neither global nor uncontrollable. Since the conduct of a therapy geared to promoting insight is going to have its stressful moments, it is important for the therapist to know, before committing himself to such a course, that a given patient's anxiety not only can be managed but can be turned to therapeutic advantage. This patient's treatment to date certainly indicates that she has responded to and benefited from the way the therapist has dealt with her initial anxiety and its behavioral manifestations.

Another important factor noted by the therapist is that the patient seems to function quite well in several important areas. In spite of her problems, she is handling her living arrangements and her educational program in a mature, goal-directed, and result-oriented fashion. This ability also speaks in favor of her capacity to profit from dynamic psychotherapy; one may hope that she will be able to cope with other aspects of her life just as successfully once she understands the misconceptions that now prevent that from happening.

At the beginning and the end of the interview the patient does display mild anxiety, which appears to be centered on the therapist. Her initial inability to find anything to say, in contrast with her productive response when the therapist encourages her, speaks for her wish to please him and her fear that she will not do so. Similarly, her suggestion that she might be too busy to come to her next appointment is seen by the therapist not as a depreciation of the treatment but as a plea for reassurance that he would welcome her attendance. Her plea, however, is couched in the now-familiar provocative style that she has developed to offset her disappointment should she find herself unwanted. Paradoxically, when she uses this defense in her day-to-day life, it assures that what she most dreads will usually come to pass; her way of testing her significance by challenging the self-esteem of her respondent makes the latter feel unwanted and quite likely causes him to react with distancing maneuvers in an attempt at self-protection. Note, however, that rather than confront the patient with his conclusions, the therapist responds directly to her need, as he understands it, by encouraging her both to speak freely and to come to her next appointment. He does this because he has formed a hypothesis, based on what he has heard so far, that Miss Banks's upbringing—with the exception of her classroom experience—was significantly devoid of opportunities to learn how to enhance her self-esteem by pleasing others. It is likely that her parents were so unhappy that they could not be gratified by their child's accomplishments: thus, the fact that she learned how to conform to their expectations did not enhance her self-concept. Perhaps behind the patient's initially arrogant, angry behavior lies the insecurity of a frightened child who would like to please but is not sure how to go about doing so. With this tentative formulation, the therapist is loath to let her flounder and, for example, is quick to reassure her of his interest when she doubts that what she has to say is worth-while.

Miss Banks's situation is not at all unusual (which, of course, is why I have chosen to use her case). It is true that she must have serious deficiencies in her ability to relate successfully, especially to men—deficiencies she will have to face in therapy; but equally significant may be her inability to recognize her own assets and to feel reasonably confident that she can use them to maintain her self-esteem. Any patient is most likely to benefit from treatment and to tolerate its difficult moments successfully and productively if he knows that the therapist respects him and finds good in him, even if he can not yet do either one for himself. It is important to understand that reassurance, guidance, and gratification of the patient's psychological demands may well be essential ingredients in the therapy of an individual who has not had sufficient opportunity in the relationship with his parents to learn how his own actions can influence the treatment he receives, and how that treatment then influences his self-concept. This approach to Miss Banks's therapy should not be confused with so-called supportive psychotherapy which is aimed at strengthening extant defenses and at covering rather than uncovering a patient's problems. The ultimate goal in the case of Miss Banks remains the promotion of cure through helping her gain insight into her characteristic behavior patterns; but first the therapist must lay the groundwork necessary to permit the patient to face herself.

Once the therapist has worked out a successful method for approaching a particular patient, the therapy develops its own momentum that carries the two of them forward. In this case, during the next ten sessions the therapist's recognition that the patient's anger expressed the fear that she would not be understood enabled him to continue to respond with curiosity rather than with hurt to her frequent and telling challenges to his self-esteem. Once assured she would not be rejected, the patient could permit the mobilization of her hope that she would be liked, admired, and approved. This hope, of course, was not directly expressed by Miss Banks: instead, in recounting some activity she would invite the therapist to depreciate her; when he did not do so, she would go on to enlarge on the topic, permitting her underlying, positive emotions to emerge. Excerpts from a session that proved to be a turning point in her therapeutic progress illustrate how she could let her hopeful feelings emerge and let the therapist know of her improvement.

Sessions 17–70

Miss Banks: My work at the agency is getting to be more and more rewarding. Even though I'm not supposed to be doing therapy, when I interview the parents I feel that they get help from talking to me about the problems of raising adopted children. [*Becoming angry*] But I suppose you feel that only you psychiatrists can do effective psychotherapy.

Therapist: It sounds like you have a genuine interest in clinical work and may well have a gift for it. Did you have a particular experience in mind?

Instead of attempting to justify himself or deal directly with her challenge in other ways, the therapist, having learned by now what she means by such angry statements, responds to this one as if she had asked, "Do you think I could be a good therapist?" and then encourages her to go on and tell him what she really wants to say. Note, however, that he does not simply interpret the meaning of her challenge as one would do with a less anxious patient, but addresses her need directly.

Miss Banks: [*Immediately calming down*] Last week there was this couple to whom we had sent a letter telling them to make an appointment for the project's follow-up interview, and they didn't respond for months. When I finally called them, they were very negativistic, but I finally got them to agree to come in. When I saw them they didn't want to talk, answered questions with only a "yes" or "no," and even though they were polite, it was obvious that they were angry at me and at the agency. I realized I wasn't getting anywhere, and not so long ago I would have panicked. But this time I just said that I could tell they were upset, and that others who had worries about how they were doing as parents sometimes felt that the agency was like an in-law who had come into the home to criticize how they were raising the baby. And did they open up! They had a lot of fears as to how to handle the situation now that their son was going to go to nursery school where people might know he was adopted, and they didn't know how to prepare him or if they should do so. They have a worker at the agency—at least they had one till she left last month—who was supposed to deal with such problems, but, it came out, they always felt on trial with her and didn't dare confess their worries. They were so relieved when I told them that their concerns were not unusual and were shared by most other adoptive parents. They were so grateful to me, even though I didn't really do all that much for them.

Therapist: You did a lot by listening thoughtfully and apparently conducting yourself in such a way that their fear of being criticized was allayed. But then you know what it's like to live with the fear that fault will be found with whatever you do, don't you?

Miss Banks: You mean with what we've been talking about regarding my father? I went home last weekend in spite of the experience the week before, and we got into it again. I just can't seem to help myself even though we've talked about it here. I guess I keep trying to get his approval and become upset when he reacts as he always does—critical of me and what I have done or plan to do.

Therapist: Mmhm.

Miss Banks: I told him about the good deal I got on the car I bought with the money they gave me for my birthday, but instead of being pleased, he decided that all kinds of things must be wrong with it. I'd told him it was checked out by a mechanic, but that didn't make any difference to him. He just spoils everything for me.

Therapist: For himself too, doesn't he?

Miss Banks: How do you mean?

Therapist: It was really very generous of them to give you such a handsome present for your birthday, but your father can't seem to enjoy your gratitude and the pleasure his gift gave you.

Miss Banks: That's true. I wanted to show him how careful I was to get a good buy, show him that I appreciated how nice he was to give me all that money. Actually, that was really more important for me than finally getting a car of my own.

Therapist: It seems to be the continuation of a long series of attempts you made as a child to win his approval.

Miss Banks: Mom was pleased at least. I ended up taking her for a ride. I think she's proud of me for being more independent, more my own person. Until now I wouldn't have dared to do what I did. I think I was waiting around all these years for Dad to take me by the hand and get me a car. I sure could have used it before. It's not the money. He just never puts himself out for me. I had to arrange all my own schooling, too. They never took me around to visit colleges when I was finishing high school, like other parents did. Then when I was looking for a graduate school all Dad did was paint gloomy pictures about the tough job market, as if it was useless for me to try to get a profession.

Therapist: You know, even though your Dad blusters angrily, I wonder if underneath all the noise he's frightened for you or scared of life generally. Behind his anger seems to be the fear that things won't work out for you—you won't get a job, your car will break down, and so forth.

Miss Banks: I never thought of that. It does make sense, though. I think if he'd had his choice I'd never have left home for college, though I will say he didn't stand in my way once I made up my mind.

Therapist: Just as with your car, when you decided to act he didn't stop you. Indeed, he then gave you the money you needed to buy it. Almost as if he were relieved that you had acted and he didn't have to take any initiative in making or implementing the decision.

Miss Banks: [*Sits thoughtfully but says nothing for about a minute*]

Therapist: So, it looks like our time is about up and we'll have to stop for today.

Miss Banks: Oh! I didn't tell you all that happened at the agency.

Therapist: Well, let's sit a few more minutes then while you do that.

Miss Banks: Oh, it's not that much really. It's just about this couple I told you about. They have no worker now, and after we talked they were so relieved to find out they weren't that much different from other adoptive parents they wanted to come back and talk over more things. I gave them another appointment, and then I cleared it with Betty (the head of the agency) that I could continue to see them therapeutically and not just for the purpose of the research. That's all.

Therapist: That's a lot. Congratulations, both on your initiative in the matter and on getting your first official therapy assignment.
Miss Banks: Thank you, it really is exciting.

Why does the patient delay—and almost omit—telling the therapist her good news about being given clinical responsibilities at the agency? Two possibilities suggest themselves: (1) The excitement of her achievement is so stimulating that she cannot handle it comfortably until the end of the session when she can report it without having to discuss it at length. Patients often leave the most important developments to the end of a session for this reason—not deliberately but owing to a temporary, unconscious defensive perceptual gap. (2) The patient may fear that the therapist will not appreciate the significance of her achievement and will, by his lack of response, leave her painfully ashamed of her own excitement. By postponing the telling to the last possible moment, she symbolically minimizes what she is about to say and prepares herself to make a quick exit—maneuvers to ameliorate the hurt she anticipates.

The therapist in this case handles both possibilities by his sincere expression of pleasure in her accomplishment and, by implication, in the victory it represents over the anxieties that have frequently prevented her from making the most of her opportunities and abilities. With a patient who had achieved greater insight and objectivity about himself, the therapist, though pleased for him, might well have remained noncommittal, only interpreting the patient's tension and asking him to examine it when the matter came up—as it surely would come up in some form—in the next session. In Miss Banks's situation he chose (I think correctly) to gratify her need reasonably and directly. This difference in approach is often mistakenly couched in terms of whether one is being "human" with a patient: the implication is that the therapist, in gratifying the patient, abandons the therapeutic posture. However, Miss Banks's therapist is not being "nice" to her as opposed to being "therapeutic." In taking her need at face value, he makes a calculated move in the treatment.

By the same token, there is nothing inhuman or inhumane about abstaining from gratifying a patient's immediate needs if the abstention is in the interest of the therapeutic goal; and if the therapist believes not only that the patient can tolerate the resulting tension, but that the treatment will benefit because optimal anxiety thus generated may enable the patient to mobilize pertinent material. The needs of the treatment—rather than the therapist's consideration of what kind of a person he will seem to be to the patient at the moment—should determine what he says or does not say.

From here on, the sessions with Miss Banks had a spontaneity and rhythm that was not present at the outset of the therapy. There was noticeably less need for the therapist to guide the hour and move it along.

It is significant that though the therapist, right from the beginning of the treatment, was careful neither to belittle nor to depreciate the patient's efforts at adaptation, she nevertheless continued to anticipate that this would happen. Each time she behaved as if she expected to be rejected, belittled, or depreciated, the therapist defused the situation with productive results for that session; yet in subsequent hours, as in the preceding example, she nevertheless manifested the same pattern—an angry, challenging attitude that covered her fear of being found wanting by him. A perceptual set reflecting a psychological trauma is not revised by benign reality alone. A so-called corrective emotional and/or re-educational experience with the therapist is not enough by itself in cases like this one to effect a character change—that is, to bring about a resolution of the perceptual set in question.

In subsequent sessions Miss Banks's relationship to her father was examined further. The therapist's hypothesis that her father was basically frightened and insecure seemed to be confirmed. From this point of view it became clear that the mother's restricted life was in obedience as much to her husband's need as to her depression. The birth of a mongoloid son had reinforced the father's feeling that safety lay in minimizing change and avoiding risks of any kind. When not supported by his familiar professional routine, he became anxious and irritable. Miss Banks now realized that it was likely that his constant criticism of her was his way of expressing his fear and, in a magical sort of way, of warding off expected disaster by predicting it.

Even before becoming aware of all this, the patient had matured considerably. As she began to see herself through the eyes of the therapist rather than through the distorting lenses of her father's fears, she permitted herself, in areas not directly involving her family, to become more hopeful about the world and her part in it, as the preceding session demonstrates. Eventually, through her recognition of her father as primarily frightened rather than angry, she was able to take a different attitude toward him as well as toward herself. Regretfully, and with some temporary depression, she gave up the childhood hope that she would somehow win her father's approval and through him finally become satisfied with herself. After giving up this phantasy as unrealizable, she lost her fear of her father's disapproval. Instead, when he started to get upset with her about something she had done or was planning to do, she learned to reassure him that she would be all right and would handle the situation and any possible complications.

Once the patient freed her father from the implied demand that he make her feel whole—a task he had not been able to accomplish for himself—his attitude toward her changed markedly. As is often the case, when adolescents and young adults with the benefits of insight won in therapy cease to demand what the parents cannot give psychologically, the relationship improves and is placed on a different footing. Paradoxically, but not unexpectedly, Miss Banks got what she had always wanted from her father once she no longer needed or demanded it. Her father, almost pathetically grateful that his secret was out at last (though he and his daughter never discussed it directly), began to use her as a confidante and friend. In the process she learned much about his past. Apparently he had been phobic and otherwise disturbed in his late adolescence and young adulthood and had managed eventually to "cure" himself by entering medical school and submerging himself totally in his work—thereby, so to speak, acquiring a new and functional identity as a physician. He became a healer and a helper rather than a patient in need of help. The shortcomings of his recovery, of course, became painfully obvious whenever he had to drop the mantle of the physician and fulfill other roles and responsibilities.

The hypothesis about Miss Banks's father as basically frightened rather than simply angry and critical was an empathic observation made about a man the therapist knew only indirectly through that man's daughter. Can one ever be certain that such a hypothesis is accurate and not simply an attractive possibility that therapist and patient have found useful and therefore accept as true? No, even if there is incidental corroborating evidence—as in this case when the father spontaneously revealed his psychopathological background to his daughter—the construct remains conjectural. But it seems to me that the way such questions are usually asked is meaningless in the context of psychotherapy. Of course we cannot arrive at a conviction of certainty in the same manner as the physical sciences do: the criteria of the physical sciences cannot be used to measure "fact," "truth," or "validity" in a field that uses a different methodology and strives for different goals. The validity of the therapist's hypothesis lies in the fact that it enabled the patient to see herself and her development in a novel way and then to use that understanding to further her maturation. Although she had been making better use of her abilities right along, now her character underwent a qualitative change. She became a significantly different person—that is, a person who saw herself differently, in terms of her past, present, and future experiences and, as a result, had new behavioral choices and new goals open to her. The obvious question then is whether some other interpretation of her father's behavior or her interaction with him might not have had the same effect. The repeated experience of failing to achieve such an outcome, no matter how well intentioned the doctor and how plausible the interpretation, convinces the experienced therapist of the accuracy of the insight when an intervention produces a result such as was obtained with Miss Banks.

As Miss Banks worked through the implications of her insight into the relationship with her father, her relationship with the therapist also changed. Once she understood that her father's critical attitude had to do more with his inadequacies than with hers, her assumption that the therapist would find her wanting waned rapidly. She no longer challenged him to dislike her but openly mobilized a long-dormant wish for a trusted parent with whom she could share her ideas and hopes. Not only her attitude but her whole appearance changed: she looked younger, and her habitual angry scowl disappeared.

One of the topics she now brought into the therapy was her manner of dealing with the men in her life. She was not unattractive, and occasionally her roommate and others introduced her to men who took her out. The sequence of events was always the same: the patient would be interested in a man, but he would stop calling her after a few dates. As she had said earlier, she felt that men respond negatively to her intelligence and self-assertion. Only persistent and insistent questioning of the patient regarding these transactions filled in details that put things in a different light. When Miss Banks first met a new man, she would encourage him to talk of his background, his ambitions, interests, and goals. Her interest was flattering and usually brought about a positive response, along with some fairly intimate revelations. Then, without being conscious of her intent and under the guise of frank discussion, she would make deflating comments attacking the man where he was most vulnerable. Inevitably a breakup would follow.

Because the patient was now able to listen to the therapist without immediately feeling unfairly criticized, it was possible for him to examine with her what she actually had said and to help her to find out not only what she was doing but also her unconscious intent in doing it—that is, to make her suitor feel attacked and belittled. This process eventually permitted the following interpretation of her behavior: in her relations to others she relived the discord with her father in hope of bringing about a happier ending, thereby symbolically undoing her trauma at his hands. Unfortunately for her, re-creating that discord necessitated her putting her respondent into a hostile and antagonistic position by undermining his self-esteem. The result, as is usual when pathological patterns are re-created in daily life, was that the trauma was repeated instead of being resolved, with the patient finding herself rejected and indignant about the injustice of it all.

Once she could see clearly what she had been doing, Miss Banks lost interest in men as suitors. Her work preoccupied her, and she was reluctant to invest the time and effort required to play the dating game; instead, she signed up for extra evening courses in clinical psychology to supplement her training.

Three months before the therapist was to leave the clinic he reminded the patient that this change was going to take place. She took the news quite calmly and said she had been thinking about it herself. Now that she had been exposed to clinical work, she said, continuing with her original plan to get a Ph.D. and spend her life in teaching and research appealed to her less and less. Instead, she had decided to get her master's degree and accept a job that had been offered to her at the agency where she was carrying out her research project. This meant she would be financially independent and could continue with treatment on a private basis. This plan was carried out.

Now in her therapy sessions Miss Banks reported on her progress and her activities, using the therapist as an appreciative audience who could validate her achievements and could, from the vantage point of his longer experience with life generally and clinical practice in particular, discuss issues and questions that came up as she found her way in the new world she was creating for herself. She was quite aware that she was using the therapist as a father surrogate who provided her with an opportunity to grow as she had not been able to do before.

Psychological issues of a historical sort were not neglected. Her anger at her mother's failings gave way to sorrow for the nature of her mother's existence and to a determination not to let herself be put into a position where she was dependent on a man and at the mercy of his psychological problems. However, the patient did not find a bitter, angry, isolating kind of resolution, nor did she vilify or scapegoat her father and the therapist, the two men now most important to her. The patient came to a thoughtful, resolute conclusion, a recognition that dependence prolonged beyond reason exacts a heavy price—one that she was not willing to pay. Along with this development came her realization that her conclusions also applied to her relationship with the therapist. Much as she now enjoyed their work together, she felt a strong urge to apply independently what she had learned and to take total responsibility for her growth. She also desired to acquire more clinical skill. Since she had been strongly influenced and favorably impressed by the two child psychiatrists who were consultants to the agency, she decided to become a physician in order eventually to qualify for such training. She was able to discuss her plans with her father and to enlist his financial support. Instead of responding with anger to his initial negative attitude, she quickly understood that he was afraid that her plan for professional independence would undermine their relationship, which had become very important to him. She was able to reassure him on that score, and she heard from other sources that he was openly proud of her ambition and initiative.

She made plans to enroll as a full-time student so as to fulfill the undergraduate requirements she needed to become a medical student, and she suggested that she would stop psychotherapy when the time came to start classes. She wanted to devote herself single-mindedly to her professional goal, and she now felt reasonably satisfied with her life and her plans for the future. Over the next few months her decision and its implications were thoroughly discussed and, since nothing came up that made either therapist or patient doubt her ability to implement her resolve, the therapy was brought to an end that summer after a total of seventy sessions.

A year later Miss Banks called the therapist to tell him that she had been accepted at a medical school and that she felt content with the way her life was going.

One might compare the therapist's recognition and interpretation of the problem that faced Miss Banks in her relationship to her father with the untying of a knot that had held back her progress in selected areas. However, unlike the neurotic patients with whom we have become familiar through Freud's writings, she was not hampered by a repressed desire to fulfill a forbidden wish but, rather, was held back by the absence of the necessary sustaining psychological environment to foster her development (Kohut 1971). Accordingly, the management of her transference and its resolution was unlike that in a classical psychoanalysis. The interpretation of the positive father transference that developed led not to its disappearance but to the freedom to use it productively. When for a brief time the patient sexualized the transference and became frightened by her thoughts, the therapist pointed out to her that she was mistakenly attributing genital motives to the love and affection she felt for him who was, through his work, giving her a chance to achieve satisfactions heretofore closed to her. She was helped to understand that her emotions were appropriate to the child who stands in awe of and wants to unite with the powerful, giving parent, and were not those of a sexually excited woman. The resolution of the transference was embodied in her going beyond the stage of working for the therapist-parent's implicit or explicit approval and praise and, instead, forming her own concept of an ideal self that she then set out to fulfill.

It may seem that the patient's wish to become a physician was only an identification with both father and therapist and an attempt to resolve a neurotic conflict through action rather than through psychological insight. I would disagree with such a judgment because it is based on theoretical preconceptions for which there is no clinical evidence in this case. The patients' sure, thoughtful manner as she went ahead with her plans, the absence of any feeling that she was being driven, and the genuine satisfaction she obtained from the process all speak against her behavior being simply an attempt at a neurotic solution for underlying conflict (see also pages 122–23).

Nor would I regard it as problematic that her therapy did not end with her riding off into the sunset with a Prince Charming to live happily ever after. Whether Miss Banks will eventually marry, and whether genital sexuality will play an important part in her life, are not only unanswerable questions at this point but, more important, are questions that need not be the concern of the therapist. Her eagerness to learn, her pleasure in her new-found independence, her willingness to move forward to see what she could accomplish with the optimistic feeling that she could enlist the world's coöperation, all remind me of the so-called latency child and the period of cognitive development between six to twelve years of age which, according to Piaget (Piaget and Inhelder 1971), is a time of mastery and adaptation to the systematic, logical aspects of the environment and the decentering of the self. In other words, it is a time when the sense of narcissistic entitlement gives way to finding satisfaction in a world where one is no longer the phantasied center and focus. Perhaps this patient will live through a "pubertal" period and a recapitulation or first awakening of an oedipal phase once she has accomplished what she needs to in this area of her belated growth. One cannot know that in advance or insist upon it. She must now have the opportunity to live with her new-found freedom, and what will eventually happen to her cannot be predicted. That she now has a viable self-concept based on an understanding of how she came to be the person who initially presented herself for treatment is a satisfactory result (Goldberg 1975).

There are, of course, many important issues in both of the cases presented so far that either have not been mentioned or need further comment. The chapters that follow will deal with at least some of them.*

*Miss Banks falls into the group of patients now classified by Kohut (1977) as "selfobject disturbances," formerly called "narcissistic character disorders." A discussion of this diagnosis and some further consideration of this case will be found in chapters 10 and 11.

VII

Introduction to Principles of Diagnosis and Interpretation

In my experience, theory is best taught in connection with clinical problems. An exposition that leaves a student glassy-eyed in the classroom suddenly makes sense to him when it is related to a clinical case with which he is concerned. The supervisory situation enables the teaching therapist to generalize from the particular aspects of a case to the broader implications of its analysis and management. Accordingly, I have used the supervisory format here to illustrate basic principles in the practice of dynamic psychotherapy.

Supervisory Session 1

Resident: I've read a lot of descriptions of various syndromes—lists of signs and symptoms that are indicative of this or that illness—but I can't seem to use them. For instance, yesterday I saw a man, Mr. Clark, referred for treatment of a depression. Two months ago he lost his wife of twenty-five years. Since then he has complained of sleeplessness and loss of appetite. He cries a lot and just doesn't know what to do with himself any more. These are all part of the textbook picture of depression, but somehow it just didn't add up for me. He said he wasn't suidical when I asked him about that, though he admitted he has occasionally thought that it might be better if he ended it all. But how do I know he isn't fooling me, or himself for that matter? Maybe I should have put him in the hospital just to be on the safe side, but that didn't seem justified when I couldn't be sure he even had a depression. Should I have prescribed antidepressant medication?

Supervisor: Let's talk about the diagnostic process in general before we get down to specifics. One of the problems in our field which you have already run into is that textbook descriptions are high-level abstractions that don't take into account the individual circumstances that usually confuse what one sees in a given instance.

That's why it's so frustrating when you try to apply these abstractions. Indeed, though in retrospect we justify our diagnoses by matching them against lists of symptoms and signs, that is not the way we actually arrive at them.

Resident: What did I do wrong?

Supervisor: Nothing, really. Actually you were on the right track. Mr. Clark was referred to you with the label "depression" already attached to him. That means you met him with a ready-made pattern of expectation—a pattern based on your past experience with depressed patients and with what you had read about this syndrome. However, when you actually saw the patient and tried to fit him into that category, you felt that somehow he didn't match the expectations that the diagnosis mobilized in you. What you have to do then is to see what *does* occur to you as you continue to talk to and examine the patient. Sometimes a testable hypothesis comes to you, and you can follow that up. Other times, as in your situation today, you end up not knowing what's going on. But it's much better to do what you did—recognize that you don't know—than to fit the poor patient on a Procrustean bed. It's better than categorizing him just to allay your anxiety and then basing your treatment on that kind of a forced conclusion.

Resident: What do you make of it? What's your diagnosis?

Supervisor: I don't think we should make up our minds about Mr. Clark on the basis of the information we have so far. After you see him again, we'll talk and see where we go. Now what I would like to do is to follow up what I told you about the diagnostic process, and give you a couple of examples that will illustrate how we actually come to conclusions in clinical situations that either confound our expectations or are unfamiliar and disconcerting.

Billy, a nine-year-old boy, had been hospitalized following a fracture of the arm. Incidentally the pediatrician learned that Billy had been having visions and hearing voices for some months. The doctor made a tentative diagnosis of schizophrenia and called for a consultation.

As I entered the patient's room, I was met by the blare of a television set tuned to a children's program, and saw a little boy sitting up in bed. He was absorbed in some sort of drawing game which he seemed to be manipulating successfully in spite of the plaster cast encasing his left arm. I said, "Hi there!" to call attention to myself. Bright-eyed, he looked up at me and with a friendly smile returned my greeting.

At this point I became distinctly aware that I had just concluded that this was not a schizophrenic boy, and I checked the referral slip to make sure I had the right room and the right patient. There was no error.

Resident: Excuse me for interrupting. You're not suggesting that intuitive hunches should be the basis for our diagnoses, are you?

Supervisor: I'm not talking about "should" or "shouldn't," but trying to describe to you what actually transpired as I reacted to Billy. Of course I didn't stop there but kept on with the diagnostic process.

I introduced myself to Billy and we had a talk during which, among other things, I asked him about his strange visual and auditory experiences. I learned that Billy could always tell when he was going to have trouble because first there would be a peculiar sensation in his head. After that he would always see a particular teacher's face in front of him and hear her voice quite distinctly, though he couldn't understand what she was saying. Then there would be people standing around him looking concerned and telling him he must have fainted. Indeed, it was during one of these episodes that he had apparently fallen down a stairway and suffered the fracture that necessitated his present hospitalization.

Resident: I see what you're getting at. The origin of the boy's pathology sounds more and more organic rather than psychological.

Supervisor: No, that's not my point. The presence of physical pathology does not rule out psychological disturbances. They are not mutually exclusive. I think it bears emphasizing that psychological diagnoses are not to be made, as is unfortunately so often done, by exclusion. It is incorrect to think that if there is nothing wrong physically, an ailment must be psychological and, per contra, if there is something organically wrong, that explains everything about the patient. Whether a psychological problem exists should be based on the findings that emerge in the interview.

As the patient was talking with me, his capacity to relate in a direct, boyishly appropriate, empathy-provoking manner confirmed me in my initial and instantaneous impression that this was not a schizophrenic child. As we talked about his interests, his schoolwork, and his activities at home, I formulated the additional hypothesis that this boy suffered from no psychological illness and did not require psychotherapy. When we got around to discussing his hallucinations, I formed another hypothesis—namely, that this boy had temporal lobe epilepsy and required a neurological work-up. Later an electroencephalogram and other tests confirmed the diagnosis of idiopathic temporal lobe epilepsy, and neurological management was instituted.

What actually happened here? How did my conclusions come about? Let's accept as a working definition that a theory is a set of propositions advanced to explain a particular experience or group of experiences. In the example just given the referring physician's mention of auditory and visual hallucinations coupled with his diagnostic impression of childhood schizophrenia oriented me toward what I had read about and seen of such children. So before I even met the patient, I had formulated a theory that I might find some variant of what your manual of nosology describes as "autistic, atypical, and withdrawn behavior; failure to develop identity separate from the mother's and general unevenness, gross immaturity and inadequacy in development."*

Resident: I can never remember all the details of those classifications.

Supervisor: Neither can I, and that's my point.

The moment Billy spoke to me I knew my anticipatory theory would not hold, but I didn't arrive at that conclusion by reviewing one by one, as would a digital computer, the criteria for schizophrenia and then comparing them with each facet of my ongoing clinical experience with Billy. My brain worked more like an analogue computer—rejecting its prejudgment because there was insufficient correspondence between the pattern of incoming signals and the pattern signifying childhood schizophrenia which, rightly or wrongly, I carried with me as a result of my then still rather limited clinical experience. Something totally unexpected came into my awareness, a wave of relief at the absence while talking to Billy of the strain imposed on a beginner of working with a nonfunctioning, unhappy, clingingly demanding or angrily rejecting child. Then followed the conclusion that, psychologically speaking, this might just be a healthy boy.

At that point I did not quickly review the various possible other causes of hallucination that might account for the history on the referral slip. Instantaneously I formed a new hypothesis: perhaps the pediatrician had been in error about the presence of hallucinations, perhaps he had mistaken a bright boy's vivid imagination and the recital of a daydream for an abnormal perception. I realized I was wrong in that assumption the moment Billy told me of his prodromal symptom. Without my pausing for reflection, the words "aura-epilepsy" occurred to me. I was then prepared to have his further recitals match the pattern for temporal lobe irritation

*Diagnostic and Statistical Manual of Mental Disorders, second edition (DSM II), American Psychiatric Association, 1968, p. 35.

which I had learned during a stint as an intern on the neurology service, and that expectation was fulfilled.*

The therapist meets a given clinical situation with a set of expectations. He matches the expectations with or compares them with what actually transpires between himself and the patient. The degree of conformity with, or deviation from, his expectations stimulates him to create a series of hypotheses about the patient which he implicitly tests for truth value as the meeting or interview continues. This process goes on until a tentative diagnosis—that is, classification and prognosis—and a treatment plan are formulated.

Resident: Sure, I can see how that would work once you have the experience, but when you start out you have to find your way without it. How do you do that?

Supervisor: Of course, in the beginning we lack the experience that would permit us to organize our thoughts about a new patient rapidly, though only provisionally, by letting his appearance, attitude, manner of speech, and the nature of his complaints remind us of other patients we have seen and studied thoroughly. We also have to reckon with the interference created by our own anxiety as we imagine how we'll look to the patient, to our colleagues, supervisors, and so on. As a result it's likely that initially we may well be focused more on ourselves than on the patient—that is, we need to know what's wrong with the patient, because we'll feel foolish if we don't.

Resident: I hate to think that I have to make every mistake in the book before I can begin to function more effectively. It sounds like a very uneconomical way to have to learn anything.

Supervisor: But don't forget that you have lived among people all your life, and that if you let yourself use it, you have a fund of information that is very helpful as you enter any new situation, including this one. Let me give you another example of this—it so happens it also involves a child.

Frank was a pre-adolescent boy who was brought to the clinic by his mother because she could not cope with him at home any longer. His behavior in the interview bore out the mother's plaint that her son was a moody, often destructive, uncoöperative child who didn't seem to be able to grow up and learn to do what children his age are expected to accomplish. In the interview this uncommunicative, bizarre boy seemed definitely out of contact with me, and there was some evidence that he was lost in a hallucinatory phantasy. The signs of manifest pathology combined with the boy's history all seemed to add up to a diagnosis of childhood schizophrenia (see page 90), but there was a complication that prevented me from feeling satisfied with my conclusion. Frank had been blind since birth.

How much of this boy's inability to live in the world was a complication of his sensory handicap, representing immaturity and resentment rather than psychosis? My supervisor,† instead of discussing my diagnostic dilemma on an abstract level, arranged for me to spend some time in a classroom for blind and near-blind children of Frank's age. Not knowing what to expect, I pictured a room full of pathetic youngsters sitting either sadly fingering their Braille books or fumbling around trying to learn how to weave baskets or make straw brooms. How, I wondered, should I, a privileged sighted person, conduct myself so as to seem neither indifferent nor patronizing when talking to these unfortunate children?

* Lest I be understood as advocating that a psychotherapist must of necessity have a medical background, let me hasten to add that my establishment of the definitive diagnosis in this case is incidental to the point I am trying to make. My job was essentially done when I was able to say with reasonable certainty that Billy had neither schizophrenia nor any other psychological disturbance that would account for his symptoms.

† Dr. Mary Engel.

As I entered the classroom, I had to struggle to keep a huge grin from breaking out on my face, and then I realized that under the circumstances I needn't bother to fight it. The teacher smiled back at me with a look that seemed to say that other visitors had had the same reaction. My smile was one of relief and recognition, for this classroom looked exactly like the ones I myself had learned in years before. The "good" students were busy with books and paper, and of course there was a "not-quite-so-good" boy teasing the girl next to him. The usual parade to the drinking fountain and to the washrooms was in progress, and the hum of active, happy, busy children served as background music for this familiar scene.

I realized that I had formed an anticipatory hypothesis of how a blind child reacts to his handicap by putting myself in what I thought was his place. I imagined that the anxiety and despair that I would feel if I lost my sight might well cause me to act in a confused, withdrawn, and/or angry fashion. So why not Frank? Once exposed to some average blind children, I realized that their manifest adaptation was quite similar to that of the nonhandicapped child, and that Frank, though blind, had more in common with sighted schizophrenic children than he did with the blind youngsters who had adapted themselves to their handicap.

Resident: If I understand you correctly, you are saying that we have to evaluate a patient's symptoms and behavior in the greater context of his background and over-all life situation. If we have seen enough similar situations, or if our personal experience helps us to understand what's happening, we have patterns of expectation that let us evaluate the situation. If we do not, there are usually ways of getting the information we need.

Supervisor: Exactly. If the patient is able to coöperate, we can enlist his aid in telling us about himself and his past and present circumstances, and thus we can get the necessary background to put his difficulties in context. Sometimes interviews with the family help if the patient is unable to participate because of age or pathology. Looking for similar situations in the literature or talking it over with colleagues who might be expected to have knowledge in an area that is puzzling to us can be very helpful. Studying the pertinent variables firsthand, as I did in Frank's case, is most instructive when it is possible.

Resident: So that's really my problem with Mr. Clark. Instead of trying to add up his symptoms, I have to establish the background against which his symptoms make sense.

Supervisor: Try to do that and let's see what happens.

Supervisory Session 2

Resident: It's been a very interesting experience. I've seen Mr. Clark twice since we had our discussion. He came in, as he did initially, symptom-oriented. He didn't feel any better and wanted to know if tranquilizers, which his wife had been taking, would help him. That was my opportunity to break out of the rut of just talking about his complaints. I asked him about his wife and why she had taken tranquilizers.

He seemed to open up at that point. He really needed to talk about her. The two of them had been nigh inseparable for a quarter of a century. He has a small business, a shoe store in a marginal area of the city, and she was his bookkeeper, saw the salesmen, answered the telephone—in other words, did all the office work.

They'd drive to the store together in the morning and lock up at night. They had no children—he is sterile—and their activities and interests were very closely intertwined.

For the past three years they both knew she could die any time, but they resolved to go on pretty much as before, and they did. The tranquilizers helped her to sleep. She was understandably anxious, fearing that she might not wake up the next morning. When the end finally came, Mr. Clark was reconciled to it and glad that she was spared further suffering, but he was not prepared for the loneliness he experienced. She was such an integral part of all he did that now, without her to talk to, his activities lack meaning. They are almost unreal for him. In addition, he is frightened about his ability to carry on the business alone. As she got sicker, they just let part of the work slide, but now the time has come when he has to get his affairs straightened out or see his store go down the drain.

I didn't have any trouble with the diagnosis this time. More accurately, I stopped worrying about what label to hang on Mr. Clark. He certainly is not depressed in the classical sense of the term. He is a frightened and lonely man. I come from a big family, so I've gone to my share of funerals and have seen how lost people are when death breaks up a good marriage.

Supervisor: Once you got over your own anxiety about how you might pigeonhole Mr. Clark, a different pattern suggested itself to you for comparison with his situation—that is, your own experience with death and loss.

Resident: Yes, and he began to look and behave differently during the interview. Once he was talking about his life instead of his symptoms, he became brighter, more alert, purposeful.

Supervisor: He sensed you could understand him, and he responded. Precisely what a melancholic or an endogenously depressed person cannot do. Were he clinically depressed, he'd have reverted to talking about his symptoms and asking you for relief, while at the same time telling you that nothing could help him, that all was hopeless, and so forth. This man is mourning his wife. Grief is not the equivalent of depression.

Resident: It was clear to me that he was not in need of hospitalization or antidepressant medication. What he needs, I think, is someone to help him cope with his loss. He has no children or close relatives, and friends have their limits. I think I was the first person whom he could tell what his loss meant.

Supervisor: Even more important, with you he probably formulated what he was going through for the first time. Having some idea of how one feels and actually voicing how one feels so as to appeal to another's understanding are two very different experiences.

Resident: I was wondering whether I should advise him to see more people, make an effort to get out. Human contact seems to help him so much.

Supervisor: Don't spoil good therapy. He'll find his way once he is free to do so. Your job is first of all to try to understand him, which you are doing with good results, and then to help him understand himself. Once you grasp what's happening to him, it seems very obvious and clear to you, but that doesn't mean he knows it yet or accepts its implications.

Resident: When I saw Mr. Clark for his third appointment two days ago, he still looked troubled but seemed eager to go on talking about his life. He even smiled a few times when he recalled some of the vacations they took. They were both avid campers and crisscrossed the country for a month in the summer when they closed the store.

Supervisor: What you are doing is fine. You are helping the patient to accomplish the work of mourning. As Freud described in *Mourning and Melancholia* (1917), as a bereaved person relives each memory, the ties to the past are loosened a little bit. The events Mr. Clark is telling you about no longer belong exclusively to the past, they are given new life by your hearing about them, and in that way the present takes on meaning. Eventually the future will do so also, and then life will seem worth while again to Mr. Clark.

Resident: How should I handle it if he brings up his insomnia or other symptoms?

Supervisor: I think you should explain to him why he's feeling this way. Help him to understand that his wife was so much a part of his self-concept that her loss leaves him with a feeling of emptiness. Without her to tell of his achievements, disappointments, and hopes there seems to be no point to doing what he's doing. He's at loose ends. What has been the focal point of his life's organization is missing, and his discomfort is to be expected.

Resident: And that alone will help?

Supervisor: Yes, it should. Knowing why you feel the way you do lessens anxiety considerably. It's only when a patient has things happening to him that he doesn't understand that the cycle of ever-mounting anxiety gets hold of him.

Resident: But surely he knows why he is upset.

Supervisor: Yes and no. He knows his wife's death precipitated his unhappy state, but he doesn't realize he's so upset because her loss deprived him of the focus around which he had arranged his life. He's like a traveler in a totally foreign country—all the adaptive measures that have sustained him at home are suddenly inoperative.

Resident: Should I reassure him that this will pass, that he'll be all right again?

Supervisor: This man is in a position similar to the one you and I were in when we first began our psychotherapy training. Everything was suddenly different, what we had learned in school seemingly didn't apply any more and yet we were expected to perform. When you came in here worried about your patient, do you think it would have helped you to hear from me that everything was going to be all right in time? Now that you have learned how to approach the situation, I can tell you that and you'll believe me. But until the possibility of a new and more meaningful order is experienced by someone who is confused, reassurances don't mean much. Mr. Clark needs to know, just as you needed to know, what the name of the game is and what the rules are so he can function again. Whether he'll win, lose, or draw depends on a lot of factors that aren't under our control, and we don't need to pretend that they are.

Resident: But some patients don't want to know the truth, do they?

Supervisor: That's so, but they signal that clearly. Don't worry. No matter what you do, those that don't want to know won't know, and I assure you they don't jump at the chance to explore what's happened to them as Mr. Clark is doing.

Resident: If I understand you correctly, successful adaptation depends on being able to compare the present with the past in some meaningful manner. If the difference between what we know and what needs to be understood is too great, then our ability to think——

Supervisor: To match patterns of experience and manipulate them . . .

Resident: O.K., if our ability to match patterns is impaired, that gives rise to psychological symptoms.

Supervisor: Yes, exactly.

Resident: That's a theory with some very interesting possibilities. Somebody ought to teach us about that.

Supervisor: What do you think I'm doing?

Resident: Oh . . .

Supervisory Session 3

Resident: Mr. Clark is doing well. I'm continuing to see him twice a week. He looks a lot better and I haven't heard him complaining about insomnia or anorexia. He is starting to use the therapy sessions to tell me about his daily activities and not just about the past and his wife. It's almost eerie. It's so obvious that he is treating me as he must have her. He tells me when he got to the store in the morning, how many customers came in, the trouble he had getting the janitor to provide enough heat last Thursday, and so on. I guess this is what's called transference, isn't it?

Supervisor: What is being transferred?

Resident: I guess I have become the lost object.

Supervisor: Have you really? In what way?

Resident: Oh, I don't mean that he has become delusional and confused me with the lady he was married to for twenty-five years, but the energy that was formerly directed toward her has now become attached to the mental representation he has of me. The energic cathexis has shifted.

Supervisor: Instead of using the language of psychoanalytic metapsychology, try to formulate what you have observed.

Resident: As I said, the patient now depends on me in the same way as he did on his wife. To use your way of describing it, I have become the focus around which he is organizing much of his life. I feel that our therapy sessions give his daily activities a meaning that they didn't have when he first came in. He looks forward to telling me what he has been doing, and that gives him a purpose, you might say, that was lacking when he first came to see me.

Supervisor: What's been transferred then, it seems, is not some mysterious "energy" but a pattern of expectations. The need to have someone understand his hopes, fears, accomplishments, and failures, which had been fulfilled in his relationship to his wife, is now transferred to you.

Resident: If Mr. Clark's unconscious goal in the therapy is to make me into his wife, should I interpret that to him?

Supervisor: What makes you think that's his aim?

Resident: Well, I told you that the way he talks to me probably replicates conversations the two of them had many times together.

Supervisor: Quite a jump, isn't it, from that hypothesis to one about making you into his wife. Anyway, what do you want to accomplish by telling him about his unconscious goals?

Resident: I guess I'm still thinking along the lines of the energy model and that he's discharging feelings that he originally transferred from his mother to his wife and now to me.

Supervisor: And if that were true, then what?

Resident: Isn't it important to get at feelings of infantile dependence and help the patient to understand them?

Supervisor: Boy! The leaps you make would make a kangaroo envious. His wife was his colleague, his business partner for all those years. He depended on her to help him work through decisions, and used her as a sounding board and advisor. It's not infantile to be dependent on another adult in such a fashion or to want to reconstitute such a relationship when it has been lost.

Resident: But I don't know anything about the shoe business.

Supervisor: Listen, and you will know about it by the time you're through with Mr. Clark. Then you'll have an intimate acquaintance with a way of life and a subculture that will stand you in good stead with future patients. However, that is of course not the point. You don't have to make business decisions for him—you can't and you shouldn't. He just wants you to understand how he feels about the events that are befalling him. If his reaction to what is happening in his business seems inappropriate to you, investigate his reasoning further. Then if you are still of the same opinion, you can help him deal with his reaction not as a job-related problem but as a psychological one.

Resident: When he told me how much trouble he had getting the janitor to give him enough heat in the store, we got around to talking about how difficult it is for him to ask anyone for anything. His wife used to make all such requests and spare him the embarrassment of having to make such contacts. He feels better when he's doing things for other people and almost dreads being obligated to anyone.

Supervisor: Good. You used this mundane incident to let him reveal more of his self. How did you respond to what he said?

Resident: I told him it must be difficult to handle by himself what he had always counted on his wife to do for him, but that I thought it was good that he was facing these issues rather than avoiding them. After all, he accomplished what he set out to do. He did get the heat in the store that he needed to make it comfortable.

Supervisor: Excellent. You are helping him ultimately to become independent of you, by reinforcing his assertive behavior with your complimentary response while, at the same time, letting him depend on you during this time of stress. I imagine that you will also learn more about his diffidence and its history, if the opportunity arises.

Resident: Isn't his dependence on me an aspect of the sexual instinct, the need to unite with me as he once was united with his mother?

Supervisor: Of course, but since everything we do can be seen as ultimately related to previous experience, that becomers a truism. You can certainly be cognizant of the origins of various behavior patterns in terms of this or that universal infantile experience, but to tell Mr. Clark at this point that you represent his mother in some way would at best not be helpful and at worst would be unsettling and counterproductive for him. Why, in the face of the fact that you are handling his dependence very well, do you think you need to establish the infantile root of his behavior and interpret it?

Resident: What I'm doing seems so superficial.

Supervisor: Your patient is undergoing a growth period—that he is a middle-aged man doesn't preclude that in the least. At the age of fifty-five he is relearning or learning for the first time—I'm not sure which—to assert himself. By letting him experiment with situations that are new to him while offering him the protection of your understanding and whatever other help you can give him, you are behaving as a good parent might. He has no difficulties with you in the transference. His self-esteem, his picture of himself as a functioning adult, demands that he conduct himself assertively, risk refusal, and accept the possibility that he might not be liked for asserting himself. At the same time apparently something in his character makes him anxious when he is in such a situation, it threatens his integration in some way. That, as I see it, is the problem. As long as he is handling it well, that should be acknowledged. If he fails, that failure should be faced and explored, but until it is clear that he is involving you in it directly, don't fish those waters. Freud (1913) pointed out long ago that we do not interpret transference as long as the treatment is moving satisfactorily. Only when the transference becomes an obstacle to progress, does it become the focus for interpretation.

Supervisory Session 4

Supervisor: Are you feeling more comfortable now?

Resident: Yes, I am. When I don't have to relate everything to childhood sexual conflicts, I can listen better.

Supervisor: So what is going on with Mr. Clark?

Resident: He is moving right along. Seems to be taking more pleasure in his work. I think he is beginning to enjoy doing the jobs his wife used to do. He is learning that he's not helpless, and that means a lot to him.

Supervisor: That's a good operational definition of what our goal in psychotherapy should be: bringing the patient to the point where he feels he is not helpless—that is, the point where he can exercise significant control over what has been threatening to overwhelm him (Seligman 1975).

Resident: Wouldn't the feeling of not being helpless be the subjective or experiential aspect of successful ordering activity, of pattern matching?

Supervisor: Yes. It's the inability to create order, or the fear that one won't be able to do so, that brings about anxiety. Order implies predictability, the belief that one can exercise control of some sort over one's future.

When his wife died, Mr. Clark felt helpless without her stabilizing influence and became increasingly anxious. When he first came to you, you saw an agitated, rather than a clinically depressed, individual. His belief that you would be able to understand him—that is, that he would find himself in the order that you created—sustained him while he learned with your help that he is able to cope with the demands now being made upon him.

Resident: He's becoming quite cheerful, as a matter of fact. He had told me he was going to look for someone to handle what had been his wife's work at the store, but the last time he was in for an appointment, he mentioned that he's going to wait for a while and see if he can't manage by himself and save the money it would cost to hire someone. Quite spontaneously he began to wonder why he had let himself believe that he couldn't do the jobs that he's doing now. I suggested that it might be related to what he had or hadn't learned to expect of himself when he was a child. He immediately began to talk about his family, something he hadn't done before. It seems he's an only child and was always babied by his mother. He had asthma and multiple allergies, and there was an awful lot he wasn't permitted to do in his early years. His mother just got him in the habit of expecting her to take care of everything that might unduly strain or excite him, and as he himself said, when he got married he let his wife take over where his mother had left off.

Supervisor: You see, if you just keep your eye on becoming better acquainted with the patient and furthering your understanding of what he presents, the pertinent material from childhood becomes available in a fashion that makes sense to the patient and, therefore, is very convincing to both of you.

Resident: It's very interesting, but what good does it do to know why he might not have trusted himself to be able to function all these years? What should he do now? Get mad at his mother? The past can't change.

Supervisor: What he has done is to get what sounds like a bit of genuine insight into himself. With that, the present has changed even though the past can't change. Where that change—his new-found understanding—will lead we don't know. In terms of your work with him, what has happened is both important and revealing. We now have reason to believe that he is in a mother transference.

Resident: You mean he sees me as being like his mother?

Supervisor: No, not at this point at any rate. You are more the mother he might have needed or wanted, a mother who believes in him and encourages his ability to grow and be on his own without, however, withdrawing her strength and support.

Resident: Hard to believe. He's old enough to be my father.

Supervisor: It's often the case that insofar as a person has a developmental arrest, he continues to experience the world at that age level. This is what Freud (1915*b*) was talking about when he said that the unconscious doesn't have a sense of time. The corollary to that statement is that in principle one is never too old to take a developmental step forward. Don't forget that Mr. Clark doesn't see himself as being quite as ancient as you do—you who are half his age. Often the very fact that one is older provides an incentive to learning and to change—there is a recognition that the future is not limitless and what's to be done must be done now.

Resident: It's true. I sense a certain excitement in him as he talks about the things he's accomplishing.

Supervisor: Then the two of you have something in common which should help you to understand what's going on within him. You are learning that you can become a psychotherapist and do the things you had only read about others doing. Mr. Clark is in the same position. Life is opening up for him as he sees himself functioning more independently and effectively in the sphere in which he has made his life's work. That there is an age difference—to say nothing of differences in background, intelligence, and socio-economic achievements—between you two shouldn't prevent you from grasping and responding to the significant similarities that exist between your life and that of your patient's.

Resident: Won't he be guilty that in a sense it's his wife's death that has freed him to accomplish all this?

Supervisor: He may never think of it that way, but it's good that you are playing in imagination with various scenarios. In a sense you prepare yourself for what you may hear. You may even have picked up some clues from him that such feelings do exist. Whether your hypothesis has to do more with you or with him remains to be seen.

Resident: So for now I should help him maintain the status quo.

Supervisor: Not the status quo. He's not standing still. If he continues to make his life at work the focus of his sessions, help him to consolidate his gains and further his progress by appropriate approval and interest. Again, don't let his age mislead you. In certain areas of his development there is a lot he needs to achieve, and it sounds to me as if he is going about it productively with your help.

Resident: It seems to be working out all right, but I must say I'm suprised to hear a dynamically oriented psychiatrist advocate what sounds essentially like behavior modification and operant conditioning.

Supervisor: You've put your finger on an interesting issue. I think the fear of being called or thought of as "behaviorist" interferes much more than is realized with the way analytically oriented therapists listen to their patients. What difference does it make if the patient talks about his daily activities rather than of memories or phantasies of the past? Who is to say that greater or more effective self-understanding will come from one rather than from the other form of association? Some patients, especially those whose character structure resembles that of the psychoneurotic, do need to resolve intrapsychic conflicts through insight before their behavior can change—that is, before they can permit themselves to learn what they need to do and implement it. Others need to pick up where their development was arrested, not because of intrapsychic conflict, but because there were conditions that made the possibilities for learning less than optimal. Such individuals, and I think Mr. Clark is one of them, use therapy as an opportunity to take up unfinished business.* Eventually the therapist can help such patients to understand what their progress means in terms of the past, but such insight can only come after adaptational change has been achieved. It is the reverse of the situation we meet with in the psychoneurotic individual.

It's a constant struggle not to be trapped and boxed in by labels, to remember that it is we who invented both the words and the categories they designate. "Behaviorism" does not have a corner on the market when it comes to dealing therapeutically with behavior, nor does a concern with adaptation preclude proper attention to furthering the patient's self-understanding through introspection.

Resident: I don't see that happening with Mr. Clark. Am I just doing supportive therapy with him?

Supervisor: Supportive treatment implies that you reinforce and make the patient comfortable with his accustomed defenses—that is, with his usual pattern of adaptation. That's the type of situation where the best you can do is to help repair and maintain the status quo you mentioned before. Mr. Clark, however, is becoming a different person in significant respects. You're not just shoring him up, so I think you have every right to call this dynamic psychotherapy.

Supervisory Session 13

For the next nine weeks the supervision of Mr. Clark's case was relatively uneventful. The patient made steady progress toward viewing himself as a capable and likable individual who did not fear that asserting himself would automatically invite rejection. He spoke less about his wife; but when he did speak of her, it was with fondness and controlled grief. He had some further recognition of how the patterns established by and for him in childhood influenced his decisions in adulthood.

The conclusion of his therapy was ushered in by an iatrogenically precipitated crisis.

Resident: I was really shocked by my session with Mr. Clark. I hardly know how to tell you what happened. You're aware that he has been doing very well, and I've had the thought that it might not be long before we ended treatment or at least reduced the intensity of therapy. Yesterday he came in and, as is usual for him now, told me what he has been doing at the store, with emphasis on his progress in dealing effectively in areas in which in the past he believed himself unable to function. Toward the end of the session, smiling, obviously pleased with himself, he announced that he must really be all right now. He gave me a conspiratorial wink and told me he went out with the boys for the first time since his wife died. I asked him to tell me about it. It seems that for years this group of men, all married as far as I can tell, has gotten together for a weekly poker game which ends after a

* Mr. Clark's basic difficulty is in the area of selfobject relationships (narcissistic character disorder) (Kohut 1977). Further discussion of these problems is to be found in chapters 10 and 11.

couple of hours, at which time they adjourn to a house of prostitution for the evening.

Supervisor: So?

Resident: Well, that's not right, is it? All these years he was married, so dependent on his wife, and then he does this to her.

Supervisor: What did you say to the patient?

Resident: Nothing, but I guess he knew from the expression on my face that something was wrong. He hastened to assure me that it was a very respectable, clean house.

Supervisor: And then?

Resident: It was the end of the session, and I just closed it with the usual, "I'll see you next week." But what should I do about this? How will I help him to uncover the guilt about his behavior and work it through? His wife is dead. He has to live with what he has done for the rest of his life.

Supervisor: Whoa, whoa! Not so fast. It sounds to me as if you're making assumptions here based on some feelings of your own rather than on anything the patient has said or conveyed to you. Judging from what you told me, he doesn't sound a bit upset. Quite the contrary. He takes the return of his sexual drive to be a good sign, which it might well be.

Resident: I don't think anybody can do that and not have a bad conscience.

Supervisor: You are committing a serious error here, one that will undermine the therapy if it is not corrected. It may very well hurt the patient and interfere with his recovery.

We all hold moral, cultural, and theoretical positions, and these inevitably color our therapeutic work to a greater or lesser degree, depending on the circumstances. It is our job to be aware of such attitudes and then to make a special effort to ensure that we really understand what the patient is telling us about himself. What does what he is saying or doing mean to him—that's what you have to find out. Once you do find out, then if you feel it's in his best interest to criticize, censure, or condemn, that's fine with me. There are times in therapy when one has to do that, just as praise, approval, and encouragement may be in order at other times. However, so far there is not one shred of evidence that the patient is conscience-stricken or in any other way conflicted about his sexuality. You may be right—he may feel guilty as hell—but explore before coming to conclusions.

Resident: So, what do you want me to do?

Supervisor: I want you to listen to yourself. "So, what do you want me to do?" The angry, sarcastic way you said that makes me believe that your mind is made up, and you are not going to be confused by facts.

Resident: [*Laughing sheepishly*] I suppose you're right. If my prejudice is involved, how do I go beyond it?

Supervisor: The same rules apply to us as to our patients. You must promote your understanding of the situation. Get the patient to help you achieve that by not hesitating to ask questions that will clarify the issue for you. If you find Mr. Clark's behavior difficult to comprehend, let him know that, and give him a chance to explain himself to you.

Resident: How should I ask him about this?

Supervisor: When you are not at ease, what ought to be very simple becomes complicated, doesn't it? What question do you have for Mr. Clark?

Resident: How could he patronize prostitutes when he had such a close relationship with his wife and professed to have such affection for her?

Supervisor: Fine, ask him that just that way.

Resident: If the opportunity comes up, I'll do so.

Supervisor: First of all, you are so concerned about this issue that I advise you to *make* the opportunity to talk about it. Secondly, I'm quite sure that your change in attitude must have registered with the patient on some level. Mr. Clark must have gotten some sense of losing the good will and benign curiosity that you have so far always brought to his situation. My hunch is that he will behave differently next time he sees you, and that it will be up to you to clear the air by discussing this issue and getting therapy back on the track.

Resident: I hope I haven't damaged things beyond repair.

Supervisor: We all make mistakes or at least *should* be making them. A therapist who doesn't have some qualms about something he has done with one or another patient on any given day either lacks the capacity for self-observation and self-criticism or else doesn't have a practice sufficiently complex to justify a specialist's attention. As Kohut (1971) has pointed out, the building of psychic structure occurs as infant and parent misunderstand one another's signals and try again to come to a better accommodation. Similarly, it is when patient and therapist struggle to overcome the obstacles to understanding that maturation takes place and conflicts are resolved. It is only unexamined errors that have catastrophic consequences. Mr. Clark cares very deeply for you and has invested you with all his hopes for a parent who won't be afraid to let him grow and will take pride in his independence and achievements. He is not going to give that up easily. He will extend you every opportunity to right what went wrong, but, like a baby or a child, he may well signal his distress at your lack of understanding in ways that are unclear and may even seem antagonistic. It is your job to interpret that to him if it occurs.

Resident: Should I apologize for what I did, or rather what I didn't do that is, listen to what he had to say without judging him prematurely?

Supervisor: Don't burden him with your confession. It's not his function to forgive you. You probably feel worse about it now than he does. The best thing you can do is just get to work with him and show him that you are ready to deal with whatever comes up—if not the first time, then the next time around.

Supervisory Session 14

Supervisor: Well, what happened?

Resident: It was very instructive. Mr. Clark came in just as he usually does and told me all the things that had happened to him. It should have been interesting because he had an altercation with a supplier in which he managed to acquit himself very well, but I found myself bored by what he was saying.

Supervisor: That is indeed instructive. What do you make of your mood?

Resident: I felt he had left me somehow, and maybe this was his response to being hurt and/or misunderstood last time by me.

Supervisor: Exactly. When you are bored by a patient, it is usually not the content of the session per se that is responsible. The loss of affective contact with the patient is what causes you to feel estranged from him. From infancy on we respond to all kinds of signals that are sent our way—tone of voice, bodily posture, the whole manner that someone has of being with us. When the patient withdraws, though he may be talking right along, the tone and the inflection that carry the message that he is speaking to us and not to a wall are missing, and quite unconsciously we tend to respond by feeling alone, isolated, meaningless—in a word, unloved. Before we realize it, we in turn have withdrawn from the patient, though we continue to look attentive and even pretend to be interested.

Resident: How do you handle a situation like that?

Supervisor: Don't permit yourself to sink into sullen passivity. Become active with the patient. Search for what might be going on if you don't know already. Don't hesitate to hypothesize aloud about what might account for the patient's silence, his aimless drifting, or his recital of seemingly insignificant details. Don't assume that if a patient is rambling on, he must necessarily be saying something that needs to be understood. And don't assume that no matter how bored you become, you have to sit out the session or sessions until the light dawns for you. When the patient is trying to say something truly important but can't make you understand, you have a different feeling. Under these circumstances you are not bored, you are excited, interested, and actively puzzled, because the patient's nonverbal communication reflects his struggle to communicate with you, not to avoid you. Then it might indeed be better to wait it out and see what happens. As long as you feel alert, something is happening, and you needn't worry.

Resident: What if your inattentiveness is due to your being tired, or occupied with some problem of your own, or experiencing some emotional upset that you are trying to deal with yourself?

Supervisor: I have found that the best antidote for preoccupation with myself is a patient who engages me in the therapeutic task. Suddenly my headache is not so bad, or whatever I'm unhappy about isn't so tragic. So I think the same principle still holds. You still have to ask yourself why you're preoccupied with your health or your problems when you're with one particular patient but not with other patients you see on the same day. The answer will usually be that the patient who leaves you time to ruminate about yourself has in some way withdrawn from you for reasons that need to be explored.

Resident: It could of course be that a patient comes in, sees you looking preoccupied, pale, or pained, and withdraws in the belief that he is intruding, and that you won't have interest to spare for him.

Supervisor: Perfectly possible, and that possibility needs to be investigated. Once that's out in the open, you are back to the patient and what his perception means to him, how he is affected by this turn of events—and that's fine.

Anyway, you were bored with Mr. Clark, and you had a pretty good idea why the patient was shutting you out. What did you do?

Resident: I decided to take your advice and not get all involved in confessing my errors and trying to undo whatever had been mishandled. Instead, I waited for him to finish, made what comments I had to make about what he had said, and then brought up the fact that I had been puzzled by an aspect of what he had spoken about last time. I said, "How could you justify your visits to a house of prostitution with the close relationship you had with your wife all these years and the mutual affection you professed for one another?" Then I waited for the ceiling to fall on me.

Supervisor: Did it?

Resident: No, surprisingly, it did not. He didn't seem to resent my question at all. He told me that although his early experiences with sex were exclusively with prostitutes, he had thought when he got married that that would no longer be the case. However, he found that his wife wasn't really much interested in sexual play, and that she resented his attempts to make their relationship more passionate. When they learned that they couldn't have children because he was sterile, his wife rapidly lost what interest she had demonstrated in the sexual aspect of marriage. It became clear to him, he says, without it ever being openly discussed, that she preferred that he take his sexual needs elsewhere to be fulfilled. It was just a matter of time before he fell back into his old pattern of seeking out prostitutes.

I still couldn't believe that that was all there was to it, so I asked him if he didn't feel to some extent conscience-stricken or guilty about it.

Supervisor: Good for you.

Resident: It was as if with that question we shifted roles. I thought Mr. Clark might get mad or defensive. Instead, he became positively avuncular. He settled back in his chair, gave me a long, kindly look, and said, in effect, that I had helped him a lot and was obviously far more educated than he, but, meaning no disrespect, in these matters his having lived longer put him in the position of perhaps teaching me something. He then told me, in essence, that he and his wife had had a very good life together, and that their marriage was an affectionate and mutually sustaining one which, he felt, it would not have been if he had continued to make an issue out of their sex life. As a young man he, too, had had an idealized concept of how life should be lived, but he found that those people he knew who couldn't compromise their picture of what things should be like tended to end up with nothing, while he and those he knew who accepted disappointment gracefully and worked around it as best they could tended to end up reasonably happy. No, he said, he wasn't guilty or upset about his weekly excursions to the house he and his friends visited. Perhaps with the years I, too, would be more understanding of how little that meant when weighed against the totality of a relationship. What had bothered him much more for a number of years was the absence of children. He would have liked to have had a son, but his wife was adamant about not adopting a child. Eventually he stopped thinking about it. He then reflected that perhaps if they had had children, he would not have been able to depend so long on his wife and would have started to do the things he's doing now much sooner. That's where we left it when the session ended.

Supervisor: I think you got a lot done.

Resident: I wonder why I got so upset at first by what Mr. Clark said about his sexual practices. Now it doesn't seem to bother me even though I personally disapprove strongly of that type of behavior.

Supervisor: Part of your upset can be attributed to your inexperience. You just didn't know that you can form a judgment of a patient's behavior without that judgment necessarily interfering with your behavior as a therapist. But deeper, and probably more important, are the unconscious feelings you built up toward Mr. Clark. You see, transference flows in both directions. I would guess that in some way you imbued Mr. Clark with attitudes and virtues that you wanted him to possess as a representative of the older generation, your father's generation. To find a man that age sexually preoccupied disturbed your sense of propriety and order, especially since he was not faithful to his wife, the representative of mother. Your anxiety, which interfered temporarily with your therapeutic attitude, sounds like the upset a boy or young man suffers when it is brought home to him that his parents are not the asexual creatures he imagines and wants them to be. It is interesting to see how, in response to the distress signals you apparently sent out, Mr. Clark changed roles with you. He became the guide and mentor and helped you to come to grips with an upsetting aspect of reality.

Resident: Do you think it hurt his treatment?

Supervisor: Not in this case. In fact, I think it helped. It served to remind him that although in certain respects he is immature and less able than he should be at his age, in other ways he is self-possessed and secure. It's good for both patient and therapist to be reminded periodically that the problematic areas of life don't represent the sum total of a person's existence. It helps counteract the notion that the patient is a helpless, crippled individual who needs to lean on the wise, strong therapist. Often patients are quite competent individuals who happen to have trouble applying what they know to a particular aspect of their lives. Sometimes the therapist may even have to face the fact that on balance he is less mature and effective than a given patient. But that doesn't preclude the patient's needing the therapist's help or the therapist's being able to assist the patient.

Resident: How can one prevent one's own blind spots from interfering with the therapeutic process?

Supervisor: To some extent it helps to be aware of one's therapeutic style and to recognize that when one's mood and behavior is atypical, it may well be a signal that a personal complex is intruding on the work. Under such circumstances one redoubles one's efforts to make sure that one really understands whatever is going on. Most important of course is the therapist's experience in his own treatment. He is likely to recognize the remobilization of his unconscious conflicts if he has worked on them in a therapeutic situation.

Resident: I sort of got the feeling that Mr. Clark's therapy was coming to an end with this last session. Maybe it's because I lost control of the situation when he took the leadership position in the relationship.

Supervisor: I would agree that his treatment has accomplished what it is able to do, but it's not a matter of loss of control on your part. You'll find that he will come in and report the day's happenings to you just as before, looking for your praise and appreciation for his achievements. The question is how productive it will be to let that continue. I think that by taking the lead in the last session, he was indicating that he can now get along by himself, and that the next and last step in the therapy should be to help him to do that.

My suggestion would be to review with him what has been happening since he first came to see you. Put into words how his wife's death made him face the need to be assertive in a way that he had not been prepared for by his past experience, how he learned in his work with you that he is not only capable of standing up for himself, but that he enjoys doing so. I would then ask him how he feels about going forward on his own, leaving the door open for him to see you when and if he needs to do so.

Resident: Do you think the grief over his wife's death has been worked through sufficiently?

Supervisor: He seems to be handling that well. The resurgence of his sexual activity indicates that he is now sufficiently free to rebuild his life. The work you have done with him certainly leaves him in a much better position to create a reasonably satisfying existence for himself than he was in before he came for treatment. It's a good time to stop. Too often the mistake is made of thinking that therapy is not over until a better life has become a reality. That leads to an interminable and frustrating kind of situation. Once the patient is ready, like a young adult, he must leave home and take his chances. Therapists no more than parents can prearrange his happiness for him.

Therapy was brought to a satisfactory conclusion two months later.

VIII

Differential Diagnosis and Choice of Treatment: Symptom Neurosis and Neurotic Character Disorders

Most of the disorders treated in a psychotherapeutic practice fall into three groups: the symptom neuroses and the psychoneurotic character disorders, the narcissistic or selfobject disorders, and the borderline disturbances. These diagnoses describe vicissitudes of development and cannot be based on the patient's appearance, phenomenology, or presenting complaint. Only an evaluation of the patient's overall character structure, especially as it emerges in his relationship to the therapist, can establish the diagnosis. However, even though a diagnosis carries significant implications for treatment and for prognosis, the categories are not hard and fast or mutually exclusive; they can overlap. Furthermore, the therapist's diagnostic impression can change either as he comes to know the patient better or as the patient matures in treatment.

Miss Gloria Delmore

Resident: The patient I'd like to talk to you about is a twenty-six-year-old woman teacher named Gloria Delmore. She came to the clinic because she has been having a lot of problems in her relationships to men. Recently she was engaged to be married, but shortly after the wedding plans were made she panicked and backed out of the arrangement. She says she realizes that there must be something wrong with her to make her develop difficulties of one sort or another with every man who likes her and seems suitable.

Supervisor: What questions do you have about her?

Resident: I'm not sure of the diagnosis. She seems to function so well in other respects, I can't figure out why she should have this problem.

Supervisor: How many times have you seen her?

Resident: Twice, two weeks apart.

Supervisor: Then let's hear what you have learned about her. How did she come across in the interviews?

Resident: She is a very pleasant and polite person. When she first came in, what struck me was that she opened our conversation by thanking me for arranging to see her late in the afternoon since she is a teacher and can't get away before 3:30 P.M. and then has a distance to travel to get here. Most people seem just to take it for granted that you'll accommodate them and never say a word about it. This wasn't just an isolated incident. There is something very decent and considerate about her.

Supervisor: You like her.

Resident: Yes I do, and I admire what she has managed to do in her life, too. She is the fourth of seven children born to a missionary family. Her father is a minister who was sent to an impoverished area of South America. She grew up for the first six years of her life in the mission and was then shipped back to relatives in the United States, so she could go to school here while her parents completed their tour of duty. The family was not reunited till she was ten years old. She remembers being very lonely for her parents, whom she saw only every eighteen months when they came home on leave. They kept in touch by letter. Her parents would write her every week, and she was expected to write them as soon as she was able to do so. Obedience to God and to one's elders seems to have been the theme that was stressed as basic for behavior, and the church and the family were the focus of their lives. As far as the patient is able to remember, she had a good childhood. The relatives with whom she stayed were kind, and she had friends and got along well in school.

She had a mild rebellion in adolescence. While at college she joined a church more liberal than her father's. Her parents accepted that, and they are still a very close family. She won a scholarship that enabled her to complete work for a master's degree in zoology. She is now employed as a high school biology teacher, enjoys her work, and gets along well with her students, her coworkers, and the administration.

All this sounds so idyllic, and she seems to be such a well-rounded individual, yet she still lives at home and can't seem to separate herself from her parents. She never lacks for men who want to take her out. They both attract and frighten her. She gets along fine with them until there is a demand for any degree of physical intimacy. Then she becomes anxious, gets all kinds of somatic symptoms—flushing, nausea, diarrhea—and soon thereafter ends the relationship. Yet she wants a family of her own and can't understand why this happens to her.

Supervisor: How do her parents feel about her being at home?

Resident: They make no bones about their wish that she would marry and settle down, even though she is needed at home. Her mother is periodically incapacitated by some chronic gastrointestinal ailment she apparently contracted while abroad, and depends a great deal on the patient during those times.

What puzzles me is that Miss Delmore quite spontaneously told me so much more than most patients are able to do in the first few interviews, and yet I can't really identify the nature of her problem or make a treatment plan.

Supervisor: When I see a patient who functions well, has good relationships with other people, and relates to me in a mature manner but has a circumscribed psychological problem that interferes with what should be a very rewarding life, then I start thinking about neurotic pathology—hysterical in this case.

Resident: Why neurosis when there is no clear-cut phobia, obsession, compulsion, or conversion reaction here?

Supervisor: You can't make the diagnosis of neurosis from symptoms. Phobias, compulsions, obsessions, and conversion reactions can accompany non-neurotic illnesses, too. These symptoms are the outcome of defensive maneuvers against anxiety and are not limited to neuroses. For example, you will find many schizophrenic and borderline patients who use compulsive rituals and obsessive thoughts to contain their anxiety. A conversion reaction can be part of a depressive picture, and phobias occur in patients with pre-oedipal character structures. The diagnosis of neurosis is a statement about etiology and should be made only if you think the patient's basic problem is oedipal.

The oedipal conflict is a frequently misunderstood concept. When oedipal pathology is focal, it implies that an individual has had a relatively undisturbed maturation until the ages of three to six, at which time what had been an essentially unambivalent relationship with his parents comes in conflict with his emerging erotic impulses directed to the parent of the opposite sex and with rivalrous impulses leveled at the parent of the same sex. Such sexual and aggressive impulses are not pathological in and of themselves but are a normal result of the competitive aspects of the oedipal phase of psychosexual development. If parents can help the child to surmount and integrate this phase by accepting his feelings while setting reassuring limits to his grandiose and frightening phantasies in a nontraumatic way, the oedipal period becomes an important maturational step in the formation of a stable and independent self (Kohut 1977). If, however, these vicissitudes of the growth process are not worked through at the time but are inadequately resolved by repression, the groundwork for neurosis is laid. By repression we mean that the forbidden wishes for which the child expects to be severely punished are not resolved but are only eliminated from consciousness and from logical thought while remaining capable of influencing behavior by indirect means. (Freud 1895; Basch 1977). Usually secondary defensive symptoms, which indicate the failure of repression, do not appear until later in adolescence or young adulthood, when the upsurge of sexuality reawakens the earlier conflict and interferes with the normal channeling of the sexual instinct. That means that sexual impulses are not unambivalently joined with positive affects like joy, interest, and excitement but also mobilize shame, guilt, fear, and contempt. Under these circumstances the fulfillment of sexual needs creates anxiety rather than satisfaction. The symptom formation that now takes place is an attempt to find a compromise that will permit sexual expression while evading consciousness of the oedipal conflict behind it. Sexual release can remain undisguised if the object is distorted: in this case a perversion rather than a neurosis is the outcome of the conflict. If the solution is neurotic, sexual expression itself becomes distorted. A so-called symptom neurosis is one in which a conversion, a compulsion, an obsession, or a phobia symbolically represents the underlying conflict and offers it a symptomatic outlet. In a so-called character neurosis the symptom takes behavioral form, and the conflict is expressed through the manner in which the patient adapts himself in everyday life. That is what I think has happened in the case of your patient.

I base my as-yet-unproved diagnostic hypothesis on the observation that although she has a block in the psychosexual area of development, she is otherwise functioning on a very high level, regards her own behavior as ego-alien, and is aware that it is she who has a problem rather than blaming other people or circumstances for her difficulties. This indicates to me that the development of her self-concept in the pre-oedipal period was reasonably normal and that the core of her personality is stable and healthy. These traits are usually associated with oedipal—that is, psychoneurotic—pathology.

Resident: In terms of her background as far as we know it, how do you account both for her strengths and for the fact that such a serious problem developed later?

Supervisor: From what you have told me of her history, she comes from a family whose sense of order was both highly developed and functional. The parents have strong convictions and conveyed them clearly to their children. This kind of background makes for healthy pre-oedipal development—that is, a sense of personal security based on having a clearly defined place in an orderly world. At the same time it may make the child vulnerable to the instinctual impulses that arise unbidden and threaten the child's sense of what is acceptable. Often there is little tolerance for what is deemed evil and unnatural in such families, and the child finds it necessary to reject a part of herself. In Miss Delmore's case I would suspect that the absence of her parents during this crucial period of development made it all the more difficult for her to deal with phantasies that could then develop without being checked by the ameliorating reality that contact with her parents—the persons who were the targets of her sexual drive—would have brought. If as a child she found it necessary to institute a wholesale repression of both her sexual and her aggressive oedipal wishes, then that might explain the difficulties in which she finds herself today, when that repression is threatened by her adult sexual needs and her drive toward motherhood.

Resident: How should I proceed with this patient?

Supervisor: My recommendation would be that she be referred and evaluated for psychoanalytic treatment.

Resident: Why can't her problem be handled in less intensive psychotherapy?

Supervisor: Based on what you have told me about her, my prediction would be that if she were taken into psychotherapy she would rapidly form an oedipal transference of great intensity. Contrary to what is often taught, my experience—and what I have seen of the work of others, as well as my study of psychoanalytic theory—has convinced me that psychotherapy is not geared to uncovering and working through repressed infantile sexual material. Even if you were an analyst, it would not help; for without the opportunities made possible by frequency of visits, the patient cannot be helped to develop the *transference neurosis* that is necessary to working through the oedipal wishes that are behind the symptom. All that would happen is that she would become very attached to you without it leading to a therapeutic resolution. It would either end up as an interminable treatment in which her unconscious phantasies would become symbolically gratified through her relationship with you, or the patient would become frightened by her feelings for you and would find reasons to interrupt therapy prematurely (see also chapter 5).

Resident: Are there circumstances in which a patient with a neurotic character structure can be helped by psychotherapy rather than by psychoanalysis?

Supervisor: Of course, very often. There are many patients with a psychoneurotic character structure who are able to create an environment that leaves them free to function effectively until something comes up that creates an imbalance and disturbs their adjustment. You may remember that this is what happened in the case of Mr. Arianes (chapter 3, 4). He had found a marital partner and a job both of which provided adult satisfaction while also meeting his unconscious, conflicted childhood needs. When his wife's attention was diverted by her sister's problems and he was no longer her sole concern, conflicts that had previously been compensated for generated anxiety and led to a somatic conversion. In his therapy he learned to understand the secondary complications of his basic problem. This helped him significantly, even though no attempt was made to effect a resolution of oedipal material.

Like other psychological disorders, psychoneurosis is not an all-or-nothing proposition. How severe the problem is in relation to the way the patient functions in the rest of his life helps the therapist to decide what treatment to recommend.

Resident: Under what circumstances would you advise that Miss Delmore stay in psychotherapy to see if that could get the job done?

Supervisor: I might have tried a psychotherapeutic approach if Miss Delmore had come to me when she first experienced difficulties in her relationship with men, before her problems reflected an established symptomatic pattern. My idea would be that perhaps she was behaving in a self-defeating way that could be explored outside the transference neurosis. Similarly, if she had come to me and complained that she felt her relationship to her ill mother and the pressure that her parents were putting on her not to leave home was keeping her from marrying someone she loved, I think I would have tried psychotherapy.

It is only when I believe that I am dealing with an unconsciously motivated pattern of self-defeating behavior that is clearly repetitive, not related to particular external circumstances, and not accounted for by lack of either experience or developmental opportunities that I would rule out comparatively short-term and less intensive psychotherapies and think of psychoanalysis as not only desirable but necessary. In my experience, the need to establish and work through a transference neurosis—that is, to mobilize and resolve the Oedipus complex—is one of the absolute indicators for psychoanalysis, though it is not the only one.

Resident: When I saw Miss Delmore I was impressed by the same things that struck you as being significant, but I could not decide whether to accept at face value the picture of herself she presented in the interviews. What if her seeming competence and high level of adaptation is only a façade, and her pleasant, accommodating behavior toward me only a ploy to ingratiate herself and hide more serious pathology?

Supervisor: What if your fears are accurate? Patient-psychotherapist relations are not of an adversary nature. If the patient needs to conceal aspects of her thoughts, consciously or unconsciously, that is worthy of note whenever one detects it, but it does not make her "guilty" of anything. It's part of the problem that you are examining. Usually this kind of a situation becomes clear over the span of several interviews, but it can also happen that one is well into a treatment program before it becomes apparent that a patient's problems and assets are not what one had thought them to be. Then the treatment plan has to be modified accordingly.

Resident: You mean if you had a patient in analysis, you might have to let him sit up and do psychotherapy?

Supervisor: Possibly, or let him remain on the couch, but modify my technique and my treatment goals. Lying down on a couch in itself does not make for psychoanalysis; plenty of good psychotherapy has been done under those conditions. It works the other way, too, you know. A patient may be in psychotherapy when you realize that he both needs and can use psychoanalysis, and you can institute that treatment.

IX

Differential Diagnosis and Choice of Treatment: Borderline Disturbances

The treatment and differential diagnosis of borderline personalities will be illustrated by the following cases taken from my own practice. I have chosen these examples because the presenting complaints are similar to the one that brought Miss Banks and Miss Delmore for treatment—an inability to maintain a functioning heterosexual relationship. A comparison of the reactions of these patients with someone under comparable stress will further clarify in practical, operational fashion the differential diagnosis between neurosis and neurotic character disorder, narcissistic or selfobject pathology, and a borderline problem.

Mrs. Tira Elbogen

I received a call from a pleasant-sounding woman who informed me that she was a friend of Mrs. Tira Elbogen who, on the recommendation of her internist, wished to have an appointment with me. No further details were volunteered, and I was clearly expected to be familiar with and impressed by the name. A subsequent call from the referring physician clarified the situation. Mrs. Elbogen, a socially prominent and wealthy woman in her middle thirties, had in recent months developed an increasingly serious drinking problem. The referral was precipitated by her having repeatedly called her physician in the middle of the night while obviously intoxicated. She would be crying, agitated, and fearful that various somatic symptoms she was experiencing (probably induced by hyperventilation) meant she would die of a heart attack before dawn.

Her incessant complaining and the physician's increasing frustration at being unable either to reassure her through repeated physical examinations or to calm her with sedatives, tranquilizers, and antidepressant medication resulted in his half hearted suggestion that she receive some "counseling". This step, it rapidly became obvious, was seen as humiliating by both Mrs. Elbogen and her doctor; and neither of them placed much confidence in it.

When I first met the patient, I was struck by her appearance. She was elegantly turned out, her face was made up with great care, and she wore a variety of jewelry which was expensive-looking but not ostentatious. Yet my impression was not of a stunning woman but rather of a pathetic child who had gotten into her mother's wardrobe while left alone on a rainy afternoon and consoled herself by playing dress-up.

At first she spoke in a manner that was meant to be charming but was actually quite condescending. She invited me indirectly to laugh with her at the silly predicament that found her in my office. All that was wrong with her, she said, was that since the termination of her engagement some months before, she had slipped into the bad habit of calming her nerves by drinking a little too much at night. What would I suggest she do? Were there pills she had not yet tried that might help?

When I told her that any suggestions I made would have to be based on a much more thorough acquaintance with her life, past and present—that only in context could I possibly understand the nature of her problem—she became angry and arrogant. She spoke disparagingly of psychotherapists who make patients slavishly dependent on them, something she did not intend to have happen to her. Her reaction was that of a frightened child who lashes out at some unseen danger. It would have made no sense to react to her implicit challenge by defending my work, so I began to question her directly about her present life. At first she answered only factually, but gradually an underlying bitterness and dissatisfaction emerged, and her voice lost its refined overtones and became an angry whine. Her parents, her first husband, the suitor who had disappointed her, her so-called friends—all had been found wanting and were assigned a portion of the responsibility for her dissatisfied state.

I told Mrs. Elbogen toward the end of the session that I felt her problem was not simple and I assured her that I did not have any medication to relieve her. I did feel she might benefit from psychotherapy, and I told her I should like to see her at least a few more times to have the opportunity to study her difficulties more thoroughly before making specific recommendations. Clearly unhappy with my suggestions, she begged off committing herself to work with me in the near future because of her plans for an extended vacation in Europe. She indicated that on her return she might see me again. Mrs. Elbogen was not amenable to my suggestion that her present condition indicated that treatment should take precedence over her trip, and she left without making another appointment.

An accurate differential diagnosis need not and often cannot be made immediately. The stress of the first interview may exaggerate the pathology. Sometimes a patient is so focused on his pain and distress that he leaves out significant aspects of his life. Although I had come to the tentative conclusion that Mrs. Elbogen had borderline pathology, I was not by any means certain of my diagnosis.

About six months, later I received a call from Mrs. Elbogen's attorney asking me to see her in consultation with a view to establishing a treatment plan. Apparently sometime before, while intoxicated, she had caused a serious automobile accident. In order to avoid more drastic legal consequences she had agreed to enter a treatment facility for alcoholics and upon her release to participate in psychiatric treatment. She was about to be discharged from the hospital and wanted me to be her therapist. I agreed to see her for further evaluation.

Over a period of weeks Mrs. Elbogen gave me more information about herself. She was the youngest of three children and the only daughter. Her father was, and is, a wealthy industrialist. During her childhood her parents were away from home a great deal of the time, traveling all over the world in pursuit of her father's business interests. The patient and her brothers—two and four years older—were raised by a series of governesses, none of whom stayed long because of the uncontrolled behavior of the boys. The patient described herself as a meek and withdrawn child who lived in terror of the next act of meanness that her brothers would direct against her. She recalls little of her childhood except that it was lonely and unhappy. She literally could not recall one incident that had given her pleasure. Although she had many expensive toys, usually brought to her by her parents after a trip, she did not enjoy any of them, and they were quickly broken. She could not recall being attached to a single other child, pet, or inanimate object. Grade school was marked from the beginning by her failure to comprehend what it was that she was supposed to learn, and by her inability to win favor with either teachers or classmates.

In high school she was asked to leave several boarding schools because of her failure to fulfill scholastic requirements. Finally she attended and was graduated from an institution that catered to the daughters of wealthy families who could not get diplomas anywhere else. The patient believed that she simply was not interested in studying. In fact, soon after starting a course she would be unable to concentrate and would become increasingly anxious about the failure she saw as inevitable. She would then act up and behave as if she did not care and had stopped studying out of rebelliousness, boredom, dislike for the teacher, and so forth.

After high school most of her peers attended college; and because she had nothing planned that interested her more, she tried it too. She registered at a school that specialized in purveying degrees to those who could afford high tuition and were not too concerned with the quality of the curriculum or the capabilities of the faculty. She did not graduate from college, however, but quit to marry a young man she met there. He came from a family as socially prominent as hers.

Once established in her own home, she was sought after by social, charitable, and educational organizations eager to have another representative of her family and her husband's family on their boards of trustees. An incessant round of meetings, charity balls, and other social activities kept her busy enough for the first few years to allow her to gloss over the fact that her marriage was a mistake. Everyone in her circle thought that she and her husband were an ideal couple, and they had convinced themselves that it was true. Actually they fought like two children, each disappointed in the other's inability to bring meaning and happiness to his or her existence.

According to the patient's report, her husband was pleasant but not too intelligent; he worked for his father, an aggressive and highly successful entrepreneur who was disappointed in his son and treated him with undisguised contempt. Her husband looked in vain to Mrs. Elbogen for validation of his worth, for understanding, admiration, and comfort. She had similar needs and felt cheated that, instead of fulfilling them, her husband made demands on her. His self-esteem was further hurt by her frigidity and her increasing distaste for sexual intimacy. He withdrew from her more and more, concentrating on his excellent tennis game which gave him a sense of satisfaction and the acclaim for which he longed. When her husband asked for a divorce after some four years of marriage, Mrs. Elbogen agreed to it. By this time she was having an affair with another man who now wanted to marry her.

The divorce did not seem to affect Mrs. Elbogen; but when her lover broke the engagement after their impending marriage had been announced publicly, she decompensated rapidly. She felt humiliated and rejected and believed that people were secretly delighted by her misfortune. Since gossip is the mainstay of many social circles, she was probably correct in her assumption. Yet there was definitely a paranoid delusional quality about her suspicions; they went beyond what would be a reasonable reaction. She could not stand to be alone, and since she had no special interests or accomplishments to occupy her, she pursued her customary round of luncheons and organizational activities; of course, these brought her in contact with the people she felt were talking meanly about her. She became more irritable, suspicious, and fearful and depended increasingly on alcohol to calm herself.

In her diagnostic interviews with me Mrs. Elbogen showed no shame, guilt, or remorse about the damage she had done to others. Her attitude was either,

"Why did this have to happen to me?" accompanied by anger at all the people who she felt should have helped her during her slide into alcoholism, or a self-pitying, "Nothing ever works out for me." She had no understanding of what it means to take responsibility for one's actions. To her the past was nonexistent; and now that she was no longer drinking, all the problems associated with drinking had also been wiped out.

The patient's lifelong history of problems—low-level achievement, compulsive socialization based on fear of being alone and never leading to genuine intimacy, inability to establish and maintain emotionally significant relationships, alcoholism, a tendency toward psychotic disintegration under stress—all seemed to confirm my initial impression that she had a borderline personality. It is possible, indeed not infrequent, that a patient who seems to be borderline, who feels that his tenuous equilibrium is threatened by human involvement of any depth, turns out to be only frightened of rejection and disappointment and, given the opportunity in a therapeutic relationship, permits his hidden longings for human interaction to be mobilized. This was not the case with Mrs. Elbogen. She resented having to come to see me, believing that since she was no longer drinking, her problems had come to an end. Although she replied to direct questioning, her answers did not lead to her becoming more introspective or desiring to understand herself better. Her mood remained tense and angry, and although she denied that therapy could help her, she spoke of her difficulties in an accusing tone as if I were to blame for her being unable to handle her life effectively.

Since her release from the hospital she had given up her apartment and moved back to her parents' home. Although her relationship with her parents was quarrelsome, her fear of dying abated now that she was no longer alone at night. Her sobriety was maintained with the aid of medication that ensured she would become violently ill if she drank alcohol. I had anticipated that her cure would not last, and was surprised that she continued to take the medicine and remained enrolled in the the treatment center's follow-up program.

One day while I was speaking to her about her hospitalization, hoping to reach her through that experience, she made the only truly spontaneous and introspective statement of her whole therapy. She volunteered that she had been dramatically impressed by the physical ravages that alcohol can cause, because of what had happened to an acquaintance—a woman some ten years older than she—who had been hospitalized with her. The woman, who had formerly been a great beauty, was now bloated, obese, and slovenly. Mrs. Elbogen had not even recognized her until her name was mentioned. My patient recalled that the one thing that made her feel her father noticed or cared about her was his obvious pride in her appearance as she grew up. He was pleased to have her by his side at social functions and reveled in receiving compliments about her.

This one and only spontaneous memory indicated that only her fear of becoming ugly, and thus losing the only worth she had for her father, inspired her to remain on the medication and abstain from drink. However, my attempts to use this opening to further her insight failed.

The patient was definitely not a candidate for dynamic psychotherapy, but I did my best to support her defenses and to strengthen them where I could. Usually she was angry about something, and I would try to help her to see the significance of her anger and to gain a realistic perspective on the situation that caused it. One day she came in furious at her hairdresser because he had missed an appointment. She felt it was a slight that she could avenge only by taking her patronage elsewhere, and she was already becoming agitated over the prospect of having to find someone new. I looked into the situation with her and found that she had been going to the same hairdresser for many years, that she had been satisfied with his work, and that he had not failed her before. I suggested that in view of their long relationship Mrs. Elbogen not act precipitately but wait to give the man a chance to explain himself, and thereby possibly spare herself the need to look for someone else and extend courtesy to a person who had served her needs for years. In the next session she said nothing about the incident until I asked her about it. It turned out that the hairdresser had been on his way to work when he was flagged down by a woman who told him that a child was drowning in a swimming pool in the yard of a nearby house. He had to scale a high wire fence before plunging fully clothed into the water to rescue an unconscious child. Sopping wet, he had rushed the victim to a nearby hospital and remained at her side till the family arrived. All this was reported in the newspapers with appropriate fanfare.

As far as I could tell, this incident had no impact upon the patient. Inconveniences continued to be taken as personal attacks, and my recalling this dramatic event was not particularly effective. Patients like Mrs. Elbogen do not seem to benefit from time and repeated exposure where their emotional lability is concerned. As a result they are always in danger of being overwhelmed by the moment, and they have all they can do to maintain a precarious hold on reality.

To say the least, this was not a satisfying therapeutic encounter for me. One cannot help being affected by the experience of being ineffective and of seeing one's efforts misunderstood. I maintained my interest by reminding myself that this case was an opportunity to study in its gross form pathology that played a part in the behavior of less disturbed patients, albeit in less total and less dramatic ways. Also I believed that the patient, though lacking insight, was acting significantly less impulsively and self-destructively because of the benign quasi-parental influence that I exercised in the therapy situation.

Since Mrs. Elbogen was continuously complaining about the inconvenience and uselessness of her appointments with me—and because I felt I could do no more than serve a monitoring function—I agreed after six months of attempts at intensive treatment to reduce the frequency of appointments from three to one per week.

Eventually Mrs. Elbogen chanced to meet one of the senior partners in the eminent law firm that was representing her in the accident she had caused. He was considerably older, a lifelong bachelor, and had been driven by the poverty of his youth to accumulate a fortune; having always been consumed by his work, he was now about to retire. He fell in love with Mrs. Elbogen, courted her assiduously, and in essence indicated he wanted nothing so much as to devote himself to her with the same zeal and exclusivity he had heretofore shown in his profession. Mrs. Elbogen felt vindicated in the eyes of her acquaintances by having a handsome, powerful, older man care for her so deeply, and she responded to him. She could not understand why he wanted to see me, but she agreed to his request, and I met the man. (It was from him that I learned something about his life.) He had come, he told me, to let me know that he in no way wanted to interfere with her therapy; on the contrary he wanted to do everything he could to see to it that she got the proper treatment. He behaved almost as if I were her father and he was asking for her hand; he assured me that he loved her and that while he knew she probably didn't yet reciprocate his feelings, he hoped that with his care and affection she would eventually overcome her disappointment with men and grow to love him.

In due time they were married and began a life that seemed to suit both of them. They owned no home but maintained a small apartment at his club which served as a base for their occasional visits to the city. Much of the year they spent traveling over the world, living in hotels or on cruise ships. The patient had no responsibilities except to look pretty and to let her husband see to her comfort. The people they met were here today and gone tomorrow, and there was no pressure to engage in anything more than social pleasantries. Whenever they were in town I would get a call from the husband to ask if it would be possible for me "to see our little girl" and to tell me how delighted he was with their relationship and how grateful he was to me for having helped her so much in her time of difficulty.

When I saw Mrs. Elbogen (as I shall continue to call her) for the first time after her marriage, her attitude toward psychotherapy had not changed. Where previously she had come to satisfy the terms of her probation, now she came to comply with the wishes of her husband. She seemed much calmer, her anger was less obvious, and she made an effort to be pleasant.

I asked her to tell me about her life. Her days, as she described them, followed a routine. She seldom got out of bed before noon; then she and her husband spent the afternoon shopping. Her evenings were taken up with lavish parties and other social events which usually lasted into the early morning hours.

(On one occasion when I saw her some years later they had been invited to a weekend party in England and were about to fly to Switzerland to pick up a timepiece they had had made as a house present for their hostess.) Although she had minor complaints about some of the inconveniences of travel, she seemed as content as I had ever known her to be, and had even developed some genuine fondness for her husband. Her problem with frigidity had been resolved. She felt that this was further evidence that there had never been anything really wrong with her and that her former husband and her erstwhile lover had been to blame for her sexual difficulties.

In periodic visits through the years she has let me known that her adjustment has been maintained; for example, in spite of ample opportunity, she has not reverted to excessive use of alcohol. On one occasion when the patient fell ill and could not come for her scheduled session, her husband asked if he might talk to me instead. He gave me a glowing report of how well his wife was doing, and he wanted my suggestions on how to manage some of the problems that did arise—for example, her great sensitivity to minor slights which might send her in tears to her stateroom, not to emerge for several days. He seemed grateful for my attempts to help him, and his visits to me became regular events. Often Mrs. Elbogen would find a reason not to come to see me and would send her husband in her place. Eventually I saw more of him than of her. His interest in his wife's psychological comfort never flagged, and he understood her needs very well. He treated her like a sensitive, fragile child, which in a way she was, and felt happy and privileged to have the opportunity to lavish on her the tender and affectionate emotions that, having been suppressed by him for a lifetime, were clamoring for release.

It is an important consideration that her husband, being considerably older, will probably predecease Mrs. Elbogen. Since therapy has not changed the brittleness of her defenses much, if at all, will she again decompensate as she did after her broken engagement? It is, of course, a possibility, but by no means a foregone conclusion. Based on my experience I think it much more likely that having found a way of life that is comfortable, she will make another, similar adaptation. She will send out messages—that is, behave—so that another man who, for his own reasons, needs to take care of a fragile, attractive child-woman will attach himself to her. The play does not change; only the actors do.

When presenting this case, I have been asked: "Wasn't her situation unusual? Would it have worked out so smoothly if the patient had not had money, beauty, and connections?" This concern is based on the fact that psychotherapists tend to get a skewed picture of life. The great majority of people with clinically significant psychological disorders do not have professional help; instead, they work out a *modus vivendi*. Whatever their problems may be—in spite of them and, as in this case, sometimes because of them—these people fit in with the needs of others well enough to become part of a larger unit—one that shelters, protects, and accommodates them. When a person does turn to therapy, it is usually because he cannot find a place for himself or has lost a place and cannot regain it. By declaring himself a patient, he finds a niche in a special system. Sometimes this can become a problem. A therapist has to be alert to see that a patient does not become too comfortable with his new-found sense of belonging—that is, of being part of a situation where he is both necessary and interesting. The therapist must assist the patient to muster the courage to move on when he is ready to do so. On the other hand, there are a number of patients for whom the role of patient is central, and it makes feasible their continued existence—often a productive one. Such a need has to be respected, and the patient and the therapist have to deal openly with the recognition that their relationship is ongoing, open-ended, and indefinite. The therapist has to overcome any guilt or shame he may have about "hanging on" to a patient year after year, and the patient has to be helped to gain as much insight as possible into the reasons for his need and to work through any threat to his self-esteem which is aroused by his prolonged dependence.*

Mrs. Farwell

The case of Mrs. Elbogen is an extreme example, and it does not mean that every borderline patient is incapable of maturing in a therapeutic relationship. Quite the contrary. As the following case shows, borderline pathology does not rule out either insight or growth as long as the patient's limitations are understood and respected (see also Adler 1979; Adler and Buie, 1979).

* In Western civilization a pejorative connotation is attached to any relationship in which childlike dependence has not been concealed sufficiently to let us deceive ourselves about its existence. In fact, however, society is basically a collection of life-support systems. Our relationships with other people, our profession, our country, our Church, and so forth, are all opportunities to meet dependent needs in situations that have at least the illusion of timelessness. In principle the productive interaction between therapist and patient is no different from any other viable social relationship. Yet we psychotherapists are creatures of the same milieu as our patients—a milieu that looks askance at openly acknowledged dependence once childhood has passed—and we have to come to grips with a certain amount of uneasiness that may be activated by our having long-term patients. Interestingly and instructively, the notion that the need for prolonged care is somehow indecent and willful is not limited by any means to patients in need of prolonged or indefinite psychotherapy. The old and the infirm often feel disreputable and blameworthy because they can no longer function independently. Physicians who care for patients in need of continued therapy—allergists and dermatologists, for example—are often looked upon as if their activities were on the borderline of acceptable practice, and their patients are sometimes depreciated for continuing a treatment that helps but does not cure. The latest addition to this group are the patients who require lifelong kidney dialysis and whose right to such therapy, which for the most part depends on public funds, is being hotly debated.

Mrs. Farwell, who was thirty-one, had become delusional after her divorce from a sadistic husband. She was quite paranoid during her first interview with me, and I suspected that she was hallucinating off and on during the session. She refused, however, to accept my recommendation for hospitalization and insisted that she would see me in the office and that she would get well. Her confidence in herself and the way she committed herself to treatment and to me as her therapist persuaded me to take a chance and accept her decision. She not only recovered from her psychotic symptoms but went on to develop a new career. Eventually she built a life that was far superior to the one she had led prior to her breakdown.

As I got to know Mrs. Farwell during her two-and-a-half years in treatment, I had abundant corroborative evidence that she had always lived on the edge of psychosis, and that her acute symptomatology was neither surprising nor inexplicable. It was clear that she could only tolerate limited intimacy and that her attempt at marriage had been a mistake. However, the psychotherapy relationship, precisely because of its limitations, succeeded where other efforts at furthering her maturation had failed.

Mrs. Farwell was an only child. Her mother seems to have been a withdrawn schizoid; her father was not only inappropriately seductive with his daughter but also had the peculiar habit of never saying anything directly and of making a joke out of everything they said to each other. As a child she had to adapt herself to each parent's bizarre way of communicating to get even a semblance of a relationship. In her adult life she was always looking for complexities and hidden meanings when there were none. In her sessions with me we looked at her present and past lives, and I was able to help her to see that her parents as well as her husband had been psychotic, or near-psychotic, and that the responsibility for the confusion in their messages to her was theirs. Through her relationship with me she was able to learn something of how one evaluates other people's intentions and communicates one's own needs. Like a child she was able to have the experience of learning about life without anything inappropriate being demanded of her—that is, her growth satisfied both of us. Eventually I was able to interpret to her what we were doing and, by helping her understand the process intellectually, to free her from dependence on me. She was able to leave therapy, returning only occasionally to get help with a specific problem or to be confirmed in a decision she had made. One could argue of course that her continuing inability to form intimate relationships speaks against her having achieved a truly therapeutic result. I think, however, that this point of view imposes what the therapist may want in his life onto the patient. Mrs. Farwell was happier than she had ever been, she did not decompensate under stress, and she could control her anxiety when it was aroused. Those around her enjoyed her as a person and benefited from her work. Yes, from the viewpoint of her pathology, I suppose I should still have to classify her as a borderline personality, but that does not mean much, because there is a lot more to Mrs. Farwell than a potential for psychotic decompensation under certain circumstances (see also page 178).

X

Differential Diagnosis and Transference

A patient's initial complaint often confuses a student, especially if the latter has been led to expect that specific signs and symptoms identify particular psychological "illnesses." Actually a therapist should not make a diagnosis simply on the basis of the main complaint, nor should he center on a patient's symptom. The therapist should consider the context in which the complaint is made or in which the symptom occurs, for it is the context that often leads to an understanding of what is going on with the patient and of what needs to be done for him. For example, the basically mature, healthy person who has a psychoneurotic difficulty and experiences its symptom as a foreign body out of keeping with the rest of his character makes a pretty striking picture—one not easily mistaken for anything else.

In practice the nature of the transference relationship is more important than the original diagnosis. To put it another way, at its best the function of a diagnosis is to forecast the sort of transference that will develop and to plan accordingly. As the patient's psychotherapy progresses, categorization becomes less significant, because in psychotherapy one is always dealing with the person behind the symptom. Although the initial complaint or other aspects of the defensive structure lend themselves to being labeled, the individual does not. People have a way of breaking out of the confines of a diagnosis.

Miss Delmore (chapter 8) and Mrs. Elbogen (chapter 9) both had difficulty maintaining a significant relationship with a man. How can we be sure that Miss Delmore is not suffering from borderline problems while Mrs. Elbogen is? Perhaps Miss Delmore is better at concealing her disturbance and simply puts up a healthier front.

Although each woman has problems in her relationships with men, that is about all they have in common. Miss Delmore gave evidence that, except in specific situations that are particularly anxiety-provoking for her, her relationships with people are varied, meaningful, and generally satisfactory. Mrs. Elbogen seemed to be distressed with everyone, and her broken engagement was just one more in a series of interpersonal failures. Furthermore, Miss Delmore was quite aware that there was something wrong, and wanted to find out what it was and what she could do to correct it. Mrs. Elbogen blamed everyone but herself for her unhappiness. That she might be responsible in some way for her misery did not occur to her, and the idea that she should make an effort, other than to take pills, to help herself seemed to her unfair and actually without meaning. Under the pressure of anxiety Mrs. Elbogen sought escape from her problems by obliterating all traces of self-awareness with alcohol and medication. Miss Delmore tended to heighten her sense of self and sought answers through self-examination. Miss Delmore was sensitive to other people's needs and to her obligations in a coöperative task, as shown by her open and considerate behavior in therapy. Mrs. Elbogen showed no such sensitivity; she expected reality to bend to her needs, and if it did not, she responded with anger. Miss Delmore's trust contrasted sharply with Mrs. Elbogen's suspicion and her conviction that if things did not go her way it was a personal insult.

It is highly unlikely that one would confuse Miss Delmore, a patient with a neurotic character symptom, with Mrs. Elbogen, a borderline personality. Mrs. Elbogen was much more disturbed; her basic character structure was seriously flawed, and her appreciation for the realities of relationships was seemingly so damaged as to preclude her finding satisfaction in any area; her only solution was a continuous search for relief through escape from life's demands. This kind of damage is certain to manifest itself in a patient's communication with the therapist; it cannot be concealed.

How does one determine what therapeutic goals to set? Miss Banks (chapter 6) seemed to bear a marked resemblance to Mrs. Elbogen, at least initially—that is, she too was angry, arrogant, demanding, mistrustful, and impulse-ridden. Yet it was decided that she could tolerate the stress of insight-oriented treatment, and the goals were set accordingly. What made the difference?

Here again it is important to realize how futile it is to make a diagnosis on the basis of appearance. There certainly were similarities between the cases in terms of behavioral content, and if one made lists comparing what each patient said and did initially, Miss Banks might look like the sicker one. The significant difference lay in the nature of the relationship each patient established with her therapist. Miss Banks immediately treated her therapist as a significant individual, albeit one who she anticipated would fail her. Mrs. Elbogen never made the therapist as a person the target of her feelings, positive or negative. Her anxiety remained diffuse, and she never could relate to the therapist as an individual who could affect her—help her or hurt her. This was the obstacle to treating her in depth.

Once a patient begins to expect something of the therapist, investing him with either hopes or fears, the therapist has a chance to examine the meaning of the patient's attitude and to observe in himself and in the patient the influence such an examination has on subsequent associations. In other words, there has to be the possibility for the development of a viable transference. It does not matter whether the mood is positive or negative, the investment of feelings acknowledges that the therapist has significance, actual or potential, for the patient. It is the patient's inability to grant the therapist some degree of influence over his self-concept and on his life that attests to the severity of his problem and to the likelihood that treatment in depth will fail.

Only if the infant's attempts at communication have been successful enough to form what Kohut (1971) calls a cohesive self—a psychic structure firm enough that its unity is not threatened even under stress—is the individual able to turn to exploring the world and to coping with change with some anticipation of gratification. There are individuals like Mrs. Elbogen, whose attempts to communicate were either so ineffective or met with such inappropriate and/or inadequate response that the matrix of effective functioning which becomes the basis for trust and security was never developed. Such patients are classified as borderline personalities because they are in perpetual danger of psychotic decompensation. Their adaptation to circumstances is fragile, and all their efforts have to be directed toward avoiding excessive stimulation and maintaining their precarious balance. Owing to their early experiences these patients react to affective feedback not as potentially sustaining but as a threat, a source of hyperstimulation they must avoid. Thus, many borderline personalities cannot and will not enter a therapeutic relationship. Insofar as therapy can serve them by sheltering them from emotional stress, they will tolerate a therapist, but will quickly distance themselves if, for the purpose of furthering their therapy, he attempts to insinuate himself into their lives as a meaningful figure.

The inability to form a viable transference relationship clearly limits the kind of therapy that can be instituted. However, both Miss Banks and Miss Delmore were able to form a transference relationship; yet the treatment approach was different. How does one determine what to do in each case, and how is the difference between the two forms of pathology explained?

Here again, the nature of the relationship to the therapist is used to establish the diagnosis and the choice of treatment. Miss Banks behaved much more immaturely than did Miss Delmore, and her petulant imperiousness at the first sessions testified to the fact that she was struggling with developmental issues from earlier than those of the oedipal period—namely, difficulties with her self-esteem and with her capacity for functioning as an independent individual. This concern with oneself to the exclusion of others is called narcissism. It was the work of Heinz Kohut (1971, 1977, 1978) that made clear that narcissistic preoccupations do not preclude or interfere with therapy, but rather provide potentially valuable information about the patient.

XI

The Developmental Base for the Therapeutic Transference

The psychoanalyst Heinz Kohut found that the basis for viable psychological human development is the organization of a unitary, stable concept of self and an adequate sense of self-esteem. Many of the demands that are transferred onto psychoanalysts and other psychotherapists are in the service of these needs. Kohut (1977) speaks of such transferences as "selfobject transferences" (initially, using classic terminology, he called them "narcissistic transferences") meaning that a patient who was never able to make certain necessary developmental steps in the formation of his self-concept now wants to use the therapist and the treatment situation to complete the task. Since the patients' needs are not conscious, and since they have been thwarted and disappointed in the past, their emergence in the treatment situation is not always obvious. As in the case of an oedipal transference, the therapist has to come to understand what these needs are from the clues the patient gives in his associations and from other behavior—not necessarily, it should be emphasized, to gratify these needs in the therapeutic relationship but, rather, to help the patient understand the nature and the significance of what he wants or feels he lacks, so that he may eventually deal with them appropriately.

Using the retrospective reconstruction made possible by the analyses of narcissistic adults, Kohut (1971) has found two parallel developmental tracks that together determine self-esteem. He calls them the "grandiose" and the "idealizing" aspects of the cohesive self. The grandiose self as it is manifested in the immature adolescent and adult refers to the expectation, which has been carried over from infancy and early childhood, that one will be the center of the universe, that everyone and everything exists only to serve the needs of the narcissist. This is expressed in its most primitive form through the merger transference: The patient tries to maintain his self-concept by treating the therapist not as a person but more like an inanimate object—a tool or a machine that the patient expects to control and use when and how it suits him. At higher levels of development the therapist's existence and separateness are acknowledged but not his individuality. The patient buttresses his sense of self by implicitly assuming that his opinions, beliefs, and goals are prototypic for the therapist. Kohut calls this the "alter ego" or "twinship" transference. Eventually, in the "mirror transference" (the mirror transference proper or mirror transference in the narrow sense) the therapist's separateness and his individuality are acknowledged, but the patient feels worthwhile and functional only when he experiences the therapist as approving. In other words, various forms of the grandiose transference recapitulate those needs that apparently were unmet when the patient was much younger and, lacking a sense of identity, depended on his caretaker's communications to impart to him a sense of being a worthwhile, appreciated, and appropriately functioning individual.

Side by side with the child's grandiose concept of the self as all powerful is the experience of being cradled and cared for by, and of looking up to, parents who are much bigger and more accomplished than he is. This lays the foundation for idealization, for a need to fuse with the other so as to possess his omniscience and omnipotence. Under optimal circumstances, as reality modifies the grandiose conceptualization of the self, the capacity for idealization offsets the ensuing sense of loss and helplessness. Alone one may not be powerful, but one's self-esteem and safety can be assured through union with an admired other.

If all goes well, grandiosity is eventually transformed into a healthy sense of self-esteem—a feeling of self-control, reasonable ambition, and a conviction that one's powers are not belittled or taken away because they are limited. The unquestioning idealization of infancy becomes modified and leads to the ability of an adult to form allegiances and to devote himself to individuals and causes that transcend the narrower interests of the self.

The resolution of the Oedipus complex is the watershed for narcissism. At the age of five, six, or seven the child becomes able to entertain the concept of separateness in the sense of isolation or aloneness. He has been able for some time to recognize himself as physically separated from other things and people, but he still sees others only as they relate to his own self. He still sees everything that happens as somehow connected with his needs and desires, either meeting or frustrating them. The challenge of the oedipal phase is to recognize that one's self is not invariably part of every human equation (Basch 1975, 1977). Having successfully mastered the anxiety of such a confrontation and come to grips with his separation and its implications, the child is able to accept realistic limitations to his power and give up the primitive versions of his narcissistic wishes without feeling destroyed thereby. Quite the contrary. In facing his own limitations, the child becomes free to funnel his grandiosity into ambition that is not destructive to others and his idealization into identifications that do not consume and destroy him.

What we know of Miss Delmore (chapter 8) indicates that she has faced the oedipal struggle successfully from the viewpoint of the self. In classic psychoanalytic terminology she can be described as having a healthy ego or displaying good ego strength. Her struggle is concerned not with self-esteem but with the conflict between unsuccessfully repressed incestuous wishes and the anxiety that would be created were she to become aware of them.

Most of the patients in a dynamically oriented practice failed in their early years to develop the requisite self-esteem to handle successfully the final disappointment of their narcissistic hopes and wishes in the oedipal phase. Their sense of "narcissistic entitlement" (Murray 1964) continues into adulthood and is responsible for people like Miss Banks (chapter 6) who, in spite of intellectual accomplishments and other achievements, are childlike emotionally and make inappropriate demands. In the past, therapists have dealt pragmatically with narcissistic character disorders and, by following their patients' guidance, have found techniques to deal effectively with this or that aspect of preoedipal pathology. However, Kohut's discovery and theoretical formulation of the selfobject transference now enables therapists to go beyond idiosyncratic therapeutic experiences and, by utilizing the concept of a developmental line of the self, to deal systematically with the evidence of narcissistic behavior in their patients.

Miss Banks's initial insistence that the therapist do what she expected and remain under her control—her panic when she could not impose her will on him—seemed to point to the development of a merger transference. If this had occurred, the therapy would have been much more difficult and probably less successful than it actually was. A patient's feeling that his structural stability is threatened by a separation of himself from the therapist makes attempts at interpretation ineffective for long periods of time. Such a patient insists on fulfillment and sees interpretation—correctly—as a threat to his need for union.

Fortunately Miss Banks's merger demands quickly abated when the therapist did not try either to fulfill or to evade them; they gave way to a mirror transference which continued for most of the treatment. As the therapist mirrored the patient through his empathic understanding of the significance of her childhood experiences, Miss Banks felt less need to evade the reality of her past and to hide from an understanding of her character problems. As usually happens, as her need for merger diminished and her need for mirroring increased, the idealizing transference became stronger. Once she could trust—and then admire—the therapist in an idealizing transference, she no longer needed to keep herself from looking honestly and critically at her father. She had built up a false picture of him and of his relationship to her mother in order to have an outlet for her idealizing needs. This pseudo-idealization was now replaced by an accepting attitude toward the reality of her parents' situation, an affection for them based on an understanding of their difficulties, and an appreciation of what they had managed to accomplish.

Her original need to dominate the therapist in a merger transference matured into the need for a relationship where the aim was not to dominate or control, but to gain strength from an association that left both patient and therapist independent and intact.

Mr. Clark's situation (chapter 7) was similar. His developmental arrest was the result not of deprivation but of such prolonged and excessive indulgence of the merger phase that he found it difficult to relinquish until fate, in the form of his wife's death, forced his hand. In a sense he had been in a lifelong merger, first with his mother and then with his wife; as a result he had acquired no confidence in his own abilities. In the therapy, as he made moves to function independently and for his efforts received the understanding encouragement of his therapist, he began to pick up where he had left off many years before. He responded to the therapist as to a mother—a mother who not only believed in his capacity to act independently but also recognized and acknowledged it with pleasure. Under these circumstances he could permit himself to mature.

Some of the best results in psychotherapy are attained with patients whose development has been arrested at the level of their need for mirroring. They often respond dramatically to finding in the therapist an understanding individual who offers neither sympathy nor indulgence but rather the opportunity to go through a developmental phase and then to move forward (Goldberg 1973).

In the last stage of Miss Banks's treatment one could see her need for mirroring fade away while the healthy, age-appropriate ambition of her grandiose self became central. She now wanted to become a therapist herself, and she shared with her psychiatrist her plans and ideas with a view to getting his agreement and support.

Was her wish to become a child psychiatrist a manifestation of identification in the transference and something that should have been interpreted rather than acted upon? In all probability this is not the case. Her decision did not seem to be an impulsive attempt to imitate her therapist, but rather a thoughtful choice, rooted in her experience outside the treatment. The fact that it lasted and withstood the problems and difficulties that such a choice entails speaks for a mature decision rather than the acting out of an unresolved transference need. Of course there was probably an element of identification with the therapist, but it would almost surely have been present whatever her career choice. When people make important decisions, they are always influenced by significant people in their lives. The therapist certainly played such a significant part in Miss Banks's life.

XII

The Idealizing Transference: Depression in an Adolescent

Once the therapist decides that a prospective patient may be helped by psychotherapy, it is neither the diagnosis—that is, the defenses the patient mobilizes against anxiety—nor the particular problem that the patient thinks he has, that determines how the therapist goes about treatment; rather, it is the developmental assets that the patient brings to the relationship which now become important. By allying himself with the patient's strengths, the therapist can help the patient re-establish a viable self-concept, with all that this implies for maturation.

Session 1

Eighteen-year-old George Gerard had asked his family doctor for a referral to a psychotherapist, giving no reason for his request except to say that he had personal problems. He is a short, bespectacled man with unkempt hair. His clothes are clean but poorly matched and ill-fitting. In answer to my greeting he smiles shyly, takes my hand but says nothing.

Therapist: So, George, Dr. Miles tells me you want to talk to a psychiatrist. What is it you would like to discuss?
George: I think I'm going crazy.
Therapist: Sounds scary. What happened?
George: I can't sleep or concentrate on anything any more. I don't seem to care about what I do. Nothing interests me.
Therapist: Why would you think that that means you are going crazy?
George: Every once in a while everything around me looks funny. I recognize it all but somehow I feel like I don't belong any more. Things are familiar but seem strange at the same time. I've read that that is one of the signs of schizophrenia.
Therapist: Oh, when did you read that?

Rather than let the patient continue talking about his symptoms, which at this point would only increase his anxiety to no purpose, I divert him. Diversion also opens the way to my getting a broader perspective on his situation, a background against which the symptom can be seen more clearly and possibly explored in context. He does not sound to me like a schizophrenic. He is clear, comes to the point, seems to be aware of me as an individual. To continue probing for evidence of hallucinations, delusions, and so on, as if I were giving credence to his suspicion, might frighten him unnecessarily and make him wonder if there were not, after all, grounds for his fears.

George: In my psych course at college.
Therapist: What school do you go to?
George: I don't go any more. I came home three months ago. That's when I first got sick. Nothing seemed to matter any more. I lost interest in studying, didn't hand in my assignments, stuff like that.
Therapist: And before that?
George: I guess I was pretty good, they gave me a scholarship. When the dean saw that I was flunking out, he called me in to see what was wrong. I told him how I felt, and they sent me to Student Health. I saw the psychiatrist there for a few weeks. He gave me pills and talked to me, but I didn't get better. So they suggested I drop out for a while and come back when I was ready. They were very nice. They let me take incompletes in my courses instead of giving me failures, which is what I should have gotten.
Therapist: Was what happened to you a big personality change or were you always moody?
George: Oh, I had my ups and downs, but I could always do my work. I liked to be busy—I was in a lot of activities. Now I don't seem to want to do anything.
Therapist: What did you and the psychiatrist up at school talk about?
George: Why I felt the way I did, I guess. I can't remember too much about it.
Therapist: Why did you?
George: Why did I what?
Therapist: Feel the way you did?
George: I got a "Dear John" letter from my girl. I never thought I'd react the way I did, though. When I left I knew there was a good chance we'd break up, that she'd find someone else. We even agreed that we'd date other people and see what happened. It's so trite. The doctor tried to talk me out of it, he told me it wasn't the end of the world and that I was young and would get over it. I knew that before I got to him, but knowing it doesn't help.
Therapist: How bad did it get? Did you try to kill yourself?

With any patient who despairs of life, it is important to find out whether he is or has been suicidal. Usually the interview offers an opportunity to ask a question about suicide; but if the subject does not arise, the therapist should bring it up: "How do you feel about life now? Do you feel you can go on or do you think suicide is an answer to your problems?" No matter how the question is phrased, the patient is usually glad finally to be able to discuss the issue with someone, and is reassured that his distress is being taken seriously by the therapist. The exact wording of the question is not important but the manner in which the therapist asks the question is. When asked matter-of-factly, it will usually get an honest answer. If the therapist is embarrassed and ill at ease about the possibility of suicide, the patient may conceal the truth. A statement like, "You're not suicidal, are you?" or "I don't know exactly how to say this, but you haven't—err, ahh—ever, that is—thought about hurting yourself somehow, have you?" is practically an invitation to the patient not to acknowledge the possible seriousness of his condition; the therapist is clearly not ready to hear about it.

George: No, I guess I'm too chicken for that. I played with the idea—"Maybe it'd be better to get it over with. Nothing means anything anyway."—but I never did anything about it.

Therapist: And now do you still feel that it might be better if you ended it all?

George: Naw. If I was going to do it, I would have done it before this. You know, it's like there's a little guy sitting in my head watching it all and saying, "What the hell is all this, George. This isn't happening to you." But it is. Do you think I really am going off the deep end, Doctor?

Therapist: The perceptual difficulty you described, feeling estranged from your surroundings, is not a hallmark of schizophrenia, in spite of what you may have read. It can be caused by other things. Chemicals, for example. Are you still on the medication that you got from the doctor at Student Health?

George: No, it didn't do any good. It was one of those antidepressants, I forget the name.

Therapist: Any drugs you're taking on your own? Uppers? Downers? Alcohol?

Questions about drug abuse and other delinquent or self-destructive behavior should be asked, like the query about suicide, at a time in the interview when it makes sense to the patient to answer them, when he can see that you need the information in order to help him rather than to judge him.

George: I'm scared of that stuff. I've smoked some pot, but not recently. Once in a while I drink a beer.

Therapist: Well, until proven otherwise we'll assume that those strange sensations were the result of emotional tension. You've got your problems, but schizophrenia isn't one of them. You're not crazy and you're not going to be crazy, but you did the right thing in coming for some help. I would like to see you again before proposing a specific treatment plan. After I make my recommendations you can decide whether you want to work with me. Do you have any questions that I might be able to answer at this point?

George: None really. As far as working with you goes, it's O.K. with me. Do you want to talk to my parents?

Therapist: Do you think I should? Is there anything they could tell me that you can't?

George: No, I just thought since my Dad is paying for it, he might want to talk to you.

Therapist: That's something else again, isn't it? If your father and mother want to talk to me, they can call me, but I will tell them, as I'm telling you, that you are the patient and what you say to me is confidential and will remain so. If they have some general concerns that I can help them with, fine, but the details of your treatment, what we say to each other—that stays between us.

George: You mean if I was going to kill myself, you wouldn't tell them?
Therapist: I believed you when you said you weren't going to do that, so it's not really an issue for us. But maybe it is important for you that I answer your question anyway. I have made a professional judgment that you are a responsible individual, and I will treat you as I would any other responsible adult, even though like most people of your age you aren't financially independent yet. If you were to let me know directly or indirectly that you couldn't trust yourself not to harm yourself, then, just as I would for any other of my patients, I would do all I could to prevent that from happening, and that could very well include notifying your parents to enlist their cooperation in doing whatever would be necessary to help you.

What about confidentiality? If a patient says he is going to kill himself or someone else, does the therapist have a right to use this information to prevent the deed? In actual practice this has never been a problem for me. When I have been consulted by a desperately ill person who was close to suicide, I have been frank with him, explaining my need to involve members of his family in planning for his recovery. As a rule the patient has agreed with my plan, relieved that the burden of the immediate future was no longer his responsibility. I am, of course, not talking about angry threats that patients make in therapy, or outside it, which are not meant to be carried out but are geared to upsetting the listener. The difference of intent that distinguishes the two kinds of suicidal declaration is usually clear; the angry threat can be interpreted to the patient and the source of his anger can be investigated.

When George asks his question, he is not really interested in the medicolegal nuances of confidentiality and privileged communication. On the surface he is baiting me to see how I will respond—that is, can I handle myself and think on my feet? On a deeper level, as I hear it, he is asking me whether I can really be depended upon to take care of him if things get worse. My answer is truthful, but I am interested not so much in clarifying my position as in addressing the underlying question that I feel he is asking. He seems satisfied with my response, and I let it go at that. If he pursues the matter and points out the seeming contradiction in a promise of confidentiality to which exceptions can be made, I would suggest that he explore the meaning of his need to put me into a bind, and I would cease to attempt to deal with his question as deserving a direct answer.

George: I guess that's all then.
Therapist: Is tomorrow at three-thirty all right with you?
George: Sure, any time. I'm not doing anything.
Therapist: See you then, George.

George clearly meets the phenomenological criteria for the diagnosis of depression. He has sleep difficulties, cannot work or concentrate, and feels that life is meaningless. But, as you notice, I do not immediately pursue the investigation of these symptoms. I do not want the symptoms to become central for therapy nor their disappearance to be the criteria for therapy's efficacy. Such an attitude would tend to create an atmosphere where the burden for improvement rests on the therapist; the issue becomes: does he or does he not make the pain go away. I want the responsibility for the patient's health to be on his own shoulders, and the therapeutic focus to be on whether the patient does the things—in as well as away from the session—that will lead to his recovery. So learning about the details of George's depression is low on my agenda. I am much more interested in the fact that while the patient is in late adolescence chronologically, he dresses and behaves as if he were considerably younger. What has his development been like? What kind of a person was he before he became ill? How is his disorder related to the developmental task of his age group? Once I get answers to such questions, a systematic approach to treatment will be possible. However, getting answers is going to take time as well as the patient's trust and coöperation; finding out such details is not a reasonable goal for the first meeting. All that needs to be established immediately is whether George is suicidal. If George's demeanor should give me reasons to doubt his assurance that he is not suicidal, treatment would have to start in the hospital. So I clarify this matter and decide that suicide is not a consideration at the moment. Later I make it plain that I will do my best to protect him from self-destructive impulses if they arise in the future.

The therapist can use the initial interviews to best advantage if he keeps to the goal of becoming acquainted with the patient. The reverse is also true. The initial interview should give the patient a chance to get to know the therapist. In my session with George once I determine that he is not suicidal and that I want to work with him on an outpatient basis, my questions and comments are made as much to let him see how I work and what kind of a person I am as a therapist as to find out about him. It is especially important not to be secretive and mysterious with adolescents. They are confused enough already without being confronted by a therapist who smiles enigmatically and leaves them to wonder what is behind the mask.

What about George's reason for coming to see me? He has apparently been depressed for quite a while but has made no move to see a therapist since coming home from college. He is now seeking help because he has had perceptual experiences that make him think he may be becoming schizophrenic. I could have allayed his fears earlier in the interview: schizophrenics, incipient or overt, do not talk in a direct and open manner; they are confused and secretive and never seem to make the point their circumlocutions are belaboring. It does not take five minutes with George to realize that he is not suffering from schizophrenia or any other form of psychosis. I do not choose to deal with his anxieties till later in the session because I want to know how he will cope with them.

Can he stand not to have an answer? Will he be so preoccupied that he cannot address any other issue? It is significant that this is not the case, and that he is able to follow my lead. To me this means that there is a fund of trust that therapy can draw upon for the formation of a therapeutic transference relationship. I volunteer an answer to his concern toward the end of the meeting to show him that I have not forgotten what bothered him, that I take his anxiety seriously, and that if I think I have answers, he will have them. The last point is important because more often than not the therapist may not be able to give a definite answer, and it helps if the patient knows from experience that when the therapist does not talk or does not answer him, it is not some ploy or trick but simply indicates that he has nothing yet to contribute.

It is especially important with adolescent patients for a therapist to make it clear early that he will respect their privacy and will stand firm if that position is challenged. When someone else is paying a patient's bill, it is not unusual for that person to feel entitled to "know what he is paying for." Whether my patient is adolescent or adult, I do not avoid his family on principle. If a family member wants to talk to me and the patient does not object, I coöperate as long as it is understood that the patient's confidence remains inviolate and that whatever a spouse, a parent, or some other informant says to me about the patient may be told to him if he wants to know or if I deem it necessary to tell him. Each situation is, of course, unique; no rule can cover all contingencies. I have learned that I can pretty much handle family members in an appropriate way as long as I am honest with myself and with the patient about what I am doing.

Session 2

When I go to fetch the patient from the waiting room I notice that he looks much less the little boy. Although he is wearing the same clothes—a jacket and pants that are both too short and an open shirt—his hair is combed and his face somehow looks older. I greet him but do not extend my hand. George nods and walks past me into the office.

George: [*In a slightly aggressive tone*] I thought I would feel better, but I don't.
Therapist: Tell me about it.

The patient already seems stronger. He has gotten something from the first interview and wants more. As for me:

1. I can't afford to be stampeded into action by his distress.
2. I won't take responsibility for his discomfort.
3. What he wants is not something I can give him but something he and I must work for.

George: After you told me that I didn't have to worry about becoming schizophrenic, I felt good for a while, but I still don't want to do anything. I had a hard time falling asleep last night and I woke up early. I haven't had more than four or five hours sleep a night since this thing started. [So the insomnia isn't all that bad.]

Therapist: You expected that these symptoms of yours would disappear?

George: I thought that what I was worried about was going crazy, and now that I know I'm not, I guess I did think everything else would be better, too.

Therapist: What I think you're complaining about is that I didn't do enough. In other words, if I was able to help you with one problem, why didn't I make the rest go away, too. However, you're putting the cart before the horse. As I understood it, the fear that you might be becoming insane was a relatively recent development. I'm glad you are reassured on that score but not at all surprised that the basic problems didn't disappear. It's going to take some work on our part to understand what happened to bring them on and what we might help you to do to improve the situation.

George: I didn't mean to complain. I'm sorry if I said the wrong thing, I didn't mean to offend you.

This is a good sign. The patient is aware of the unspoken interpersonal nuances that, much more than verbal content, determine the degree of success of a given transaction. A patient who is able to deal with the therapist only on a concrete level ("but you said . . .") will be confused by any attempt to send him multiple messages in an interchange. When it comes to conversation, George is an adolescent in the way he can conceptualize as well as in age (Basch 1977). Equally important, he is able to use this awareness to draw closer to me. He does not automatically classify an adult as the enemy, but is able to accept one as a potential helper and friend. This capacity indicates that he can develop an idealizing transference—an important factor for the psychotherapy.

Therapist: Far from being offended, I am pleased. We can get somewhere only if you say what you're thinking without disguising it or dressing it up. Everything hinges on your continuing to do that, and that includes feelings and thoughts about me and our work together.

On the unspoken level I send George the message: "You want to win my favor and good will? You can do so by continuing to do exactly what you are doing, thereby letting me do my job." This is what positive reinforcement of behavior is all about. As I have pointed out, such techniques are not the private property of behaviorist psychologists but are a statement of how society fosters growth. If a patient's development has been so distorted that the love, affection, or appreciation of another is not seen as either rewarding or attainable, the therapeutic task becomes much more difficult, perhaps impossible.

George: Maybe I was complaining but didn't know it. My mother says I have an accusatory tone in my voice that drives her up the wall.

Better and better. He is spontaneously introspective and makes connections between his experiences.

> Therapist: That is what I was responding to and made the basis of my inference. You say it bothers your mother?

Now that the subject of his mother has come up in connection with something he is experiencing in the therapy with me, it makes sense to encourage him to talk about her. We will learn very different things from what would have come out if he had been asked apropos of nothing in particular, "Tell me about your mother."

> George: Mom is the stiff-upper-lip type. She feels there's nothing you can't do once you put your mind to it. I think she's pretty disappointed at my coming home this way, but she just says that whatever it is that's bothering me will pass when I decide I've had enough of it.
>
> Therapist: It was a shock to her, I suppose, to have you drop out of college when you must have shown a lot of promise to get that scholarship.

It is a serious mistake to try to curry favor with an adolescent by siding with him against his parents. No matter what he says, he wants you to respect them and their viewpoint even if he himself does not do so at the moment.

> George: I don't like it any better than she does, but that doesn't help me get over it. What would you say is wrong with me anyhow? I mean, what's my trouble called?
>
> Therapist: I'd say you have a depression.
>
> George: But I'm not sad or crying all the time. It's just an empty, useless feeling. Like nothing matters. What used to be important just isn't any more.
>
> Therapist: It is that feeling of meaninglessness which is basic to depression. Some people cry a lot and get very sad in reaction to that state, but others don't.
>
> George: Then the psychiatrist at school was right to give me antidepressants. Should I try another kind?
>
> Therapist: I'd like to wait with that. In my judgment your situation can be explained and dealt with psychologically. Let's see how far we get on that assumption.
>
> George: How do we go about it? You said we would work out a treatment plan.
>
> Therapist: I would like to see you three times a week for the time being—the frequency of visits to be adjusted upward or downward as your situation warrants. As I have already started to tell you, we'll proceed pretty much as we have so far. You say whatever is on your mind, just as it occurs to you, and that will give us a chance to hear together the data on which an understanding of what happened to you can be based.
>
> George: That's a lot of times to be coming. At school I only saw the doctor once a week.
>
> Therapist: Hmm, anything else?
>
> George: Wouldn't I get too dependent on you? I don't want to have to come here for the rest of my life. Sorry—you told me to say what I was thinking, and that was it.
>
> Therapist: Since you're counting on me to get you out of the grip of whatever it is that's hampering your life, I don't think there can be any question but that you'll

be depending on me, on our work, and on this situation. If that bothers you then we'll look at that just as at anything else that comes up. But you keep apologizing for doing exactly what I hoped you would be able to do—putting the cards on the table.

George: I'm afraid you won't understand that it's nothing against you personally, and that you'll get mad at me.

Therapist: And then what?

George: Won't want to help me, I suppose.

Therapist: Maybe that's why you are afraid of your dependency feelings. If you need someone a lot, then you can get hurt if that person's affection or good will is withdrawn.

George: That's the way I felt about my girl, about Nancy. For a while there we told each other everything, and then just to get a letter saying everything is over—that just wasn't right. [*Begins to cry quietly; after about a minute smiles sheepishly through his tears*] I feel like apologizing again, but I'm not going to this time.

Therapist: Right. Just continue to say whatever comes to your mind.

George: It's not as if I had a lot of friends. I was a loner in high school. I wasn't particularly athletic, and the kids thought I was weird because I liked to read and got good grades. I got to know Nancy at the library. She is very pretty, and I figured that she wouldn't want anything to do with me, that probably she had some football player taking her out. She was the one who talked to me first, actually. Then I knew I might have a chance, once she showed she liked me. We went together for three years. She had been lonely too, I found out, but once we had each other it didn't seem as if we needed anyone else.

Therapist: When you graduated you went to different colleges?

George: I wanted to stay here and go to State with her, but my mom said I'd be a fool to throw away a chance to go to an Eastern school, especially since it seemed to want me so much. I was going to be a lawyer, and graduating from a college like that would have given me a crack at some of the top places in the country. [Has he given up the idea of law? Of college?]

Therapist: So, let's set up our schedule for regular appointments now. I was thinking of Monday, Wednesday, and Friday, if it's O.K. with you.

George: Fine with me. Will I see you on Friday this week still?

Therapist: Yes, we can get together then.

It is not the affective state that determines whether a patient is depressed. As I explain in part to George, the hallmark of depression is the sense or the attitude that life is meaningless—an indication that the perception of the self is no longer a unifying focus for ambitions and ideals. In the resulting condition the goals that ordinarily organize behavior seem to have been lost (Basch 1975).

The myriad symptoms of depression are an attempt to circumvent helplessness and to enlist assistance in restoring some meaning to life—that is, to recapture a sense of direction for the self. The nature of the symptoms varies depending on the patient's character formation and his level of maturity. Symptom removal should not be the primary therapeutic goal in the treatment of depression, nor does the elimination of symptoms and discomfort necessarily signify the end of the illness.

The answer to the depressive's call for help lies in aiding him to regain his ability to engage in goal-directed behavior that is self-constructive and not self-destructive. Clinically speaking, this means that the patient's development of his grandiose and idealizing self has to be understood, remobilized, and possibly redirected. These developmental factors, not his symptoms, must govern the diagnostic investigation and the management of the therapy.

In some nonpsychotic depressions—especially but not exclusively those associated with the menopause, the climacteric, and old age—there seems to be an organic factor that is at least partially responsible for the interference with the goal-directed functioning of the brain. Usually an organic depression is not related to a particular loss or disappointment; it is endogenous rather than reactive. One must consider in the differential diagnosis, however, that an endogenous or somatic depression may be precipitated by—although not caused by—an external change; it need not be an upset or a failure but is as likely to be a success or an achievement. In such cases, as in psychotic depressions (Redlich and Freedman 1966; Freedman et al. 1975), biological and physical therapies, in addition to psychotherapy, are indicated.

To use an analogy, if the problem lies in the computer's hardware, chemotherapy or electroconvulsive treatment is likely to be of help; if the programs themselves, the software, are the source of difficulty, psychological treatment is indicated, and medication will usually not help. I have had a few cases where the need for psychotherapy was clear, but the patient could not utilize his sessions until chemotherapy was added to the regimen. By the same token, the relief given these patients by medication was not sufficient to restore them to effective operation; psychotherapy was still necessary.

In George's case there is no doubt in my mind that his difficulties are reactive to his recent experiences of loss—that is, separating from his family to attend college and losing the emotional support provided by his girl friend. Therefore, medication is not indicated at this point.

Sessions every other day should give the patient and me an opportunity to establish a relationship that will support him as he is helped to investigate the problems responsible for his distress. It brings us into sufficient contact to let me serve as a transference figure with whom he can work through a renewed attempt at becoming an independent and mature individual.

Session 3

George: Since Wednesday when I saw you last, I haven't been able to sleep at all, and I think I've lost some more weight—no appetite.
Therapist: What do you do all night?

Again, the emphasis should be placed on his activity not on his symptoms.

George: Mostly I lie in bed and listen to my stereo. I still can't concentrate enough to read anything, not even the paper.
Therapist: What do you listen to?
George: Oh, jazz, blues, the oldies. I've been collecting records since I was twelve. I don't like this modern stuff, though.
Therapist: What do you think about while you're listening to the music?
George: Oh, about myself, and what's happened. Nancy and I used to spend a lot of time playing records and talking. What should I do about not sleeping and eating?
Therapist: Getting started in treatment may have stirred things up a bit. It sounds like you have a lot on your mind, and the best way to deal with it is to talk about it here. I would expect that its expression will reduce the ability of whatever is troubling you to disturb your natural functions.
George: Another thing I've been thinking is that maybe I never wanted to be a lawyer. It wasn't really my idea. My grandfather was a lawyer, my mother's dad. She thought the sun rose and set on him. I never thought he was that great. He died when I was eight years old, but I remember he was always critical of me. I was only a kid, for Christ's sake, and he expected me to have the manners of an adult. If I didn't, he'd complain to my mother, and she'd be mad at me. Anyway, my mother's been on me for years that someday I'd be a lawyer and go into Grampa's old firm. The only way I could ever get her to act like she liked me was to talk about what law school I'd go to someday, and get prizes on the debating team, or win the American Legion essay contest, stuff like that. It sort of got to be taken for granted that that's what I would become.

What was nice about going with Nancy was that she liked me for what I was, not for what I was going to be. . . . [*Pause*]

Therapist: Yes?
George: I'm sending for my clothes.
Therapist: How's that?
George: My clothes. The stuff I have in the dorm at college. When I left I didn't take it with me. One day I just got on a plane in what I was wearing, blue jeans and a T-shirt, and came home. What I've got on now is old stuff. It doesn't fit any more, but it's all I've got right now. Yesterday I called my old roommate, and he was very nice about it. He's going to pack it all in my suitcases and send it to me. I'll pay for the delivery charges of course.
Therapist: So you're home for good. [It sounds as if he has committed himself to an extended therapy with this gesture.]
George: Mom's pretty upset about it. I guess she figured that any day I would just pick up again and get on a plane going the other way to take up where I left off. She tried to rile up my dad, saying she didn't want me idling around the house and that I'd have to go get a job if I wasn't in school. She tried to get you into it, too, by saying this couldn't be doing me much good, that I was going backward since I started coming here.
Therapist: What did your father say to all that?
George: Tried to calm her down like he usually does. But he did say that even though he didn't understand it all, if I thought I had to come to you to get better, then that's what he wanted me to do. So that got Mom angry. She always thinks in terms of who is on whose side. Then she told me if I was going to live there, I had to help her more around the house. She has gone back to work three days at the law office. They always have called her in when they were short of secretaries, but now she's going on a regular basis. I thought that was fair, and I did agree to do more of the housework, but I could tell she wasn't satisfied by that anyway. I'm

just not in any shape to figure out what I want to do with my life right now. She doesn't understand that.

Therapist: O.K. then, George, I'll see you on Monday.

Sessions 4–21

For the next six weeks George told me his life story. It came out in bits and pieces, one memory stirring another, and I made no attempt to make him follow a chronological order. Sometimes he told of incidents whose significance escaped me because I did not have enough background to put them in the proper context. However, since he was proceeding on his own, clearly welcoming the opportunity to talk out his thoughts, I kept my questions to myself for the most part, confident that as he went on what was puzzling me would soon become understandable. It was more important for me to see the affective links that were revealed by the sequence of his associations than to have everything neat and orderly.

I learned that George was an only child. His mother, because of complications at his birth, had to have a total hysterectomy shortly after his delivery. It was wartime, and his father was serving overseas in the military during the first three years of George's life, while George and his mother lived with her parents. He has few memories of those days but does recall resenting the presence of his father, who had just returned home, at his third birthday party.

Through the years George often heard from his mother how disappointed she was that when his father was discharged from the army, he did not carry out his plans to become a lawyer. The father felt that he could not adjust to being a "college boy" again after his wartime experiences, and also he wanted to become self-supporting so that he could move his family out of his father-in-law's house. He and a friend saw an opportunity to make money buying and reselling war-surplus equipment, and left college to do it. Eventually they started their own manufacturing company and enjoyed a modest success. However, George's mother apparently never forgave her husband for not fulfilling the hopes she had built up for him. She had first met her husband when he was working during the summer as an office boy in her father's law firm, where she was a legal secretary. It seemed clear that she married him in good part because it was a foregone conclusion that he would join her father as soon as he passed the bar exam.

George described his mother as often bitter, tending to withdraw from emotional contact and to occupy herself with household and other tasks. She prided herself on efficiency and a job well done, and always expected George to live up to her standards. George enjoyed her approval and worked hard to earn it. Everything was fine as long as he was performing well, but she had little patience with him when he was in trouble, and he learned not to come to her at such times but rather to rely on adults outside the family.

His father came across in George's description as a quiet, decent man who never had much to say to his son but who participated actively as coach, counselor, troop father, and so forth, in George's many after-school activities.

Mrs. Gerard did not hide her disdain for her husband's occupation, especially when he came home from his business with machine oil on his clothes. She berated him for appearing in such a state before the neighbors, most of whom were professional men. As a young boy George was puzzled by her attitude for he was quite proud of his father and of the way his father was consulted when anyone had a mechanical problem. On weekends George would sometimes go along when his father went to help out a friend or neighbor who could not start his car or whose furnace was not functioning. In other people's houses George saw his father treated like a welcome and important person—important because of his knowledge—while at home that knowledge was treated as something to be ashamed of. When he was about ten years old, George mentioned this paradox to his father, who just said matter-of-factly, "Your mother always wanted a lawyer. Now you're elected."

Although he was well fed and well cared for, there was a chill around the house which made him seek outside activities. He also read a great deal because his mother approved of reading and would not be critical of him if she saw him doing it, whereas watching television or fooling around with his friends would get him a "sermon" about the value of time and the importance of self-improvement.

He and Nancy met when he was fourteen years old and she was fifteen. She, too, felt she had no one to talk to about herself, her past, and the thoughts that were crowding in on her. The two were kindred spirits and reveled in the warmth of their new-found friendship. Although George was aware of his sexuality and had an extravagant phantasy life when alone, with Nancy he was physically reserved and limited himself to an occasional kiss, although she let him know that she would not mind if he became bolder.

The night before he left for college he overcame his shyness and became more passionate, but they stopped considerably short of intercourse. Although they had agreed that they would be free to date others, George had no desire to meet other girls after he arrived at college. In the past he had struggled mightily to control his masturbatory habit, but now he found that he had ceased to have a need for such release. His phantasy life, too, had disappeared. George pursued his studies mechanically and experienced none of the pleasure he had formerly had in mastering a new subject. Letters from Nancy were the only thing he looked forward to, and the only activity that still interested him was writing to her. Although he maintained the frequency and emotional intensity of his side of the correspondence, Nancy's letters became fewer and increasingly noncommital. The handwriting was on the wall, but he refused to see it.

Throughout these eighteen sessions I said little except to encourage him to go on if he faltered and—when he began to wonder whether I could be interested in what he was saying, especially when he was repetitious—to assure him that I was far from bored.

Even without interpretations from me, the opportunity to tell me about himself seemed to have a salutary effect. He seemed to forget about his initial complaints, and one day he mentioned with some surprise that he was eating and sleeping normally. He mentioned reading he was doing, and I assumed that he was also able to concentrate again.

Although the content of the sessions provided innumerable opportunities for me to make clever interpretations, it would have been a mistake to try them on him. He was talking at this time to make himself understood, to let me know him. He was being drawn into a transference, but until it was established and its nature understood, interpretation was premature. The beginning therapist especially must resist the temptation to "earn his keep" by showing that he can make connections between various events in the patient's life. Only if the patient gets confused and can not go on is it helpful for the therapist to point out to him the sense in what he has been saying. Interpretation, when it becomes possible, should be made in the framework of the patient-therapist relationship, and then it may or may not be tied in with the historical material. At this period George was painting a picture of himself for me, and I was going to let him finish it. Then he and I could step back and together look at and comment on this or that detail, add finishing touches, or perhaps erase large parts of the canvas and start afresh. But all that would come later.

At this point in the treatment the therapist can, in the privacy of his thoughts, place what the patient is saying in the context of the developmental phases in which it occurred; he can also reflect on what it all means to the patient as it is reviewed and relived at his present level of maturity. These reflections will lead to predictions about the transference which can alert the therapist to what may happen in the near future and prepare him to act accordingly.

It became eminently clear during George's associations in these weeks that the seeds of his depression had been planted long before his adolescence. Although his leaving home as well as his separating from and then losing his girl friend precipitated his symptoms, these events did not explain them. I felt that his mother's seeming need to control his life in the interest of her own needs and ambitions and the relative absence of a strong male figure with whom he could identify may well have left George unprepared for the maturational phase he was entering. His depression struck me as a retreat from a job that he found overwhelming. If this assumption proved true, the therapeutic task was to help him identify and understand the significance of his developmental deficiencies.

XIII

The Idealizing Transference: Resolution of a Developmental Arrest

Session 22

George: I've been thinking that you haven't said much lately, Doctor. Don't you ever get tired of hearing all this stuff?

Therapist: Not a bit. What you say is all very important for me as I try to understand you and your life.

George: Boy, I don't know if I could do what you do for a living. Listening to people's problems day after day. Did you always want to be a psychiatrist?

Therapist: I think it's the only career I ever considered seriously. I made up my mind to become a psychiatrist at the age of sixteen, even though I had never met one and wasn't at all clear what was involved. I've often wondered how I happened to make that choice. All I can figure is that something I read or heard must have convinced me that this would give my life the meaning that it seemed to lack or maybe provide the answers I was looking for. I am aware of the steps I took after that to learn more about what was involved in that profession, how I turned an inner conviction and ambition into a reality over the years, but I never have learned what that initial deciding incident was.*

George: That's what's meant by the unconscious, I suppose.

Therapist: Yes, very often the most important factors in our lives are not in consciousness and we know them only through their effects.

George: Even in your own analysis you didn't learn about the origins of your decision?

Therapist: No, not that I know of any more, at least. If it ever surfaced, it was pulled down into the depth again, and I know nothing of it.

George: Gee, I had the impression that in psychoanalysis you were supposed to

*I realize that the introduction of a personally revealing anecdote may sound a dissonant note because it is inconsistent with published case reports and with classroom teaching. My rationale for this maneuver is discussed further on pages 144–45 and again on page 177. Indeed, the introduction of personal anecdotal material for therapeutic purposes is not unusual. My sources of information are patients who had other therapists before I met them and colleagues who have been frank in their discussion of cases with me. It sounds strange only because much of what really happens in the actual therapeutic interchange is seldom either written about or taught to students.

uncover everything, and when you got done you'd know everything about yourself.

Therapist: No, you never get to that point, or anywhere near it—fortunately, I think. If you get a reasonable result, you do end up with enough insight into how and why you often make yourself unnecessarily unhappy. Then you can use your knowledge as a tool either to prevent a repetition when the temptation arises to make old mistakes or perpetuate former misunderstandings, or, if you're already in the soup, to get yourself out of it quicker and with less damage to yourself and others than you would have been able to do before analysis. Now that may not sound like much compared with phantasies of a perfect life governed by unlimited self-knowledge, but it really is a great deal. It makes all the difference in the world.

George: I'd like that for myself.

Therapist: As I see it, that's what we're working toward.

George: You are a psychoanalyst, too, aren't you?

Therapist: Yes, why do you ask?

George: I read about different forms of treatment in my Psych course. Psychoanalysis is supposed to be the one that goes deepest.

Therapist: Yes?

George: How come I'm not getting analyzed? You know, four or five times a week on the couch over there.

Therapist: If I had decided you needed analysis, we wouldn't be doing anything different from what we are doing now. With a person of your age who has the problems you've told me about, I think our present psychotherapeutic approach can do a fine job, especially when I have the kind of coöperation you have given me so far in looking at your personality and its development. All I can tell you is that I wish I had been sitting where you are when I was eighteen, it would have saved me a lot of grief.

A few more words about the myth of the therapist's anonymity are in order (see also pages 4–5 and 7–8). The notion that the therapist should try to remain an unknown quantity for the patient has become dogma, a formula that is taught religiously although its original function has long been forgotten. (Fortunately the rule is not followed as consistently as it is given lip service.) The therapist need not be afraid to inject a personal note when that seems to be the appropriate therapeutic move. The purpose of keeping the details of the therapist's own life secret from the patient is to give the latter's imagination as much freedom as possible to reveal his unconscious mental life through the phantasies he attaches to the person of the therapist. This reticence is an important aspect of treatment when the therapist is trying to recover and bring to consciousness a patient's repressed wishes. In the case of George, my aim was just the opposite. I did not particularly want George's phantasies about me to be stimulated, but rather I wanted to give him the opportunity to identify, if he cared to do so, with the searching adolescent that I once was. It was clear to me that George was coming to see in me the understanding, helpful, and admired mentor that adolescents need and that he had not previously found. I was perfectly willing to lend myself to the role now that his depression had resolved itself and further growth was once again a possibility for him. My reminiscing with him, taking him into my confidence, was my way of agreeing to serve this purpose. It was also my way of acknowledging that his efforts in therapy had borne fruit, that our relationship had been raised to a new level. Furthermore, by telling him something of my own search, I hoped to foster the more mature aspects of the transference rather than a merger based on union with an imaginary omnipotent, omniscient therapist-god.

But what if George needs to see me as an all-powerful being with whom he wishes to merge? Has my comment ruined the possibility of that development? Not at all. I have learned that whenever I go wide of the therapeutic mark, the patient indicates in some way that he has not registered the meaning of what I have said—that is, he disavows my comment or interpretation and goes on to use me in a way that makes sense to him. Usually no harm has been done. There is an unrealistic grandiosity and an untoward therapeutic ambitiousness behind the notion that everything we therapists say is of such moment that patients' lives hang on every statement we make. A mistaken interpretation or thoughtless comment is not going to destroy everything. Not only our patients but we, too, have to learn that we are not that powerful. When our words make an impact, they do so not because we are so omniscient or omnipotent, but most likely because we have had the good sense to read the patient's signals correctly and tell him what he is ready to hear.

George: At least you knew what you wanted to be. I thought I was going to be a lawyer, but I'm not sure now that I even want to go to college. Everything seems so pointless.

Note how the patient uses what I said about myself as a stimulus to search more within himself. It is exactly what I had hoped for and a good therapeutic sign.

Therapist: Right now everything is colored by the way you feel about yourself. One time, though, you seem to have enjoyed reading, writing, and debating—all interests that seem compatible with the study of law.

George: Maybe I just thought I liked those things because my mother wanted me to like them, and the same for my decision to be a lawyer.

It is best that the patient himself brings up this consideration which, of course, has been in the picture from the start. It is only if the patient does not make the obvious connection that the therapist has to point it out to him. The making of connections should not be confused with interpretation—that is, the clarification of repetitive patterns in the transference which the patient cannot be expected to achieve unaided.

Therapist: I am sure that that did play a part in forming your decision, but regardless of its origin you may have built up a genuine interest in the field—an interest that is now yours and not your mother's.

By setting yourself up as devil's advocate, you force the patient to think and talk matters through more thoroughly than he would if you just fell in with the obvious explanation—In this case that his need for his mother's approval may well have coerced him into believing he wanted to be a replica of her admired father.

George: I do like reading and public speaking, but when I worked at the law firm last summer, I can't say I was all that thrilled with it. I didn't want to dig in and find out all about what was going on there, I just ran the errands they sent me on and whatever else they gave me to do. I figured that when I knew more about it, maybe I'd get excited about court calls, writing briefs, and filing motions. Anyway, I had four years of college ahead of me before law school, and I could always change my mind if I found something better for me. Right now I haven't found anything better, and I don't want to go on with pre-law either.

Therapist: Was there ever a time in your life when you were doing something you really did enjoy? Anything that exercised sort of a gravitational pull on you?

By helping the patient to recall what meaningful activities have engaged his interest, I help him escape circular rumination about his present condition, while still dealing with the subject he has raised.

George: Did I tell you I worked in Dad's shop after school and on vacations for a couples of years?

Therapist: No, you haven't told me that, as far as I remember.

George: Funny, I guess I forgot all about it till you just said that about "gravitational pull." I did like that work. I like machines and have sort of an aptitude for mechanical things that I must have inherited from Dad.

Therapist: What did you do at the factory?

George: At the shop? Oh, I was a helper, sort of. At first they just had me sweeping the floor and carting away the trash. Then some of the older guys let me try my hand at running some of the equipment, and when I showed them I could do it without ruining a job, they let me take over when they went on breaks or if somebody was sick and they needed stuff in a hurry.

Therapist: How did your father feel about your work?

George: He never says much. When he saw that I wasn't just putting in time, he'd show me things once in a while. He more or less told me that he'd take me off the floor and let me work in the office the next summer to let me see that side of the business, but I didn't go back after my junior year in high school. That summer I worked in the law office.

Therapist: How come you changed jobs?

George: I had this course in social science, and the teacher talked a lot about social justice and the inequities of the capitalist system in oppressing minorities. It got me to thinking a lot about the exploitation of the working class. I mean, if I wanted to I know I could go into the shop and someday be an owner. But it doesn't seem right that just because I am the son of the boss I should be in line for the top job while someone else has to spend his life behind a machine. Oh yeah, now I remember, that's when I decided maybe being a lawyer wouldn't be bad.

With a law degree I could work for social justice, not just talk about it. Civil liberties, consumer protection, antitrust—it all seemed pretty glamorous to me when that teacher talked about it.

Therapist: [There is something missing here; his argument does not sound quite right. Do the facts support it?] Working on the floor of your father's shop you had the opportunity to see discriminatory or demeaning practices firsthand. Did the men complain much? Was there prejudice against minorities? Were things so bad?

George: No, I can't say I heard anything except the normal amount of grousing that always goes on. Actually the men were pretty happy, and I don't think they put on an act for me just because I was the boss's son. They knew that Dad could do anything they did and that he understood their problems from having worked the equipment himself. Dad never discriminated. Even when black people couldn't work at skilled jobs anywhere, at least in this town, Dad always hired them if they were capable of doing the job. He said if blacks were good enough to share foxholes with him overseas they were good enough to work with him stateside.

When I was at the shop he turned me over to Al, one of the foremen, a black guy about six foot four and two hundred fifty pounds. Al told me the story of how the organizer from the union came around and wanted to make the place a closed shop. I guess he told my dad that if he didn't let them put their people in and get rid of the blacks, he might get hurt. Dad listened to him and then called Al into the front office and said, "Al, take a good look at Mr. —— here. He tells me I should get rid of you and let a white man who deserves it have your job. It seems if I don't go along with him it might affect my health." Then he turned to the organizer and told him: "Mr. ——, we know who you are and we know where to find you. If anything happens to me or to the shop that shouldn't be happening, I'm holding you responsible." "Al, if something does happen and they get to me before I can kill this son-of-a-bitch, I want you to do it for me. Now take him to the front door and see that he leaves my property. If he ever comes back without an invitation you have my permission to throw him out on his ass." This guy, the way Al tells it, was a sort of pudgy, short fellow, and while Dad was talking, he kept looking over and up at Al, all the while getting paler and paler. He left without a word. They never heard from him again and didn't have any trouble either.

Therapist: From what you said I would think you would be for the union.

Here I was playing devil's advocate again.

George: I guess there's unions and there's unions. Dad pays union scale and higher, but he doesn't want to be told how to run his business and whom he can hire. He really doesn't see himself as that different from the men. He's on the floor as much as he is in the office.

Therapist: Now when you are talking about him, you sound very proud of your father. I'd never have suspected this side of him from your previous description. He seemed to be sort of a nice guy but a nonentity.

George: He's easygoing, but he'll stand up for what he believes is right.

It sounds as if George's identification with the underprivileged masses was a convenient rationalization for his emotional ambivalence toward his father. It is likely that he was torn between an idealization of his father and an urge to be like him and an adolescent drive toward independence through rejection of parental ties. I might have pointed out to him that there was no basis in fact for painting his father as an ogre who exploited the masses and that his leaving his father's business must have had other reasons. I do not bring up this issue because it is no longer germane. He is clearly proud of his father, and I am more interested in seeing what he will do in that relationship now than in trying to get him to second-guess the past. Furthermore, he is in the midst of developing his transference to me, and I feel that to focus on conflicts with his father may, at this point, interfere with that process.

Session 23

George: You know, I found it hard to believe when you told me last time that something really important like your desire to become a psychiatrist could disappear from your consciousness, but then I realized that something very much like that has happened to me.

Therapist: Hmm.

George: It's as if I had forgotten all about those two years that I worked off and on at the shop. Of course it wasn't exactly like what happened to you because if anyone had asked me directly about where I had been working during that time, I could have told him. It's just that I never thought about it or what it meant to me. That conversation with Al about my dad, for example, that was very important.

Therapist: Any idea what the reason for that might have been?

George: Well, my mom never did like my working there. She didn't say anything directly against it, but I knew not to mention it when I was around home. She wouldn't come right out with it, but she'd hint that I wasn't spending enough time at my homework. There wasn't much she could do, though, because I always got top grades and made the honors list every time.

Therapist: Even though you weren't prevented from working with your father, you didn't feel that you could talk about your experiences and opinions at home. In a way that lends an air of unreality to that part of your life and makes it seem as if it is not something that even happened. Important parts of your life can lose their meaning that way even though they are not forgotten.

George: I always felt as if I had to do a balancing act at home. Certain things just couldn't be discussed.

Therapist: That's why Nancy was so important, I imagine. You two could tell each other anything and everything without having to worry about being misunderstood.

George: Yes, I really miss that. It's funny, though, I don't miss her that much any more—I haven't thought much about her in the last month or so. Maybe it has something to do with coming here—I get a chance to tell you whatever concerns me, and talk it over. I wonder if I misjudged Nancy, though. I thought we were so close, and then when she found someone else, just to drop me wasn't right. She made me feel like I wasn't good enough for her.

Therapist: I wonder if that was the way you saw your mother looking at your father—not good enough for her, a disappointment.

George: I've thought about that. I don't know how he has taken it all these years.

It's too bad her hopes were disappointed, but, Jesus, he can't live his life for her. I wonder why I never saw that all these years till now.

Therapist: You needed and cared for both your mother and your father and wanted them to be a unit. It's difficult emotionally for a child to feel two ways about a parent. Very often the unpleasant aspect of his feelings is dissociated, split off in such a way that he doesn't have to reckon with it consciously. As you get older you learn to deal with conflicting emotions. You are now able to look at shortcomings you think your parents have, without thereby rejecting them in any total way.

George: Yes, I really feel more sorry for them than for me. At least I have a life ahead of me still, they don't. [Further confirmation that the depression has lifted.] It all seems so pointless, why couldn't they have been happier? It's not all mother's fault either. Sure, she was dissatisfied and pretty vocal about it, but Dad could have stood up for himself more. Maybe then she would have woken up to the fact that there was nothing to be ashamed of in being a businessman's wife, especially when he's a successful one.

Therapist: Maybe, but I tend to think that it would have taken professional help to get her to come to grips with the fixation she seems to have on her father. You know, I tend to think that even if the war hadn't interfered and your father had become a lawyer, she would not have been satisfied. He still wouldn't have become her father reincarnate.

George: You mean it's one of those Oedipus complex deals. She wanted to turn her husband into her father?

Oh! So that's why she wants me to be a lawyer! I feel sick.

Therapist: It's a painful thought.

George: It's nauseating.

Therapist: It's a side of life we don't ordinarily look at, but it is a part of everyone's life for all that.

George: It makes me feel cheated. I want to be myself, not some mannequin she dresses up with her phantasies.

Therapist: Well put.

George: It must be ever so much worse for Dad. He can't win. The only way she could want him is if he wasn't himself.

Therapist: We know what's going on in your mind, but not what's in the mind of either one of your parents. Your father, for instance, doesn't sound like such an unhappy man.

All these ideas flooding in on you are understandably unsettling, to say the least, but you can't equate your feelings and experiences with those of your father on a one-to-one basis.

George: I guess that's right. They don't act that unhappy with one another. She doesn't like his work, but I've never heard her say she doesn't like him.

It is usually the case, as it is with George, that when a therapist helps a patient to face an undeniable psychological difficulty in a parent which had a serious impact on his own development, such a confrontation—far from turning the patient against that parent—leads to a better understanding and to a more sympathetic view of him or her. It helps to understand something even if it cannot be changed and seems to be unnecessary and unfair. One cannot, of course, be too cautious in making sure that the facts are what they seem to be and purging one's interpretation of anger or condemnation that one may feel through identification with the patient in his past or present condition. Indeed, when the therapist feels impelled to explain something of this sort to a patient, the identification should be with the parent in question, as if the therapist were saying to the patient what the parent would say if he or she had the requisite insight to make himself or herself and his or her motives understood.

Session 24

George: I had a bad dream last night. Do you want to hear about it?
Therapist: Of course. It's what you're thinking about, isn't it?
George: I don't know who the people were. All I can remember is that there was some woman in it. She was kissing me, and it was nice until she turned into a man. Then I woke up and felt disgusted.
Do you think this means I'm a homosexual?
Therapist: Say what occurs to you.
George: I never thought I was. You hear about guys playing with each other or being approached by older men, but nothing like that ever happened to me. If it did, I think I would just be upset and turned off by it.
Therapist: A woman changes into a man. Anything more occur to you about that?
George: No, nothing other than what I said—homosexuality.
Therapist: What about our last session in which we mentioned that the freedom you had in talking to Nancy is now something you experience with me.
George: I had forgotten about that.
Therapist: Doesn't that tie in with your dream?
George: I worried about being dependent on you before, do you remember?
Therapist: Yes.
George: Well, maybe what happened in the dream is what I worried about all the time. If I got those feelings as I got more dependent on you, then I would be a homosexual, wouldn't I?

Note patient's developing capacity for thinking psychologically about himself.

Therapist: No, you'd be just what you are now—a young man who is afraid that feeling close to another man means he is a homosexual.
George: Doesn't it?
Therapist: Under normal or average circumstances every boy has affectionate feelings toward his father as well as toward his mother and expresses them physically. That closeness lays the groundwork for later relationships with men—friends, mentors, his own male children, and so forth. Your love for your father does not make you a homosexual.
George: Yes. I never thought of those other relationships you mention as homosexual. But in the dream I was kissing this woman who then became a man. Kissing a man—that's not just friendship, is it?
Therapist: That depends. There are plenty of cultures in which men kiss in friend-

ship, just as women do in ours—but, more to the point, you may have been expressing longings that belonged to your own boyhood in relation to your father.

George: My father isn't like that. He's not a physically demonstrative person in general, and I don't recall him being so with me. I kissed my mother at bedtime but not Dad. He just sort of waved to me and said, "Good-night."

Therapist: I would wonder if you didn't long for more physical contact with him, without your necessarily realizing it consciously. So now when you feel understandably close to me as our work progresses, you experience with me those urges to be close with your father.

George: I can't remember if it really happened in the dream or not, but as you were talking it seemed to me the man in the dream said something, and it sounded like your voice.

Therapist: Now that you are an adult you tend to cast your longing in adult terms, but I suspect that what's getting mobilized within you is a boy's wish for affection and intimacy with his father.

George: I told you Dad was away in the war during my first three years, didn't I?

Therapist: Yes, I remember very well.

George: That might have made a difference in how we related to one another.

Therapist: You also mentioned that your first memory, or one of your first memories, was the resentment you felt at your father's presence at your third birthday party. Understandable as it is that you might have seen your dad as an intruder on the special relationship with your mother that you had enjoyed till then, still your negative reaction to your father—who probably had imagined a very different scenario—may have put him off and made him hesitant about becoming more physical with you.

George: It's hard to know what happened. Dad is sort of shy, if he doesn't feel welcome he backs off quickly. I've seen that.

Therapist: Of course you had plenty of opportunities for physical closeness with your grandfather in those early years.

George: Are you kidding? They still talk about how Grandpa thought of babies as dirty little things that he didn't want anything to do with. He dressed very fashionably, even around the house, and was always afraid that any babies or pets might get him dirty. He didn't touch his own children till they were five years old, and I'm sure he didn't make any exception for me. I sure don't remember anything physical with him.

Therapist: It's interesting to speculate, even though that is all it is, that your grandfather's aversion to relating to his children physically may explain your mother's preoccupation with the law. It is perhaps her way of still trying to get close to her father.

George: That makes sense, but we'll never know. Boy, you not only get shoved around by your own unconscious but by that of your parents, and they're under the influence of their parents. It goes backward to God knows when, doesn't it? I might be beting influenced by some character from the Middle Ages, for all I know.

Note the patient's increasing ability to speculate creatively. My own excursions into the realm of phantasy about what might have happened are in the interest not so much of trying to establish what actually took place as to show him by example how one can go about using one's hypothetical capacity, how one can play with ideas.

Session 25

George: I found out something very interesting. When I got home after last time, I decided to ask my parents about some of the things we had been talking about. I was especially interested in my behavior toward my father when he came home from the war. They told me that I didn't even condescend to notice him for the first few weeks he was back. Then I let him get a little closer, but I'd wriggle off his lap if he wanted to hold me. If he tried to hug or kiss me, I would get very upset, holler and scream, and hold my breath till I turned blue. It wasn't Dad who started that business at bedtime, it was me. I insisted he "say good-night like Grampa." As I told you my grandfather didn't want me near him for fear of getting dirty, and apparently waved at me from across the room when I was taken upstairs.

I guess there is something to this reconstruction of the past, as you call it.

Therapist: Well, it is interesting to get such corroboration for what we hypothesized. Often the actual events don't correspond so nicely with the reconstruction. However, we're not after a moving picture likeness of your development anyway. It's the attitudes about life that motivate you now that need to be understood in the context of the past. What we want to know is not so much what really happened as how the past can clarify what you're going through today.

George: Now what?

Therapist: Now what, what?

George: We figured out what my dream meant, now what do we do with it?

Therapist: We figured out what your dream didn't mean. It doesn't mean you're a latent homosexual. That is already not nothing.

George: Probably one of the reasons I was afraid of homosexuality is that I've never really done anything with a girl. I've often wondered if that makes me abnormal. Other guys my age have had all kinds of experiences already. But, like I told you, with Nancy I never seemed to want to get much past the kissing and hugging stage. My sex life has always been more in my head—there I am a great lover, but always with women I don't know. Someone I saw on the street, or a picture in a magazine.

Therapist: Have you been having sexual phantasies again? Has your interest in sex returned?

George: In the last couple of weeks, yes.

Therapist: Is there a particular drama that you stage for yourself in the theater of your mind when you have sexual phantasies or masturbate?

George: Do I have to talk about it in detail?

Therapist: No, you don't. At least not before you're ready to do so.

George: Oh, what's the difference, I've told you everything else. I meet the girl, usually she's a woman older than I am, and she lets me know that she's interested in me. Then we talk and she makes it clear that she'd like to make love to me. We go to her place, a fancy apartment like I've seen in movies, and she undresses me. That's usually when I come. I've tried to go on with the phantasy sometimes, but I can't. I suppose because I never have done anything, I really don't know what such an experience would be like.

Therapist: It sounds to me as if here again we have an earlier need that has become fused with adult sexuality. Rather, an early still unsatisfied need takes precedence and subordinates sexuality to itself. The basic theme that I detect in your story is that of being shown that you are wanted and desirable. In your dream you were being kissed by the man, in your phantasy you are being undressed by a woman who has let you know she wants you. You recall that in real life the only girl you became close with, Nancy, approached you in the library and let you know that she liked you.

My guess would be that the being kissed and held and tenderly undressed were things that your mother did, perhaps in those years when you had her all to yourself before your father came home. These memories remain permanently fixed in some form as a source of comfort to which you return, disguising them to suit the occasion, when the present seems not to offer warmth and receptivity.

Holding, hugging, and kissing. These are some of the ways in which a child is shown that he is worth-while, a precious being. From that comes a healthy self-love—identity, self-esteem, self-respect—call it what you will. If we're not satisfied that we truly are worth-while, we can spend the rest of our lives looking for that affirmation in whatever we do. It's a hidden agenda that is operative in all our behavior, unbeknownst to us. A need that must be fulfilled before we can go on to reach other emotional goals.

So I think we can hazard an answer to your question about your sexuality. It's not a matter of homosexuality versus heterosexuality, but a matter of priorities. There's something you have to get done first before you can fulfill adult needs. You must settle for yourself the issue of whether you are a worth-while, desirable person. You will look at whomever you're with, regardless of gender, and in whatever situation you find yourself, for an answer to that. And because it is an issue from many years ago you'll want it answered in the way you would have needed it then. Will they hug me, hold me, touch me, and kiss me, or at least let me know by how they look at me that I am precious to them? Or will they abandon me to my own devices to cope as best I can, literally and figuratively, untouched in my loneliness?

George: [*Laughs*] Sorry, I'm not laughing at what you said.

Therapist: I know, everything fits doesn't it? From infancy on when what was disorganized or confusing falls into place and lets itself be understood, we laugh with pleasure.

George: I hated college from the day I got there. There were so many people, and no one seemed to care what happened to me. Nobody said, "George, we've been waiting for you." When I got into trouble, then the dean said, "We want you," but by that time it was too late. It didn't warm me up. Nancy was all I had, and I must have wanted her caring to pull me through. When she didn't, it was the last straw—but I felt betrayed by the college before I felt let down by her. Unless someones shows me I'm wanted, I just can't function.

So much makes sense now. I feel lighter.

Therapist: I'm glad. You worked hard.

The fear of being a homosexual is voiced by many people who do not seem to have any tendencies in that direction. For them homosexuality is simply the most shameful thing they can think of, and they are saying that they are afraid that something will come out in the treatment to make them feel terribly unacceptable. Like George, what they usually fear is their need for closeness and affection which has in the past been significantly disappointed, leaving them under great tension and ashamed to have wanted so much and been able to recruit so little. They feel unacceptable and terribly lonely in their need, and in later life "homosexuality" symbolizes that state perhaps because, at least until recently, it is the paradigm for a situation where a compelling urge must be kept hidden and only secretly fulfilled to the accompaniment of fear, shame, and guilt. It will be interesting to see whether society's seemingly changing attitude toward homosexuality will lead patients to create a new collective symbol for expressing tensions felt to be shameful.

George has managed to clarify for me the reason for his depression, why the challenges of adolescence were too much for him. My hypothesis is that he could not go on as long as he felt unwanted and unacceptable. While he was still in his parents' home, geographic proximity and the daily routine sustained him in a feeling of belonging and being cared for. Once he left, the loneliness and isolation he felt was not so much for his parents per se but rather for what he had not been able to get from them—a sense of being a loved and worthwhile self.

Once he was away from home and from Nancy, he no longer felt held and, in terms of the little child he still is in significant respects, no longer felt whole. In his relationship with me, words are now the equivalent for him of being held, and in that context he can examine himself and grow.

Sessions 26–55

In subsequent sessions George became interested in re-examining his life and behavior in the light of this new-found concept. We arrived at the conclusion that he had remained isolated and aloof when he really always wanted to be friendly, because he became quickly disappointed with the limits of friendly relationships. He became jealous of his friends' other friends and felt hurt that his friends were not devoted to him exclusively—probably a throwback to his wish to possess his mother's total affection.

I discussed with him, and we explored, the possibility that when his father came home from the military, George perceived him as a new sibling, a brother, a full-grown accomplished rival, who came between George and his mother, while the stern, forbidding grandfather retained the father-surrogate position. This situation could well have been fostered and perpetuated by his mother's depreciation of his father when he chose not to resume his pre-law studies. This, combined with her obviously worshipful attitude toward her own father, could well have made it difficult for George to make his father the target of his idealizing needs. George's desire to please his mother and become a lawyer seemed, on further consideration, to be a bid to be mother's favorite "child," rather than an attempt to win mother away from father in the oedipal sense.

Although the accuracy of these reconstructions could not be established since they were not based on interpretations of transference manifestations, they were valuable in continuing to stimulate George's introspection and in bringing him to reflect on his condition. The ideas that his present-day feelings and behavior were multiply determined, and that he could think through the various factors involved, gave him a sense of control over himself as well as an acquaintance with himself he had not had before.

While these discussions were going on, George, who was now essentially symptom-free, made moves to resume his acquaintance with some of the young men he had known in high school and who were now home from college for summer vacation. He became part of a group that went swimming, hiking, and golfing. We had plenty of opportunity to observe how George reacted to the inevitable tensions that developed under such circumstances. He was easily hurt by any sign that he and his ideas were not given preference. Now, however, he was, with my help, better able to observe himself instead of withdrawing from situations that made him anxious, as he would have done in the past. I would usually acknowledge his feelings but then place his upset in the larger context of his personal history—a procedure that moderated his pain and made it unnecessary for him to overreact.

He began to have occasional dates arranged by his new-found friends, but he didn't care much for any of the girls he was introduced to. He went out with them in order to fit in with the rest of the group. The end of the summer was drawing near, and soon his companions would be leaving to return to school. George had thought about returning to college, perhaps switching schools to be with his friends, but he decided against it since he still had no wish to resume his pre-law courses or to take up any other field of study, for that matter. Not wanting to sit around any longer with nothing to do, he made up his mind to work again for his father. Since George was quite well acquainted with the business, his father assigned him to the first shift at the factory in a minor supervisory position, checking production and bringing records from the day before up to date. He would get up around 4:30 in the morning, eat breakfast at an all-night restaurant on his way to work, and report for duty at 6:00 A.M. He was finished in the early afternoon and so could get back to town and keep his appointments with me.

Session 56

Therapist: That's a nice suit you have on, George. Is it new?

George: No, I got it last year before I went away. You just haven't seen it before. I wore it today because Dad had me come along with him to have lunch with some customers.

Therapist: How come?

George: I think it's his way of introducing me to the sales end of the business. I've been on the floor and in the office, but the selling part is new to me.

Therapist: How did it go?

George: Pretty good. I'll say this for Dad, he never makes me feel like I'm a fifth wheel. He is always nice to me. These two fellows who were in today account for ten percent of our business, and they want to do more with us if we can meet their delivery schedule. When Dad introduced me to them, he said I was there because I'm closer to production than he is now, and could give them some of the answers they're looking for. That's not really true. He knows exactly what's going on in every department, but it was nice of him to say so. During lunch he'd turn to me and ask my opinion about anticipated output and so on.

Therapist: Working at the shop you're getting to know your father, too, and not just the business, aren't you?

George: Yes. I never knew there was so much to learn and what goes into what Dad does. There's something else, though. I'm glad to see you today because I've got myself a new problem.

Therapist: If I can help, I will.

George: You remember that waitress I told you about at the restaurant where I eat my breakfast?

Therapist: Becky or Betty, isn't it? The one whose looks you like and who you thought was flirting with you?

George: Betty. Her real name is Beatrice, but she wants to be called Betty.

Therapist: What about her?

George: Well, you know I'm there real early when there aren't many people in the place, so most of the time we get a chance to talk. She's only a few years older than I am, but she's already been married and divorced. She tells me stories about the guy she's going with now. He sounds like a very sharp operator. She was gone for a week, they'd gone to Mexico for a vacation. She came back, and they must have had a fight because she told me they had busted up while they were down there.

Therapist: So?

George: We've always kidded around a lot, and I sort of suggested myself as a replacement. She took it seriously and said she'd meet me after work tomorrow.

Therapist: To do what?

George: Awhile ago we were talking, and I told her about the picnic Chuck, Pete, and I had at the zoo last summer and how great it was. At the time she said it sounded like fun and she would have liked to have been there. So from then on I'd tease her saying, "When are we going to go to the zoo," or "How about meeting me tomorrow night at the lion house?" She was going with Harry then, so it was only kidding.

Therapist: Half kidding. "Going to the zoo," the way you say it, became a suggestive quasi-sexual overture.

George: Now she took me up on it. I mean really to go to the zoo. She wants to drive out there tomorrow.

Therapist: That's not so terrible, is it? You obviously like her, find her physically attractive, and enjoy talking to her.

George: It's one thing to be kidding around at the restaurant for a couple of minutes every day. This is something else.

Therapist: You sound scared.

George: Sure. She sees me as a pretty confident guy with a good job who knows what he's doing and where he's going. But you and I know the truth. I feel like a kid with her. She's had all kinds of experiences. She'll find out what a jerk I am compared to the men she's used to.

Therapist: You've been to the zoo before. Why should you look like a jerk taking her there?

George: But afterward. What if we go up to her place? What will I do? If she finds out I'm a virgin, she'll laugh me out of her apartment. I'll be so humiliated I'll never be able to face her again.

Therapist: You're taking a lot for granted and letting your imagination run away with you. Maybe Betty, who after all has just broken up with her boy friend, isn't that eager to hop into bed with anyone. Maybe she just sees you as a nice fellow who it would be fun to spend some time with so she can get her mind off her upset. It's just possible she wants to go to the zoo, period.

George: And if she wants to do more? You're the guy who is always saying I should let my imagination go and think "What if this or that happens?" Well, that's where my mind is going and scaring the hell out of the rest of me!

Therapist: Remember all the worries you had when your dad put you in charge of the first part of the first shift? How you thought you'd be made fun of for being young and relatively new at this business? All the terrible things that were going to happen to make you look like a fool?

George: I remember.

Therapist: What happened? Do you remember what we talked about and how you handled the situation?

George: I know, what I feared didn't come to pass. But this is different. The same rules don't apply.

Therapist: Oh yes, they do. You figured out then that if you didn't come off defensively like a smart aleck, but kept your eyes and ears open to see what you could learn, and asked questions when you didn't know the answers, people would give you a chance. And they did.

I think the same will hold true for Betty. You are you, not Harry or Larry or anybody else. You don't drive an expensive car and take weekends in Las Vegas. But you are a nice guy with whom she wants to go to the zoo. Why don't you give yourself a chance? It's no disgrace to back off politely if demands are made that you're not ready for yet.

George: O.K., I feel better. Thank you.

Therapist: You're welcome. I'm glad if I helped. Have a good time.

Usually so-called sexual problems have little to do with genitality per se. It seems to me that George is experiencing the possibility of having sexual intercourse as an occasion for a performance that will find him wanting. I feel his anxiety is too high to make a direct interpretation of this profitable for him. I choose instead to support him by helping him to realize that it is not likely that he will be called upon to perform, and that even if he is, he need not comply if he does not feel ready to do so. My intervention is intended to accomplish the following:

1. Reduce his anxiety and restore his adaptive capacity.
2. Prepare him to deal with potential feelings of inadequacy in whatever area or situation they may occur—that is, teach him that there are ways of protecting one's self other than retreat.
3. Demonstrate that sexual questions can be dealt with like any other problem.
4. Strengthen his confidence in my ability to help him and thereby deepen the transference relationship between us.

Session 57

George: You were right.
Therapist: Hmmm.
George: I feel foolish about all that I thought was going to happen. She really did want to go to the zoo, like you said. We stayed till closing time. You know, she never had been to a zoo of this size. She was just like a little kid. We took all the rides twice, ate hot dogs, fed the elephants. It was fun.
Therapist: Good.
George: I drove her home and I could tell she was really grateful. Like you had predicted, she thanked me for letting her get her mind off her unhappiness and letting her know she could enjoy herself again. She said good-bye to me at the front door. I gave her a kiss. She didn't seem to mind.
Therapist: That was nice.
George: I still feel foolish for thinking the way I did.
Therapist: When our phantasies come up against reality, it is usually a humbling experience. All I can tell you is that it happens to the best of us. You're in good company.
George: We made a date for next Saturday. I'm taking her to a show. . . .

Though Betty was only two-and-a-half years older than George, she had been away from home and on her own since age fifteen and was much more adult than he. Even more important, she did not share his rigid character structure. George had been raised to be a perfectionistic, obedient little boy who worked hard for approval, and in adulthood he was filled with rage and shame when he failed to achieve preferment and recognition. Betty was much more easygoing, able to enjoy the moment, and take pleasure in a situation for itself. Unlike George, she did not take herself so seriously and react to every situation as if it were a mirror that showed her in either a favorable or an unfavorable light.

As they continued to go out with one another, George learned to relax somewhat and to have fun without continually needing to prove himself. He felt comfortable with Betty because she was obviously impressed with his intelligence and conversation.

For a number of weeks the physical aspect of their relationship was minimal; holding hands and kissing good-night at the front door was about the extent of it. George did not make overtures for greater sexual intimacies, but in phantasy, as he told me, he usually saw himself as her lover.

Session 66

George: I've been telling you all about Betty and me, but you haven't said much about it. What do you think I should do?

Therapist: Do about what?

George: When I'm not with her, I get all charged up. You know, I've told you how many times I've made love to her in my head, but then when I'm actually with her, I'm more of a pal than a boy friend. We have a great time all right, but it's more like being brother and sister. Maybe she thinks there's something wrong with me that I don't try anything, but I just don't feel like it.

Therapist: In my opinion you are doing the right thing by heeding your feelings and not trying to force the issue. After all, the two of you do have a lot of fun together, and one needn't quarrel with that.

George: How come I get turned off that way even though I think of myself as a passionate, or at least a potentially passionate, kind of guy?

Therapist: Most likely in the actual situation when passionate behavior becomes a possibility, some fear enters and interferes with the sexual feelings you have for Betty.

George: Sometimes I wonder whether I really have sexual feelings for her or whether it's just in my imagination.

Therapist: That's where all our feelings and experiences are located. Sex is in the head not in the genitals. Your sexual thoughts are blocked at critical times by some other thoughts, and this prevents the translation of the former into physical arousal. But let's not overlook the fact that for the first time the girl of your sexual phantasies and the girl you're going out with are one and the same. The fears must have been even stronger before to make you rely on imaginary companions for your autoerotic activities.

George: I sure am still scared, just as I was originally, that if I were to have intercourse with her, or try to, I'd mess it up and look like a fool. I wish I could put that fear out of my mind.

Therapist: That would lead to trouble if you could do it. Putting the fear out of your mind is not the same as resolving it. That fear, whatever it may be, would assert itself in disguised form. Your sexuality would still be subject to interference, leaving you just as miserable—or even more—with the added problem of not knowing that you were frightened. This way at least you know what the immediate problem is, and have a chance of looking at it and investigating its cause and method of operation.

Instead of putting it out of your mind, let's take advantage of your knowledge. Perhaps we can get more specific about the nature and form of your fear.

George: I'm scared to start anything with her for fear I won't be able to function. What if I get to the point where I should be having intercourse and can't get it up?

Therapist: You're afraid you won't be able to perform, and then what?

George: If I let myself phantasize about sex with her, I get to that point, and then I hear her laughing, and I get chills and break out in a sweat just as if it really had happened already.

Therapist: How do you know that's what would happen with such certainty? Do you laugh at people who prove unable to perform when they first try something? You tell me all the time about Betty's unfamiliarity with many of the things you take for granted, like concerts and museums. Do you laugh at her if she doesn't understand what's going on or how to conduct herself in these new situations?

George: Of course not. It gives me pleasure to be able to help her and see her excitement when she catches on.

Therapist: So?

George: This is different.

Therapist: I'd say the only difference is that this time you'd be in the role of apprentice rather than teacher, and that more than sex per se is what frightens you. For someone else to see that you don't know something is a blow to your pride. The laughter you put in Betty's mouth is a projection of the contempt you would feel for yourself under such circumstances.

Many times that fear of yours is an asset. Remember how when you went to work at the shop you'd take the manuals home and go in on Sundays to practice up? Your pride drove you, as it did in grammar and high school, to feats of mastery that brought you a lot of rewards from those around you. But pride has its limits. Some things you can master on your own, but others require participation with other human beings. Truly satisfactory sex—and I'm not just speaking about genital intercourse—is certainly a prime example. That's when your usual way of dealing with your own ignorance or inadequacy doesn't work and you become convinced that all is lost. The problem seems to be that you cannot trust anyone to understand you.

George: I never looked at it that way. I suppose I think of people behaving the way my mother did. She never had much patience for me when I didn't catch on. I think she expected me to just know what the right thing to do was.

Therapist: From what you say, your grandfather was a pretty intolerant person, too.

George: My dad though, he's not that way. He doesn't say much, but he never got mad at me that way or embarrassed me if I didn't know things. I told you how he was Scout master of my troop. When we went camping he was always nice. Not just to me, to all the boys. He'd let us do as much as we could, and when we got stuck he'd help out without criticizing. We all learned a lot that way. The other boys thought I was pretty lucky to have Dad for my father.

Therapist: That's very true, and I think his influence did ameliorate the effects of the other type of experience. However, he was not there for the first three years of your life, and it's in those early years that our concept of the way the world operates is laid down. Frankly, what puzzles me is why, based on what you remember of your mother's and grandfather's perfectionism, this is not a bigger problem. You are by no means devoid of trust in other people. Certainly you had no big problem in relating to me. Actually you were able to give me and our work together a chance from the very outset. That tells me that a foundation for trust was laid down early—a foundation that we were able to build on.

George: I never told you about my grandmother, did I?

Therapist: No, you didn't.

Sessions 67–70

George's relationship with his maternal grandmother was another significant area of his life which he had disavowed. No mention had been made of her in all his recollections of early childhood which, as previously recounted, centered around the stress engendered by his grandfather's intolerance for the vicissitudes of childhood and his mother's demands for achievement. He now recalled that throughout his childhood his grandmother was both an oasis in the emotional desert of his early years and a port in the storm when the anger of the other adults broke around him.

His grandmother was a quiet, retiring person, with an ample, comfortable figure and a distinctive German accent in spite of her having come to America when she was still a young girl. She lived in the shadow of her domineering husband who frequently bullied and humiliated her. She would retreat to one or another room of their big house and busy herself with the interminable household chores that seemed to occupy her night and day. It was at these times that George, while still a small boy, sought her out. Once they were alone, his grandmother became a different person—cheerful, often singing, even talkative. George came to her knowing that if he talked, she would listen and if he was upset, she would soothe him. He was now able spontaneously to recover a number of early memories that clearly testified to his attachment to "Omama" and all that she meant to him. Their special relationship continued until he was about nine years old. It was she who would bake him a special birthday cake and see to it that he got the part of the turkey he particularly liked on Thanksgiving. It was Omama who would tell him stories and read his favorite books to him when he came to visit after he no longer lived with his grandparents. It was to her that he proudly demonstrated his beginning reading skills when he got into kindergarten. They would play Chinese checkers according to rules known only to the two of them, rules that assured his invariable triumph; Omama would always feign surprise and chagrin at having been defeated once again by her grandson's superior skill.

Shortly after George's ninth birthday his grandmother had a stroke from which she never fully recovered. Overnight this alert, spry lady became senile and incompetent. After she was placed in a nursing home, George asked to be taken to visit her. She did not recognize him. He never asked to see her again, and he recalled that when she died four years later, he felt no emotion at her funeral.

As we talked about the relationship and the importance it must have had for him, he was able to experience some belated mourning for her death. It was clear to me—and I interpreted to him—that his grandmother had actually died as far as he was concerned when she was unable to recognize him in the nursing home. For a number of days after this discussion he found himself getting angry at the slightest provocation and went so far as to pick a fight at a traffic light with another driver who had cut him off on the road. I interpreted that the anger he was expressing now was anger stirred up by his grandmother's "leaving" him by having a stroke; I explained to him that young children take the illness or the incapacity of a beloved adult as abandonment and rejection of their need. He went through a period of mourning again, this time for himself and the loss of the one individual who had accepted him unquestioningly and seemed to understand him perfectly.

Some time later I told George about a two week vacation that I was planning four weeks hence. He took the news with seeming equanimity.

Session 73

George: [*Arriving ten minutes late for his appointment, unusual for him*] The goddamned parking lot was full, and I had a hell of a time getting rid of my car. What are all these damn people doing driving downtown anyway!

Therapist: You're angry.

George: Well, wouldn't you be if you had to keep circling in this rotten traffic till you finally got into a lot? They charge you an arm and a leg to let you park, and you can't even get in when you're in a hurry.

Therapist: Sure, but I get the sense that your anger is out of proportion to the provocation and, furthermore, the way you say it, it sounds as if you're angry at me, not at the parking lot attendant.

George: I've been irritated all day. Why do I have to be the one who has to straighten out everything that goes wrong on the other shifts? You should have seen the incredible mess the time cards were in. They just dump them on my desk and expect me to have the payroll ready on time anyway. And I'll tell you something else. I didn't much feel like coming here either—it feels like it's just one more thing I have to do that I don't have time for.

Therapist: You know that you have handled similar irritations in the past without becoming so angry.

George: Well, why do I feel this way then?

Therapist: I think your anger might be in reaction to my impending vacation.

George: What vacation?

Therapist: The one I announced last week.

George: Oh yeah, I remember. I must have forgotten it.

Therapist: I think you had to disavow the effect of my message on you by dropping it from consciousness, but the emotion it stirred up is coming out in other areas of behavior. Instead of letting yourself be aware of the anger you feel at my leaving, you found other things to get mad about.

George: But I'm not angry at you. You're entitled to a vacation like anyone else.

Therapist: As an adult I am sure you mean that sincerely, but we are never all grown up. The child that still lives in each one of us makes its demands—in your case, angry disappointment that I should be leaving you.

[*At the end of the session, just as the patient gets to the door, he stops, slaps his pocket*]

George: Darn it, I meant to pay the bill and bring you your check, but I left it on the table at home.

Therapist: [*With a little laugh*] But you're not angry at me.

George: [*Grins sheepishly, waves in my direction and leaves*]

Session 76

George: [*Looking very angry*] I shouldn't even have come here today.

Therapist: Why?

George: You know damn well what you did!

Therapist: I can see you are very angry, but you had better explain what you mean, because I really don't know what you are talking about.

George: I waved to you and gave you a big hello, and you just sat there and looked right through me. That's what I'm talking about and you do know it!

Therapist: I did not do any such thing. Can you imagine that I really would do that to you.

George: Do you drive a blue Buick?

Therapist: No, I do not.

George: Oh . . . I pulled up at a stoplight right near the courthouse, and I could swear that that was you sitting in that Buick Electra waiting for the light to change. It wasn't you?

Therapist: No.

George: I was so sure it was you. I guess I owe you an apology.

Therapist: You owe yourself an explanation. What do you think happened to make you misperceive this way?

George: I suppose I have to admit you were right about the anger. I must have been looking for another excuse to be mad at you.

Therapist: You were in a rage.

George: Even though I believe you that it wasn't you in that car, you know, I can still feel myself being sort of mad at you.

Therapist: Of course. It's the vacation that you're mad about, and that hasn't changed by having your error corrected.

George: Why can't I be aware of that and face it head on? It's ridiculous. You've done a lot for me, you deserve a break.

Therapist: The undiluted ferocity of your anger, the way in which you are totally in the power of that feeling, puts a time stamp on it. As children that's how we react. We are totally consumed by the moment and its emotion. I believe that your relationship with me and its coming interruption has touched on some aspects of your childhood that you are now reliving.

George: But why couldn't I face my anger as a kid?

Therapist: Two possibilities occur to me. It's especially difficult in childhood to cope with anger at someone you need. An eye for an eye, a tooth for a tooth. If you get made at me, the therapist, then I'll get mad at you and won't want to help you. Since you do need me and care for me, you can't take a chance on that happening, so you do your best to bury your anger, as you did when you were much younger—but, as we know, it keeps creeping out around the edges. Another possibility is that the intensity of your anger frightens you. As a child you may have felt you really were angry enough to kill when you felt disappointed by being left—and, of course, you then had to dissipate your anger in other ways.

George: When I first got the letter from Nancy telling me it was all over, I kicked the shit out of the furniture in the room. I almost broke a toe. If it had been her there instead of my desk and chairs, she would have been dead.

Therapist: Maybe, then, it is the fear of the strength of your anger and the fear of what you might do that makes it necessary to defend against it. If the phantasies are so frightening that they cannot either become or remain conscious, then you can never deal with and dissipate your anger through adult reasoning.

George: Why would I be so upset about your leaving on vacation? You're coming back.

Therapist: True, but to children the future is not a viable concept. There is only now. Children can't miss someone and long for his return. They feel abandoned and bereft of something they need and it makes them desperate and angry. So if you've got problems in that area that haven't been worked out, you can expect trouble now, too. You are behaving as if I were going to abandon you, leave you to deal with your problems alone. My vacation is experienced as a rejection, a turning of my back on you and your needs. That is what you played out in the drama with the man in the Buick. Even though he was physically present, I think your grandfather's inability to respond to you was like being left by the then most important, indeed only, man in your life. When you put me in that Buick, like grandfather I was there but not for you. That's what my vacation feels like to you.

George: But I didn't stay angry long at Nancy when she left me. I got depressed.

Therapist: Depression is like retreating and shutting down the plant. If there is no way of dealing with the problem, you go out of business. You couldn't get Nancy back and you couldn't deal with your anger by working it through consciously, so you stopped functioning—something like going into hibernation for the winter.

George: You got me out of the depression, out of hibernation. The first time I saw you I was feeling bad, but I remember thinking that you would understand me. It didn't help me then, but I suppose it kept me coming until it registered.

Therapist: So now I am going to leave you, and you feel threatened by the loneliness of once again not feeling understood. Your first reaction is to get angry. Like babies that kick and scream when they are hungry and wet and nobody has come to help them, we tend to respond with some form of anger. That's a message. It says, "You can't do this to me. You must be here for me."

George: When the anger passes, will I get depressed again?

Therapist: What do you think about that?

George: It's not really the same thing as with my grandmother—I mean, with my grandfather—because I'm not a kid any more. And it's not the same thing as with Nancy because then I was all alone and felt lost at college. Now I've got my work and Betty. So maybe even though you do leave, I won't react the same way. I hope not.

Therapist: Also, in addition to what you mentioned, the anger is not so unconscious. We are talking about it and any other reactions you may have, so maybe it won't be necessary for you to go to such lengths to avoid the anxiety that your feelings generate. Instead of depression, we can substitute insight and understanding—solutions that are not self-destructive and are also more effective. By the way, did you notice that you caught yourself saying grandmother when you meant to say grandfather?

George: Yes, is that supposed to mean something? One of those Freudian slips?

Therapist: Maybe you were telling us not to forget that as long as we are talking about reactions to being left, not to forget what happened with Omama.

George: You mean her leaving me when she died?

Therapist: As I said before, I think you felt you had lost her when she became senile and couldn't recognize you. As far as your mind was concerned, she had rejected you, turned her back on you. The only person who you felt had really understood you.

George: But I didn't get angry or depressed then as far as I can recall.

Therapist: I wonder, though, what it cost you emotionally to amputate that part of your life and simply not think about it any more. My guess is that it left you vulnerable in the sense of making you reluctant to form relationships again.

George: I told you I was a loner in high school.

Therapist: Till Nancy came along, and then she disappointed you. I think that was the last straw. You felt you had opened yourself up once more, only to be left again. Now there was no way out but to retreat from activity into helplessness as expressed in depressive symptoms.

George: It makes sense, doesn't it? Do you think that my not being very sexual with Nancy was because I wasn't seeing her as anything but someone who could make the good feelings I had with my grandmother come back?

Therapist: That hadn't occurred to me, but I think you are right on target with that, George.

Sessions 77–84

The sessions remaining before my vacation gave us the opportunity to continue to explore what my leaving meant to him. I explained to him in various contexts that a person's concept of self, especially in the early years, is very much dependent on the messages he gets from those around him. To be left alone can mean that one is faced with what seems to be an overwhelming task in childhood—that is, to maintain one's sense of integrity and cohesion, to do for oneself what one had depended on others to do. One is faced with the anxiety of wondering, "Am I really ready to do that?"

Although he was never left untended physically, when his grandfather indicated that he could not tolerate the child's physical expression of emotional needs, psychologically George felt as if he had been left because he was in someway unacceptable. With his mother, the feeling that her approval and affection were contingent on what he did at a given moment interefered with his being able to develop a sense of a positively tinged continuity of self which could sustain him during difficult times.

During this time he drew closer to Betty. They saw each other more during the week and became more intimate physically. We discussed—and he understood—that his sense of loss about my leaving was bringing this about.

At our last appointment before the vacation George asked where I was going. I told him and volunteered the address and telephone number where he could reach me if he cared to or needed to in the next few weeks.

I did not hear from him during the time I was away.

The question of whether to tell a patient where you are going when you absent yourself from the office cannot be answered with a formula. If you believe the anxiety of not knowing your whereabouts will be a productive stimulus for a patient, it would be incorrect to short-circuit that possibility by giving him factual information. In George's case I felt that it was most important that he understand that my absence did not mean I was unavailable to him. Although he only asked for general information about where I was going, I provided specific details and invited him to let me know if he needed me. There are also situations where it would be a depreciation of the patient's capacity for independence to tell him where you will be, and there are patients who would misinterpret such data as indicative of *your* dependence on *them*. Furthermore, as treatment progresses, you may want to deal differently with a patient's curiosity about your leaving. Just because you tell him your whereabouts one time does not mean that he should know the details on another occasion. The fears of a two-year-old who sees your absence as a threat to his integrity are handled differently from the fears aroused in a six-year-old who becomes afraid of his own phantasies when you are away but is not in danger of seeing his self fall apart. Like other issues in therapy, your assessment of what the focal developmental issues are at a given time determines how you should handle information about yourself, your vacations, and other matters.

Session 85

The first time I saw George after returning from my vacation, I greeted him in the waiting room and offered him my hand. He shook it vigorously.

George: You look good. You got a nice suntan.

Therapist: Thank you. I had a very nice time. You look like you've been in the sun, too, George.

George: Yes, I took a few days off. I thought I might as well as long as you weren't here. It was O.K. with my dad. I had a week coming and I was covered at work.

Therapist: Did you go away?

George: Yes, I did . . . we did.

Therapist: Hmm?

George: That is, Betty was going to visit her brother and his wife for a while down South, and I offered to drive her. She'd never been in the mountains before, so we took a few extra days and went the long way around.

Therapist: How was it?

George: What? Oh, the drive. Very nice. Doctor?

Therapist: Yes.

George: I suppose I should tell you everything. It happened . . . ahh . . . we slept together.

Therapist: Slept together?

George: Well, you know, had sex.

Therapist: That is a momentous occasion, isn't it, that first time.

George: I was afraid you'd be mad at me. Not talking it over first, I mean. I'm glad you understand, but I should have known you would.

Therapist: If you want to talk about it now, we can.

George: Before you left I told you we were doing some pretty heavy necking. I didn't tell you that a couple of times we had our clothes off when we were doing it. But somehow I never got up the courage to go all the way. I swear, I really didn't think any more would happen when we traveled together. Understand, I wasn't suffering. It was fun, and I figured I wasn't ready for the rest.

As we were driving, before we got to the hotel, I mentioned to Betty that I'd try to get adjoining rooms for us, but she said no, one room would be enough.

Therapist: How did you feel at that point?

George: I got scared. Not so much of the sex part, but having to register at a hotel as Mr. and Mrs. I'd never done that. Right away I thought that the room clerk would know we weren't married and refuse to give us a room. . . .

Therapist: In a stentorian, disdainful voice that would ring through the lobby——

George: You get the picture. Of course nothing like that happened, although I must say I don't remember exactly what did happen. I must have behaved all right, but I was so nervous I don't recall anything except that we ended up in a room which, I was able to ascertain later, had a very nice view. By the time we got cleaned up and went down for dinner, I had calmed down a little, but not much. Everything about this whole business was new to me. I didn't know how to behave and had to figure it out as I went along.

By the time we got to bed I was so worn out from worrying about the details that sex was just another hurdle to get over. There was nothing exciting about the prospect at all. I think Betty knew what was happening to me. She was very sweet and just held on to me when we went to bed. We hugged and kissed awhile and then went to sleep. Towards morning we woke up, and I don't exactly remember what happened then, but we ended up having intercourse. The first time I came too quickly, but after that it worked out very well.

We had a nice couple of days after that.

Therapist: It sounds as if you had a very fine introduction to adult sexual life.

George: It must have been pretty obvious that it was my first time, but she never treated me like the fumbling fool that I felt I was. [*Blushing*] She told me I was a good lover.

Therapist: A gracious lady. You were very fortunate.

George: It couldn't have been nicer. I'm glad you're taking it this way. You're not mad at me that I didn't talk it over with you first?

Therapist: It was your decision to make, and you made it. It may well be that you waited, unconsciously, to make this move till I was gone because you realized this and felt that it was something you had to do on your own responsibility.

George: I do feel more of an adult since all this happened. As if I've passed a test. I want you to know about it, but I didn't want to ask permission like a little boy.

Therapist: Certain thresholds in life must be crossed alone.

During the three weeks that Betty was visiting her brother and sister-in-law, George seemed to mature on many fronts. It was not that he did anything dramatically new, but that he went about his daily activities with a more adult attitude. In his sessions with me he took more responsibility for examining his thoughts and feelings in addition to reporting them. Understandably, a considerable amount of time was spent in discussing his relationship with his lover. He questioned what Betty meant to him. Though he remained grateful to her for the experience they had had, he worried that she might expect more from him emotionally than he was prepared to give. However, when Betty came back, it was he who found himself making demands on her for a degree of devotion and exclusivity that she was not willing to grant. Their sexual relationship continued to be satisfying, and they enjoyed each other's company, but he spoiled his pleasure by the jealousy he felt if there was any indication that she was interested in anyone except him, no matter how innocent her interest might be. In therapy I pointed out to him the parallel between his feelings now and the feelings that he might have experienced when his father came back from the war and made his emotional claims on George's mother. However, I think that time and circumstances, rather than insight gained in therapy, eventually resolved what threatened to become a sticky situation. Betty decided that as long as she remained a waitress her future was limited, and that she wanted to resume her education with a view to becoming a nurse. In order to have enough money to pay for her education, she decided to leave the city and move in with her brother during the time she went to school. George was encouraging and supportive while she was making this decision, even though it meant their being apart geographically. Faced with her leaving, he briefly toyed with the idea that he might be in love with Betty, and he thought about marriage. He realized, however, that these thoughts were motivated more by his anxiety about being alone and having to form new relationships than by an emotional commitment to her. He was able to monitor his feelings effectively and accurately during this period and felt that, though he experienced a sense of loss, this pain was certainly preferable to the anger and depression he had felt after he and Nancy had parted.

After he had gone through this phase, he asked that his therapy sessions be reduced to two per week and eventually to one. He was making most of his decisions for himself but still valued my impressions of their significance for him and his future. He no longer needed me as a parent; now he relied on me as an older friend whom he could trust. Eventually he decided that he wanted to return to school to study business administration with a view to taking a leading role in his father's business. He decided not to leave town but to go to a local university which had an excellent department of business administration. He did not want to leave his father whom he had come to see in a very different light. They enjoyed each other's company and the common meeting ground of the family business. He was quite active socially, developing a circle of male and female friends of his age group. He had some casual sexual relations but declared himself satisfied to put off into the indefinite future thoughts of a permanent attachment. Two years after beginning therapy he decided that he could manage well on his own. He asked that he be permitted to come for consultation when and if his situation warranted it, and I readily agreed with that arrangement. We parted with mutual good feelings and with George's thoughtful expression of what his relationship with me had meant to him.

Among the many questions I had at the completion of George's therapy, two stood out. Was his choosing to remain at home and to go into his father's business a retreat from independence or a step toward it? Arguments in favor of each position could be made, and George and I talked about some of them together. It did seem a sign of maturity that he was no longer threatened by closeness with his father but could enjoy it and to some extent make up for what he had lacked as a child. His involvement in the work at the factory was genuine, and his energetic and creative approach to his job hardly spoke for a pathological career choice.

More problematic was his relationship to Betty. He needed her to love him, and she did not have much of an existence for him beyond his need. Not that he was unkind, callous, or mean. Quite the contrary. It was a step forward for him that when she chose to further her own career, he could let her go without feeling rejected and, indeed, could even help her to make the decision that would part them. Yet once she was gone, it was in some ways as if she had never existed. It reminded me of the way he had dealt with his grandmother's illness and death. It was too early to tell whether his relationship with Betty was a necessary though flawed steppingstone to greater and more meaningful intimacy, or whether George's early experiences had placed a limit on his capacity to love whose resolution would require future therapeutic work. In the latter case, it would have been pointless to drag the issue into therapy before George was ready to deal with it. Time will have to pass, and in the interval George is much better off finding his way without continued dependence on a relationship with a psychotherapist.

George's case illustrates that, though the presenting symptom picture may fit the category called "depression," that in itself tells little about what the patient's problem may be—that is, what has made him depressed. If the depression is reactive rather than organic, it remains to be established whether intrapsychic conflict (neurosis) or developmental arrest (selfobject relationship disorder) is responsible for the symptom picture. George could not function independently and reach adulthood until he had first had the benefit of a relationship with an idealized other who could validate his worth and thereby permit him to modify defenses that impeded his progress. His depression lifted rapidly once he could experience the therapist as that longed-for person. Treatment was then a matter of helping him to maintain a cohesive concept of self when his inner structure threatened to fail him in various stressful situations. In operation, love is a state of being in which one gives another power over one's self-esteem. The therapeutic transference is a form of this state. Once established the transference permits the therapist to speak for and to the patient's self, to encourage, reassure, and sometimes guide the patient when his attempts at organizing what is happening to him threaten to fail.

George's therapy illustrates the fairly easy, typical, and ultimately productive and rewarding treatment process that one can anticipate when the patient is hungry for an idealizing transference relationship. The history of past achievement, the capacity for adaptation, the striving for perfection, and the desire to please are the hallmarks of an adolescent who, again typically, comes to a therapist because of a depression that has followed a failure in his ability to take the next step up the developmental ladder.

XIV

Summary and Conclusion: A Theoretical Foundation for Psychotherapy

The preceding chapters focused primarily on the method and the clinical principles of psychotherapy. This chapter will draw together these principles and give them a theoretical foundation. It is to be hoped that such an explanation will help the reader retain what has gone before and will make its application more meaningful.

Although the psychotherapist is sometimes called a "problem doctor," solving problems is one thing he definitely does not do—at least not in the usual sense. What he can do, as the clinical examples have illustrated, is enhance a patient's problem-solving capacities. Then the patient not only can do something about the problem that brought him to therapy originally, but also is better equipped to operate in all areas—to get more from and to give more to life.

No matter how good a driver someone is, if he does not read a street sign and heads the wrong way on a one-way street, chances are that the outcome will be disastrous. People who come to us for help are in a situation comparable to the driver's. A patient's presenting complaint is usually the end result of a chain of failures to understand and to organize signals that he has continuously been receiving. His having difficulties is not surprising. What is surprising—and more interesting to investigate—is why he is not in even more trouble. As the patient talks about what he believes is the reason for his unhappiness, he unknowingly gives clues about the true source of his difficulties. The therapist must be alert for the information and must allow time for it to accumulate. He cannot afford to be stampeded into activity by demands that he do something about the patient's immediate complaints. The therapist has to convey the idea that his priorities are of necessity different from the patient's. As is so often the case in psychotherapy, the best and easiest way to say this is to be straightforward. Fear that the patient will respond negatively to the truth simply reflects the therapist's fear of disappointing. In fact, I can't remember ever having had a patient leave me because I acknowledged that I could not straighten out an unhappy marriage, or help someone find himself professionally, or alleviate someone else's depressed feelings. People seem readily to accept the notion that the therapist's ability to help is based on the patient's letting the therapist get to know him, and that the patient's symptoms will make sense only in the context of his life, past and present.

By addressing the patient's knowledge—often unrecognized but nevertheless present—that his problems are based on a lifelong inability to understand himself and make himself understood, the therapist actually gives hope and holds out a promise that the patient's cooperation in therapy will bring him a much greater return than the symptomatic relief that he was ready to settle for initially. This is the reason that a patient is willing to settle down and work with a therapist. Indeed, once a patient realizes that he does not have to be in desperate straits to hold the therapist's attention, and begins to explore the broader implications of his discomfort, the problem that precipitated his coming tends to fade into the background.

This way of working is called "insight," "psychoanalytically oriented," or "depth" psychotherapy because it is based on Freud's recognition that psychological problems are developmental, and that only by obtaining insight into the process that gives rise to them can a resolution based on cause be reached. However, unless we therapists first modify Freud's conclusions in the light of today's clinical experience and integrate Freud's findings with what we now know about the rhythm of psychological growth, Freud's speculations about the specifics of that development (they were derived from the study of the neuroses and described in terms of the biological and physical models of his time) don't help very much.

I think it is useful and accurate to use the terms "mind," "mental life," and "thought" to refer to the problem-solving activity that is carried out throughout life (Basch 1975, 1976a).* By "problem solving" I mean the necessity of dealing continuously with stimulation from within and from without that must be organized in such a way as to let the individual generate appropriate responses. In this light, so-called mental diseases or emotional problems are, in effect, the manifest aspect of disturbances in the ordering function. While listening to a patient tell his reasons for entering therapy, the therapist should ask himself, What in the precipitating incident interfered with the ordering process and made this patient anxious?

*The theoretical framework presented here is one I have developed in some detail over the years. Rather than burden this summary statement with either its details or its justification, I will, from time to time, refer the reader to articles by me and by others that expand upon particular issues and cite pertinent references.

Different organ systems have different ways of signaling disturbed functioning, thereby letting a doctor locate and, if possible, correct the trouble. A stomachache says that the gastro-intestinal system has gone awry. Joint pains indicate trouble in the musculoskeletal system. When the brain cannot perform its ordering function, the particular subjective state that it generates is called anxiety. The experience of anxiety is usually described as a nonspecific dread, the fear that something terrible is going to happen, heightened by the fact that the "something" is not identifiable. There are, however, other ways of responding to disorganization. For example, a person describes the experience in behavioral terms: he is unable to concentrate; he finds himself irritable, tense, and easily angered; he has difficulty sleeping. In other words, the brain can no longer carry out its ordering function effectively.* Anxiety may also show itself in the patient's attempt to create a temporary illusion of order by dulling or pacifying the brain chemically. When there is excessive, sometimes uncontrollable, ingestion of food, alcohol, or other drugs, this excessive use, rather than its cause, attracts attention. Whether anxiety is experienced as such, manifested by defects in functioning, or signaled through symptomatic behavior, all these conditions are the result of an individual's inability to bring about harmony and to maintain what for him is the customary orderly hierarchy among stimuli. A patient comes to a therapist not because of his ostensible problems, though he believes he does, but because he feels threatened on a deeper level with a more or less permanent disorganization and subsequent disintegration. In other terms, a patient's sense of self is so threatened as to make him doubt that he can continue to function effectively without help.

For example, in the case of Mr. Clark (chapter 7) it was not simply his wife's death that caused him to become agitated and seek help; but without his wife to serve as a buffer he felt himself confronted by demands with which he could not cope, and the resulting anxiety brought him to the clinic. George Gerard (chapter 12, 13) blamed his girl friend's defection for his depression; but it soon became obvious that losing her was so threatening to him because of his unconscious belief that without the emotional sustenance he drew from the relationship, he could not face the demands of young adulthood. The retreat from anxiety into depression stabilized him temporarily, but after his return home the recrudescence of anxiety, in the form of thinking that he was "going crazy," led him to seek treatment.

In these, as in other cases I have discussed, the precipitating event that brought the patient to therapy had special significance because it confronted

* Sleeplessness, irritability, and inability to concentrate are often listed in psychiatric texts as indicators of depression. Since depression is one response to anxiety, it is not surprising that the loss of goals and the attendant hopelessness that is fundamental for depression (Basch 1975) is mingled with the symptoms of the antecedent condition.

him with a task that he unconsciously expected would prove to be more than he could handle. In fact, however, the patient whose treatment was successful was able to do what was necessary to improve his life once he became aware of what he had been avoiding, and why. In each case, the problem was not an inability to function appropriately, but the patient's unconscious belief that he would not be able to do so—that he could not be other than he was.

Of course some patients, like Mrs. Elbogen (chapter 9), cannot be helped to understand what prevents them from facing and coping with their difficulties. They can only search for and find conditions that will permit them to function even as they continue to ignore the source of their anxiety. However, a person who actively seeks out a psychotherapist or is relieved to be referred to one—Mrs. Elbogen fell into neither category—is indicating an unwillingness to settle any longer for a life circumscribed by his unconscious problems.

But what are unconscious problems? For practical purposes they are concepts, attitudes, beliefs, memories, and images that are subject neither to reflection nor to maturation. They create islands of arrested development which interfere with effective problem-solving. Mr. Arianes (chapters 3, 4), who was usually responsible, productive, and reasonably contented, responded, without being aware of it, like a hurt child when his wife became preoccupied with her sister's problems and ceased to cater to him. When I hear a story like his, I ask myself, How would I feel under similar circumstances? We have all had experiences analogous to Mr. Arianes's. A spouse, a close friend, or a colleague on whom we depend is suddenly too busy for us and our problems. Of course we feel hurt, perhaps angry too, and we may do something petty to avenge the injury. But we soon put an end to such unpleasantness by coming to our senses, realizing how unreasonable are our demands for priority, and feeling ashamed for not being more considerate of the other person. Mr. Arianes could not make such a recovery. His behavior was causing his relationship with his wife to become progressively worse; this in turn aggravated his psychological tension and his somatic symptoms.

I would expect someone like Mr. Arianes to behave no worse than I would under his circumstances; but if he does behave worse, I assume, until proven wrong, that something in the course of his development must have prevented him from bringing to bear on this problem the maturity he has achieved in other areas, and impels him to behave instead like a child. Usually an emotional upset is inversely proportional to the patient's degree of insight. Children are at the mercy of their feelings because they cannot yet take an objective position vis-à-vis their experiences. Insofar as an adult is arrested in his development, he reacts like a child, even though he is expected to and expects himself to act in an adult manner. This triggers a vicious cycle. Anyone caught in such a bind finds his difficulties escalating. The more immaturely he behaves, the more he is rejected by those around him, and the more inadequate he himself feels. Unable to look at himself and see his behavior for what it really is—an immature attempt at alleviating some distress—he rationalizes his position. Instead of bringing adult reasoning powers to bear on the problem, he justifies his feelings and behavior—often in a clever, sophisticated, and superficially convincing way—and becomes increasingly entrenched in an unproductive, self-defeating, and misguided attempt at resolution. His suffering is all the more poignant because the target of his immaturity is usually someone who means a great deal to him and is very important to his well-being.

When the patient first comes for therapy, he fully expects to have to continue his self-justification and to persuade the therapist of the inevitability and the correctness of his position. But the therapist's attitude undercuts such behavior. By taking it for granted that the patient must have good reason for behaving the way he does even though it gets him into trouble, the therapist implicitly and explicitly conveys to him that he, the therapist, is not condemning him out of hand. In this way one helps the patient to focus on the emotions involved in his presenting complaint. Once a patient is able to experience the therapist's interest and feels free to talk about his own feelings, he almost invariably finds himself connecting his present situation with his past. It is affective experience that from infancy on forms the basis of one's concept of self, and to explore one's emotions is to wonder how one came to be the kind of person one is.

Infants cannot reason in the sense of logically analyzing what is happening to them, but they can and do respond to the emotional tenor of the interaction with parents and others who are around them. This is not a mindless or unsophisticated reaction on a baby's part, but represents the selective responsiveness of the involuntary or autonomic nervous system which is active from birth (Basch 1976b). As illustrated so dramatically by Spitz's (1946) observations of depression in the first year of life, infants need to communicate with other human beings to sustain themselves just as much as they need food, water, and air. They are not passive recipients of whatever stimulation happens their way, but are actively on the lookout for novelty in their environment and for human contact (Basch 1977). The activity of the infant and the response he elicits lays down those nonverbal, imageless, sensory-motor patterns of perception, action, and reaction which form the matrix of the personality of the adult-to-be. For the rest of our lives, though we tend not to be aware of it, the need to communicate on some level with other human beings—that is, to make ourselves understood or understandable, and in doing so feel cared for, safe, stimulated, and appreciated—remains the prime motivator for all that we do or don't do. Informed direct observation readily confirms Kohut's retrospective psychoanalytic reconstructions (see chapter 11) regarding the continued significance of the appropriately attuned affective transactions between children and those who care for them. The transition from infancy to childhood is marked by the possibility for self-awareness—that is, the toddler can now begin to step back mentally and regard himself as an individual among individuals. What he thinks of that self continues to be greatly dependent on the kind and the appropriateness of the responses of those around him. The implicit hypothesis of psychoanalytically oriented psychotherapy is that only significant failures, disappointments, or shortcomings in the affective transactions shaping the self-concept can give rise to characterological defects or dispositions that in adulthood cannot be resolved by reason and/or experience, and, therefore, require professional assistance.

In the case of Mr. Arianes the opportunity to think about his problem in the larger context of his life soon led him, to his surprise, to consider those aspects of his early relationships which made him especially vulnerable to interpreting his wife's behavior as a personal injury. Similarly, Miss Banks (chapters 5, 6), once her anger was sufficiently under control, talked about a time in her development when she was not appropriately supported emotionally and was in the position of having to (or at least acting as if she thought she had to) hold her family together. Her seemingly irrational anger and her supercilious disdain for others made sense when seen as a reaction to her expectation that history would repeat itself, that she would meet again the incomprehension to her needs which greeted her as a child. She was expressing that expectation, though she did not know it at the time, when seemingly out of the blue, she attacked the credibility of the therapist on her very first visit and did all but beg him to be mean and to reject her in turn.

Just as it would be an error to accept a patient's presenting complaint as the problem to be dealt with in psychotherapy, so would it be a mistake to point to the patient's childhood situation and say that it in itself was the issue to be resolved. Frequently there is a misguided attempt to cure patients by attempting to substitute in the therapeutic situation what they lacked in earlier life—that is, by supplying a so-called emotionally corrective experience. However, one cannot "love" a patient into health. First, the therapist is not his parent. Second, the patient is no longer an infant or a child, and much has happened in his life to complicate matters considerably. And, finally, if love, attention, or understanding is all the patient needs, he can find any of them outside the treatment situation and will not need a therapist to supply them. Furthermore, a therapist meets people who have suffered childhood problems similar to or much worse than those of his patients, but without the same detrimental consequences. Thus, the therapist should focus neither on the presenting complaint nor on the patient's early trauma, but rather on the patient's reaction to whatever misfortune befell him. In other words, long-lasting damage is effected not by the emotional trauma per se but by the manner in which a resulting developmental arrest may affect one's problem-solving ability, and it is to this aspect that therapy must address itself.*

The ordering function, or problem-solving ability, the capacity to communicate effectively both as a receiver and sender of messages, the self, development, or maturation—all are the same concept seen from different angles. Development is never complete. Guided by parents, teachers, and other mentors in one's early years, in adulthood one assumes responsibility for one's continuing maturation within the framework provided by society for its fulfillment. A new patient is saying, in essence, that he fears he cannot meet that obligation. It is not the therapist's job or within his purview to bring the process of maturation to completion, but, rather, to identify for the patient the impediments to the goal and to help him to see that with effort he can surmount them. No one can turn back the clock for a patient and redo his early life, but onto the person of a therapist the patient can transfer the fears, the disappointments, and the unmet hopes of his early years so as to re-experience and reexamine them. The transference of affect is a normal process that takes place throughout life whenever anyone finds himself in a position of dependence on another person. If the therapist does not undermine or misunderstand it, a workable transference will be part and parcel of his relationship with a patient. How one manages the transference depends on its nature and its manifestation. Gedo and Goldberg (1973) and Gedo (1979) have designated the functions of the therapist as: pacification, unification, optimal disillusionment, and interpretation—all potentially culminating in a patient's self-awareness. Each term refers to a function that the empathic parent carries out at some stage of early life, and that, in the transference, the therapist temporarily supplies for the patient. Not, as said previously, to try to make up to him for what he has endured or to undo the past, but to give the patient a chance to remove the impediments to maturation that precipitated his complaint and brought him to therapy.

Pacification, the soothing function whereby the therapist temporarily absorbs the excessive positive or negative emotions directed toward him in the transference, permitting them to dissipate so that they do not overwhelm the patient, is

* The exceptions are the cases where substitution rather than insight is the only feasible answer. For example, although Mrs. Elbogen's husband was not her official therapist, he essentially acted as one by supplying her with the love, the concern, the total devotion, and the around-the-clock availability that an infant needs. Mrs. Elbogen indicated by her response that this attitude was what she had been waiting for; previous experience had shown that nothing short of such reinfantilization could stay her in her self-destructive path. There are certain organizations, like Alcoholics Anonymous, that offer lifelong emotional support to a person who has explicitly acknowledged both his problem and that he is forever helpless to face on his own life's stresses and temptations to regression. A substitutive and/or supportive kind of treatment is indicated for the patient who has suffered such great damage in the earliest phases of development that his capacity for a healthy self-concept has seemingly been damaged beyond repair or retrieval.

similar to what a mother must do for an overstimulated baby. It may come early in the therapy, as with Miss Banks, or later, as with George Gerard who did not show the extent of his rage until it was time for the therapist to take a vacation. Of course, one cannot hold and soothe the patient as one would a baby, but the therapist's willingness to listen without responding punitively to provocation is the equivalent of that maternal behavior.

Unification involves the therapist in temporarily taking over the patient's ordering function. Mr. Clark's therapist played this role when he helped the patient to reorganize himself by listening to him go over the day's events as Mr. Clark had been wont to do with his wife. In my case, telling George Gerard how I not only survived my adolescence but ultimately prevailed, was in the interest of unification—that is, of helping him to see how order can come of the chaos and confusion of adolescence.

Optimal disillusionment refers to the necessity of confronting a patient with aspects of his character that he either does not recognize or whose effect he misunderstands. Miss Banks, for example, believed that her attitude toward men was motivated by a refusal to be put down by them, a modern woman's readiness to assert herself and insist on the respect due her intelligence and achievement. When it was possible and proper to do so, she had to be confronted with the rage, the arrogance, and the destructive intention that she was expressing in this behavior. Such confrontations are always painful, even though they are usually made at a time when the therapist can also give the patient an explanation for the origin of his behavior. It is distressing for a patient to face how he has been hurt, but ever so much more devastating to find out that he has become a person who hurts others. We all admit that we have faults, but not the ones that others ascribe to us. For instance, Mr. Clark's therapist found my supervision painful when he had to face the fact that his self-righteous attitude toward his patient concealed problems of countertransference. That it did. But often only when a person is confronted with the problematic aspect of his behavior does he realize that, although someone has seen him at his worst, the relationship has not ended. Learning that one does not have to be perfect in order to function reasonably well is very important for people who have gone to great lengths to disavow the negative aspects of their personalities and, as a result, have little or no control over those attitudes.

Interpretation involves the explanation of the meaning of behavior in terms of past or present relationships. Psychoanalysis has emphasized genetic interpretation, linking the meaning of present behavior to affectively significant events in the patient's past. (Such interpretation is amply demonstrated throughout this book.) But the concept of interpretation should also include the process of clarifying to the patient the deeper meaning of his relationships in the here and now. For example, the therapist's explanation to Mr. Arianes of his significance for his nephew Bobby was an interpretation insofar as the patient was helped to see the meaning of that relationship in a new light.

There is not a hierarchy of therapeutic interventions, and one need not follow the other in the course of treatment. As usual the therapist has no such set guidelines. The manner in which he uses these techniques can and does vary with each patient and with each session with any particular patient. Nor is the choice of technique necessarily matched to the level of the pathology. Mrs. Farwell's treatment (chapter 9), although she was deemed to be suffering from borderline pathology, was conducted primarily through interpretation. She was unusually open to recognition of the implications of historical connections and had a clear, detailed recall of the incidents of her early life. Once she understood the significance of her past life for her present behavior, she seemed able to make the changes that enabled her to function at a much more satisfactory level. Little other therapeutic intervention seemed necessary or advisable in her case.

Self-awareness by the patient—and the ability to use it productively, even in situations that have not been discussed in some form in the therapy—is, of course, the desired result of insight psychotherapy. When the patient demonstrates self-awareness, it is often a sign that the formal aspect of the treatment is fast drawing to a close. Perfection is not the goal of therapy. The capacity for self-scrutiny is not an absolute. The fact that the patient still has blindspots and immaturities after the treatment has been brought to an apparently successful conclusion attests only to his humanity. A more valid indication of a successful treatment is the patient's ability to learn from those incidents that involve residual problems or problem areas. If he can grasp the meaning of an anxiety-provoking incident or a regressive move and can then reverse the self-defeating process, he demonstrates that he has acquired a useful tool through the therapeutic experience.

The mobilization of the transference in dynamic psychotherapy permits the re-creation of a situation analogous to the traumatic one of the patient's childhood. But this time—since the patient now possesses adult faculties and experience, and the therapist is prepared to understand what is happening—the trauma is not so intense nor does it have the same consequences: arrest and regression. Instead, reliving it spurs maturation. By understanding what has happened to him the patient is prepared to face and resolve his difficulties. The therapist does not solve the patient's problems, nor does he supply what has been lacking in the patient's upbringing—only the patient can make up to himself what he has missed. The therapist serves only as a midwife for the birth of a patient's self-esteem and for the development of a more adequate self-concept.

Although I have maintained that the transference of affect arises spontaneously in the process of a properly conducted therapy with a suitable patient, is it really spontaneous, or does the therapist's suggestion make it appear? It seems to me that one does not rule out the other. Of course, the therapist's attitude toward the patient, the questions he asks, and the manner in which he slants his comments are all geared to having the patient pay attention to horizontal and vertical affective connections—that is, to how his emotional needs run like threads through the cross-section of his relationships today as well as how they tie the past to the present. This may be seen as suggestion. However, as Freud pointed out in connection with dreams, a therapist can suggest that a patient dream but not *what* he dreams. Similarly, in every case I have discussed, the nature of the transference and what it revealed about the patient's past relationships came as a surprise to both patient and therapist; this information and the insights made possible by it was not something that the therapist had expected to find and prodded the patient into "discovering." Indeed, my rule of thumb is that any facile connections that can be made between a patient's conscious memory of his past life and his present difficulties are either trivial or wrong. Only in the crucible of the transference and in the glow of reawakened affect can the participants in the therapy become aware of how the past informs the present.

A final question concerns how to reconcile my therapeutic approach with different methods. Other therapists put emphasis on such points as conditioning the patient's behavior, on his decision making, on the mobilization and expression of immediate emotions aroused by present-day difficulties, on an examination of the transactional aspects of a given problem situation, and so on. These therapists can and do point to good results and often use these results not only to advocate their forms of treatment but also to conclude that the psychoanalytically oriented approach is unnecessarily involved and extended, needlessly burdening both patient and therapist. My answer is that the approaches advocated by these other schools of therapy are very much a part of a properly conducted dynamic psychotherapy. Many examples attest to that in the cases I have used as illustrations. For example, with Mr. Clark, the therapist used the patient's discussion of his daily activities to reinforce the behavior that tended to move the patient in the direction of self-sufficiency and independence. George Gerard's therapy made a great deal of use of the cognitive approach in helping him to look at how he was solving his problems and assisting him to develop more effective techniques for decision making. The ventilation of emotions was part and parcel of therapy with all the patients, and the benefit of such catharsis is undeniable. Similarly, the nature of personal relationships was not neglected: a patient's attempt to ignore the fact that he lived with people and that his behavior affected them, was seen as a defensive maneuver to be pointed out and dealt with appropriately. Rather than choosing among various therapies, I should like to suggest that we therapists can learn from one another's variations in emphasis to pay attention to factors we might otherwise overlook. Our differences are more in language than in practice. Therapists with different orientation may be doing the same thing but calling it by different names. I hardly think, for example, that the experienced behaviorist overlooks the whole person any more than my colleagues and I do. We don't forget that the patient is, by the way he behaves, creating the world in which he lives, and I doubt very much that the behaviorist forgets that today's behavior has a past history. I think the transference exists as much as a therapeutic tool in other forms of therapy as it does in dynamic psychotherapy. I believe that the successful therapist with a nonanalytic orientation probably uses the transference in sophisticated fashion without daring to call it by name, similar to the reluctance of some psychoanalytically oriented colleagues to admit that they influence their patients through anything other than genetic interpretation.

Factionalism strikes me as unnecessary and unproductive. I hope that what I have written has made psychoanalytically oriented psychotherapy less mysterious to those who are already committed to learning and practicing it, and that my book has given them the feeling that their work is something they not only can do but can enjoy doing. I hope, too, that what I have written has helped the student who is being trained along different lines to recognize that there is in our work a common denominator that makes communication between all of us both possible and desirable.

REFERENCES

Adler, G. 1979. The myth of the alliance with borderline patients. *American Journal of Psychiatry* 136:642–45.

Adler, G., and Buie, D. H., Jr. 1979. Aloneness and borderline psychopathology: The possible relevance of child development issues. *International Journal of Psycho-Analysis* 60:83–96.

American Psychiatric Association. 1968. *Diagnostic and Statistical Manual of Mental Disorders,* 2nd ed. (Washington, D.C.: American Psychiatric Association).

Basch, M. F. 1975. Toward a theory that encompasses depression: A revision of existing causal hypotheses in psychoanalysis. In E. J. Anthony and T. Benedek, eds., *Depression and Human Existence* (Boston: Little, Brown) pp. 485–534.

Basch, M. F. 1976*a*. Psychoanalysis and communication science. *The Annual of Psychoanalysis* (New York: International Universities Press) 4:385–421.

Basch, M. F. 1976*b*. The concept of affect: A re-examination. *Journal of the American Psychoanalytic Association* 24:759–77.

Basch, M. F. 1977. Developmental psychology and explanatory theory in psychoanalysis. *The Annual of Psychoanalysis* (New York: International Universities Press) 5:229–63.

Freedman, A. M.; Kaplan, H. I.; and Sadock, B. J. 1975. *Comprehensive Textbook of Psychiatry,* vols. I and II, 2nd ed. (Baltimore: Williams & Wilkins Co.).

*Freud, S. 1895 [1966]. Project for a scientific psychology. *Standard Edition,* 1:281–397.

Freud, S. 1912 [1958]. Recommendations to physicians practising psycho-analysis. *Standard Edition,* 12:109–20.

Freud, S. 1913 [1958]. On beginning the treatment (further recommendations on the technique of psycho-analysis I). *Standard Edition,* 12:121–44.

Freud, S. 1915*a* [1957]. The unconscious. *Standard Edition,* 14:159–204.

Freud, S. 1915*b* [1958]. Observations on transference-love (further recommendations on the technique of psycho-analysis III). *Standard Edition,* 12:157–71.

Freud, S. 1917 [1957]. Mourning and melancholia. *Standard Edition,* 14:237–58.

Freud, S. 1937 [1964]. Constructions in analysis. *Standard Edition,* 23:255–69.

Gedo, J. E., and Goldberg, A. 1973. *Models of the Mind* (Chicago: University of Chicago Press).

Gedo, J. E. 1979. *Beyond Interpretation* (New York: International Universities Press).

Goldberg, A. 1973. Psychotherapy of narcissistic injuries. *Archives of General Psychiatry* 28:722–26.

Goldberg, A. 1975. Narcissism and the readiness for psychotherapy termination. *Archives of General Psychiatry* 32:695–99.

Grinker, R. R., Sr. 1959. A transactional model for psychotherapy. *Archives of General Psychiatry* 1:132–48.

Kohut, H. 1971. *The Analysis of the Self* (New York: International Universities Press).

Kohut, H. 1977. *The Restoration of the Self* (New York: International Universities Press).

Kohut, H. 1978. *The Search for the Self: Selected Writings of Heinz Kohut: 1950–1978.* Paul H. Ornstein, ed. (New York: International Universities Press).

Murray, J. M. 1964. Narcissism and the ego ideal. *Journal of the American Psychoanalytic Association* 12:477–511.

Piaget, J., and Inhelder, B. 1971. *The Psychology of the Child* (New York: Basic Books).

Redlich, F. C., and Freedman, D. X. 1966. *The Theory and Practice of Psychiatry* (New York: Basic Books).

Seligman, M. E. P. 1975. *Helplessness* (San Francisco: W. H. Freeman).

Spitz, R. A. 1946. Hospitalism: A follow-up report on investigation described in Volume 1, 1945. *Psychoanalytic Study of the Child* 2:113–18.

*All the Freud titles cited are from *The Standard Edition of the Complete Psychological Works of Sigmund Freud,* translated from the German under the general editorship of James Strachey (London: Hogarth Press). The dates in brackets denote this edition.

INDEX